Leading Voices on People Positive

The global building and construction industry is one of the largest and most foundational pieces of our economy, and yet somehow it is woefully detached from its core purpose: to shelter human beings. People Positive brings us back to that core purpose in a highly digestible format that will prove to be a must-read for any designer or builder who truly cares to improve lives with their work.

Lindsay Baker | CEO, Living Future Institute (ILFI)

People Positive challenges conventional assumptions about value creation and offers a fresh, actionable perspective on how organizations can better align business outcomes with human wellbeing. Gayathri skillfully connects sustainability, social impact, and operational decision-making into a coherent framework that leaders can apply in practice. Her heart for our work in sustainability shines through. This book has the potential to reshape thinking around performance, responsibility, and long-term success.

Myrrh Caplan | Board Chair, mindful MATERIALS; SVP Sustainability, Skanska; LEED Fellow

We taught the market to count carbon and the market moved. Systems like WELL taught it to count the occupant. We started on the supply chain and stopped at the loading dock. Nobody counts the installer on his knees or the custodian at midnight. Gayathri Unnikrishnan follows one cheap line item, a substituted floor, through both, then shows you how to catch it before you sign. This is the measurement we owe.

David Gottfried | *Co-founder, U.S. Green Building Council; Founder, World Green Building Council; Author, Regen360: An Operating System for a Regenerative Earth*

Gayathri Unnikrishnan's People Positive explains why we externalize the social costs of business and how we can proactively change. It is not in our hearts; it is in our heads. This new guide brings together some of the early lessons from the Green Building movement with business acumen and the systems thinking required to make durable and lasting changes within complex structures. If you wonder how your work can better align with improving the butterfly effect of human rights, give this book a read. As we have found in our collective race to decarbonize, we can turn heads and improve what we can measure, resulting in more ethical business practices.

Arathi Gowda | *Principal at Perkins&Will; Founder of Yes Praxes; Adjunct Faculty at Howard University*

This book reveals how our systems of sustainability do not sufficiently include human dignity. This is a lack that many of us know and feel. Gayathri Unnikrishnan invites us -- and empowers us with language and logic -- to include people more intentionally. Together, intervening in the system within our scopes of influence, we can shift the global transition.

Kira Gould | *Strategic Communications Consultant,* Kira Gould CONNECT; *Co-host,* Design the Future *podcast; Author,* Women in Green

People Positive identifies the need for a lens that bridges across systems for integrated and informed decision making, an approach that works across departmental and budgetary silos, as well as time, to ensure our capital infrastructure investments are well positioned to serve our shared humanity.

Julie Hiromoto FAIA | *Partner and Director of* Integration, HKS Inc

We know that where you sit and who you sit next to shape your health in profound ways. People Positive extends that insight beyond the occupant to everyone a building touches — the workers who build it, the suppliers who stock it, the communities that absorb what's left over. Gayathri makes the human ledger visible, and once you've seen it, it will change your perspective on just how important healthy buildings are to everyone, everywhere.

Rachel Hodgdon | *President and CEO, International WELL Building Institute (IWBI)*

I've watched Gayathri turn 'what if' into 'what now' for years, and People Positive is the fullest expression of that gift. She writes with the clarity of an engineer and the heart of someone who has never stopped asking who gets left out of the room — a question I've carried from boardrooms into pulpits. This book is an invitation to build spaces, and a world, where every person is counted as worthy of thriving.

Kimberly Lewis | *Chief Equity Officer, Havenz Network*

As I read, I found myself snapping my fingers in recognition. The book resonated deeply.

It felt almost like an out-of-body experience: a moment of clarity in which the larger pattern became easier to see.

From that perspective, it was clear that we, as systems changers, have not failed.

Rather, the changes we are working toward are often difficult to detect when measured only through transactional metrics. They become more visible when viewed through a human consequence lens.

Gladys Ly-Au Young | *Partner, Side x Side Architects*

"We live in a world where every day, we face climate, not as a distant future but a lived reality. Driving meaningful climate solutions for our cities is not a technical challenge, it's a human challenge. The climate transition is reshaping our cities at extraordinary speed, but a low-carbon future is not automatically a liveable or equitable one. People Positive *gives us a systems thinking framework, to connect climate solutions into lived experience, for the people who build, operate, use, and inherit our places. Gayathri Unnikrishnan moves the conversation from aspiration to action, from* Inspiration to Implementation, *illustrating a systems thinking frame work, where human impact can work alongside the same briefs, budgets, specifications, and decisions that already shape our built environment today. For anyone working on the future of cities, this is an important and timely body of work with actionable guidance."*

Farah Naz FCIBSE | *Author,* Net Zero Cities *and* Mission Zero; *Global Climate Advisory Director, SJ Group*

I have spent my career watching good intentions get value engineered out the moment they meet a budget line, no matter whether the decision sits inside a project plan, a product spec, or a program budget. People Positive gives leaders the language and structure to keep human impact in the room where decisions actually get made, not just in the vision statement that gets filed away. This is the tool the field has been missing.

Sarah Robinson Enaharo

Being a sustainability advocate means constantly bringing together varied stakeholders to address ecosystem issues through everyday decisions. In People Positive, Gayathri presents a comprehensive yet very approachable framework to ask such a profound yet simple question – who is impacted by a decision, named or implicit. In this moment of climate and technological transition and uncertainty, the protocol allows us to create a decision tree to define and communicate social value to any audience. This book will make you pause and think about how each one of us can use shared language and create change, one question, one discussion, and one decision at a time.

Divya Vedartham | *Managing Director, Energy & Sustainability;*
CBRE Global Workplace Solutions

People Positive

Building the Human Dimension of Sustainability

Gayathri Unnikrishnan

122 Press

People Positive

Building the Human Dimension of Sustainability

Published by 122 Press
An imprint of Gaya Labs LLC
Redwood City, California
makeitliveable.com

ISBN 979-8-9972076-0-1
Library of Congress Control Number: 2026920211

Cover illustration and design by Nvard Yerkanian
Interior design by Nvard Yerkanian
Author photograph by Sandeep Menon

First edition, September 2026

Permissions, commercial use, and bulk orders:
peoplepositivebook@liveable.earth

For my grandfather, and for my parents, Amma and Acha—
whose hands cleared bramble and thorn,
so mine could hold a pen.

TABLE OF CONTENTS

Gamochonia, 1899 – 1904,

Ernst Haeckel

INTRODUCTION

We live on a planet where octopuses sometimes collect curios, shells, shards of glass, pieces of ceramic, and arrange them outside the entrances to their dens. I wondered, as perhaps you do, whether these objects protect them, disguise them, or mean something else entirely. The truth is, we do not know. Researchers have offered possible explanations, but none have settled the matter.

And maybe that mystery says less about the octopus than it does about us, about the smallness of a word like "purpose" when placed against a mind so unlike our own.

Dolphins use distinct names to communicate and locate their loved ones over long stretches of water, with those called responding. Bumblebees fall asleep inside flowers, dusted in pollen, and some of those flowers fold shut around them for the night, following their own inner clock and the falling light, and open again at dawn to release both flower and bee. Elephants greet friends they have not seen in years with an acoustic rumbling so excited that field biologists compare it to teenage boys laughing. Migrating birds cross entire continents using the stars as a map, operating without an external blueprint or a localized navigation system.

Yet for a long time, we disregarded intelligence if it differed from our calculated, transactional reasoning, labeling it mere instinct.

This was our civilized way of saying that because we could not measure it with the instruments we had, it had no value on the ledger of performance.

That is one of the oldest and most enduring mistakes we humans have made and continue to make: **we confuse what we can recognize with what is true.**

And we commit this exact design error in the corporate world we have built for ourselves.

Our blind spot

Neither the octopus tending its garden nor the dolphin summoning others is a random act. They are responding to the world through forms of intelligence our instruments are not always equipped to read. Nature survives through relationships, context, memory, and feedback, most of which cannot be reduced neatly into a spreadsheet.

But our modern industrial systems have been engineered to strip that context away.

Some executives today now dedicate their entire workdays to the buying and selling of billions in stock, driven by tiny price fluctuations, while the workers, households, and communities impacted by these choices are seldom factored into the equation. Even though corporate spaces are designed down to the millimeter, there's usually no feedback system to ask the cleaning staff if the lighting causes them chronic headaches. The lobby of a high-end commercial tower is designed to impress an investor arriving exactly once, but fails the security staff who work in its freezing air every day. Where a global supply chain is fine-tuned across a thousand distinct mathematical variables, but the actual human hands making the physical product do not appear among them.

We closely monitor material costs, delivery schedules, space dimensions, and energy efficiency with exceptional accuracy. Organizations often track pieces of human experience too: ergonomics, safety, well-being, accessibility, diversity, responsible sourcing, and community feedback. But the harder question is whether those measures carry enough weight to influence budgets, specifications, procurement, timelines, and operations before the decision is made.

We built vast, efficient systems that span continents and cultures. And somewhere along the line, we forgot to put ourselves in them. We built for what our tools could measure and left the rest to a growing pile of assumptions.

Nature teaches us that living systems rely on connections, signals, and feedback our instruments do not always know how to read. When we screen out the human impact to keep our spreadsheets clean, the cost doesn't disappear. It just forces the human beings inside the system to become the one unmeasured variable carrying the weight of the entire structure.

This book begins with that omission. The cost of not counting people does not stay theoretical for long. It returns as attrition, rework, failed projects, broken supply chains, and budgets that balloon in the second act because the first act did not ask the right questions.

Our current task is to integrate human impact considerations into the existing discussions on cost, schedule, carbon, risk, and performance. This book discusses how to incorporate human impact into the decision-making process and reveals what opportunities arise when people understand the human cost before deciding.

Buildings are the chief lens for this book because they make these systems visible. A building is a long sequence of choices made physical. Decisions about capital, land, labor, materials, contracts, and operations become the air people breathe, the routes they walk, the work they perform, and the conditions a neighborhood lives with for decades. Products and organizations appear throughout the book, but the built environment allows us to follow a decision from intention, through the documents that govern it, to its consequences in the physical world.

Inside the systems

I learned how good intentions disappear from budgets, specifications, and final decisions by working inside the systems that shape the built environment. My education spans three continents, and my career has taken me through very different building cultures: India, Dubai, New York, California, and global standards work with teams around the world. And each place taught me to notice a different part of the same problem.

Long before I helped build a widely used standard for healthy buildings, I watched human evidence lose to a budget line on a hospital project, in a meeting I describe in Chapter 4. I did not yet have the language for what I was seeing. I have spent the years since building it.

My engineering education in India instilled a deep respect for the parameters a system must accommodate, including load, failure, tolerance, cost, and consequences. In Sweden, lighting design taught me that a space can meet every technical requirement and still miss the person living or working inside it. Years later in the United States, studying corporate innovation at Stanford Graduate School of Business, I recognized the same pattern operating at organizational scale: good ideas fail because there is nowhere in the system for them to go. That observation has shaped my work since.

Working across product development, manufacturing, design, standards, certification, strategy, and advisory work. This has allowed me to observe project decisions from multiple perspectives, including design, positioning, specification, value engineering, defense, installation, maintenance, and explanation. I have sat at the tables where good intentions become requirements, and close to the places where they disappear.

The systems we work inside did not develop by accident. They continue because some organizations benefit when minimum protections remain weak and the resulting costs are pushed onto workers, suppliers, communities, or public systems. Appeals to empathy cannot resolve a problem held in place by commercial incentives. Under the current rules, ignoring human impact can appear financially reasonable, even when the consequences are negligent.

That is why this book is not primarily a moral argument. Statements of care are already common. Capital will continue to follow the choices that protect cost, speed, and return unless human impact is built into the rules, budgets, and decisions that direct it.

Who this book is for

This book is written for the people working inside those ordinary, high-pressure rooms where the decisions actually get made. It is concerned with the distance between the intentions we state in strategy sessions and what we go on to fund, build, and repeat once the room empties. If human impact is going to survive its passage through the brief, the budget, and the procurement process, it has to stop depending on appeals to empathy and start being written into the tools themselves.

People working on projects usually do care about their social value. We see it when someone asks how a compressed schedule will affect the site team, whether a new material is safe to install, or who will carry the cost of a decision after the project moves on. The issue is what happens next.

The cost of the omission

A value may be written into the vision statement, repeated in a public commitment, and raised with genuine conviction in a meeting. Then the project enters the brief, the budget, the procurement plan, and the delivery schedule, and the concern loses its place. Usually, no one owns it, no line item pays for it and no requirement protects it. By the time the work begins, the commitment has become difficult to act on, even for the people who still believe in it.

We already know how to give structure to other forms of seemingly intangible value. We model energy use, calculate carbon, track waste, and benchmark financial returns. These tools have changed what organizations notice, fund, and reward. Human impact rarely travels with the same force. The people affected by a design may be discussed in a workshop or described in a report, while evidence about their health, time, safety, or dignity usually never reaches the budget meeting where the decision is made. That gap is built into the way many projects operate.

When a human outcome has no field in the spreadsheet, no line in the budget, no owner in the process, and no metric in the report, it is easy to support in principle and difficult to protect in practice. *People Positive* began with that problem.

So the solution then is to bring human impact into the same disciplined systems already used for cost, carbon, risk, and performance. That means carrying it from intention into the brief, from the brief into the decision, and from the decision into evidence that can shape what happens next.

A people-positive approach works alongside financial discipline and environmental performance and it widens our sense of what they can achieve. Organizations do not become People Positive by caring more loudly. They do it by building systems that carry human impact from intention into decision, from decision into evidence, and from evidence into change.

Why now

None of this is new.

In the winter of 1855, in a British military hospital at Scutari, Turkey, the building was killing more soldiers than the war was. Florence Nightingale is remembered today as the lady with the lamp. But what she actually did was count and measure. She recorded the deaths, sorted them by cause, and then she drew them: a diagram in wedges, one for each month, the deaths from wounds in one color and the deaths from preventable disease in another. The second color swamped the first. Turns out, the men were not dying from gunshot wounds. They were dying from the conditions around them: the sewer beneath the floorboards, the foul air, and overcrowded wards.

She was right about what and wrong about why. Nightingale believed in bad air rather than germs, and the theory she was working from is one no epidemiologist would defend today. It did not matter. She had measured the outcome instead of arguing about the cause, and the numbers were strong enough to move the British Army, which had every reason not to be moved. A sanitary commission was sent out. The sewer was cleared and the wards were ventilated. The mortality collapsed.

A few years later she was elected the first woman member of the Royal Statistical Society.

That was 170 years ago. We have known since then that the room you put a person in is not a neutral container. It is part of the treatment, or part of the disease.

So, the fair question is: why this book, and why now?

The law stepped back

For a few years, it looked as though regulation would do this work for us. The European Union had assembled the most serious instrument the field has ever had, the Corporate Sustainability Reporting Directive, which required large companies to report on workers and affected communities, and the Corporate Sustainability Due Diligence Directive, which required companies to identify and address human-rights and environmental harms in their value chains. Then, in February 2026, the Union cut them back. The due diligence directive's scope was reduced by around 70% and the reporting directive's by around 90%, the EU-wide civil liability regime was removed, and application was pushed out to 2029.

When I began writing this book in 2022, the European due diligence directive was settled. It had been fought over for years, it had passed, and the question inside the industry was no longer whether it would arrive, but how much work it would take to comply with. I wrote the early chapters on the assumption that the floor was about to be raised for everyone at the same time, and that mine would be the easy argument to make.

Instead, the tides turned. Whatever human consequence gets counted over the next decade will be counted because somebody inside a company created the systems to count it, and not because a regulator obliged them to.

And the politics turned

The regulatory retreat is part of a wider political shift. As I write in 2026, social responsibility itself is a political target. In the United States, several states restrict how public funds and contracts can take ESG factors into account. Federal policy has turned against diversity, equity and inclusion (DEI) and toward tighter immigration enforcement, while companies are removing DEI language from public commitments and disclosures. Some are also reducing sustainability teams or quietly withdrawing earlier promises. The European rollback is not happening in a vacuum.

That may seem like a poor moment to publish this book. I think it makes the work more urgent, for two reasons, and neither is a moral argument.

The first concerns the people still doing the work. Wealthy economies continue to rely on migrant and contracted workers to build, clean, care, drive, and keep essential systems running. Restrictive migration politics do not remove that dependence. They raise the cost of speaking up, especially when a worker's job, visa, housing, or right to remain depends on an employer or sponsor.

The second concerns where a commitment must live if it is going to survive. A promise on a website can disappear in an afternoon. A requirement written into a scoring matrix, payment term, specification, budget, or review gate has to be removed deliberately.

If the language has become politically vulnerable, the answer is to stop relying on language alone. Human impact has to be built into the machinery of the work.

We are building the next 50 years right now

The largest deployment of capital into the physical world in living memory is under way in the name of the climate transition, and it is being run through instruments that can see carbon to two decimal places and see people in fragments. Clean energy investment alone has climbed past $2 trillion annually, part of an unprecedented reallocation of capital that will require an estimated $4.5 trillion a year by the early 2030s.

The minerals for the batteries are being taken out of the ground somewhere, by somebody. The retrofits are being installed by hand, at pace, often by people who were trained for the work in a hurry because the work arrived faster than the training did. A specification written this year will govern how a building is operated, cleaned and maintained for the next 40.

Climate change proved that it could be done

25 years ago, this book could not have been written, because there was no evidence that a diffuse, contested, morally loaded consequence could be given a boundary, entered in a spreadsheet, and made expensive to ignore.

The Greenhouse Gas Protocol changed that. Published in 2001, it gave organizations a shared method for deciding which emissions belonged inside their accounts. Scope 1 covered emissions from sources they owned or controlled. Scope 2 covered purchased energy. Scope 3 extended the boundary across the wider value chain, from raw materials and suppliers to the use and disposal of what the organization sold.

The Protocol is not perfect, and its critics are right about many of its limits. Its achievement was to make a vast, distributed problem administratively legible. Once emissions had agreed categories and reporting boundaries, they could enter inventories, targets, procurement decisions, investor disclosures, and eventually financial scrutiny.

I do not think that proves human impact can travel in exactly the same way. Human experience cannot be reduced to a single interchangeable unit. But the Protocol removes the argument that a consequence is impossible to account for simply because it crosses departments, property lines, and supply chains.

And the excuses have run out

"We can't measure it" was a reasonable thing to say in 2005, when the tooling was expensive, the data was scattered, and the exercise would have consumed a department. It is not reasonable now.

It costs almost nothing to categorize a workforce survey down by shift and contract type, to follow a supply chain past the first tier, to put a sensor in a service corridor, or to walk down to the loading dock and ask the drivers where they are supposed to wait when the bay is full. The instruments are cheap, they are available, and most organizations already own several of them without having pointed them at anything in particular.

So, the conditions have arrived together. The law has stepped back, the language has become dangerous, the money is being spent this decade, the counting has been shown to work, and we have the technical tools.

None of that adds up to a movement, and I am not going to pretend it does. What it adds up to is a window, in the specific and unglamorous sense that the documents governing the next 50 years of the built world are being drafted right now, by people who are busy, and who could put something in them.

How to use this book

This book is built on a single, stubborn principle: every person can change a decision.

It is easy to look at the machinery of real estate, global supply chains, or corporate governance and think, no, I do not have that kind of power. I do not control the budget. I do not even work in that department.

I have heard some version of this from talented people at every level of the industry, and I disagree with all of them, because the leverage does not disappear when the authority does. It changes shape.

If you hold authority, your path is direct. If you don't, your power lives in your capacity to ask questions. When you ask who is carrying the unmeasured burden of a compressed timeline, or why a vendor's bid came in so far below the others, you introduce friction into a system engineered for unthinking speed, and you force the spreadsheet to acknowledge what it was formatted to ignore. A single question requires a verbal answer. A repeated question forces an administrative response. Over time, compounding questions alter the boundaries of what a system carries.

This book is set up to give you the vocabulary, data, and logic to ask those questions in your next meeting, and to act on them at your next opportunity. It does this through four sequential parts:

Part One: Acknowledge explores the omission: why human impact is often present in our language but weak in the systems that guide decisions.

Part Two: Assess helps you find where that omission appears: in People, Place, Product, Partners, and Public Good.

Part Three: Adopt shows where change can enter: through plans, policies, standards, specifications, gates, levers, and measures.

Part Four: Amplify shows how change travels: through evidence, language, reporting, and proof that gives the next person permission to go further.

You do not need to fix the entire system at once. Start with the decision directly in front of you in the ordinary imperfect places where systems decide what they will notice, fund, protect, and repeat.

This book is an invitation to widen what we count, what our instruments can see, so that human dignity has a permanent place in the systems we build.

PART 1

ACKNOWLEDGE

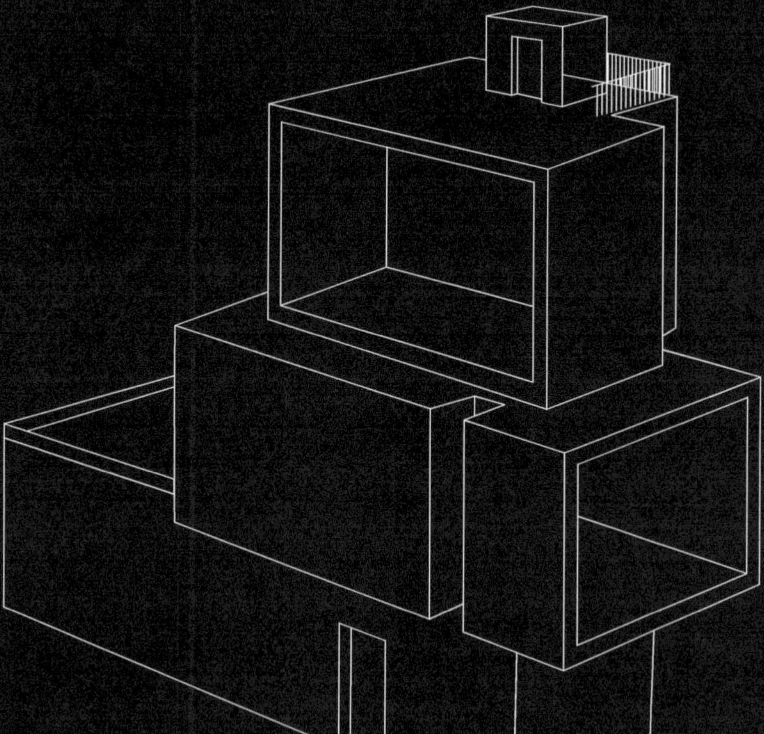

Before social value can be improved, it has to be seen. The first part of this book looks at the accounting gap underneath so many modern decisions: the belief that a human consequence which does not appear in the main ledger has effectively disappeared. It has not.

Costs move through buildings, products, workplaces, supply chains, and communities long before they return as delay, turnover, risk, distrust, or repair. These chapters are about learning to recognize that hidden movement, less to assign easy blame than to understand what our current instruments were built to see, what they were built to miss, and why human impact so often disappears while the process appears to be working.

The trouble with a blind spot

The trouble with a blind spot is that it does not feel like one.

I spent my early years in the industry looking for the villain. Disney movies had trained me for this, so I knew what I was looking for: someone at the back of the room with a sinister smile, waiting for his moment. I looked for years. They never showed up.

What I found instead were tired people working to a deadline somebody above them had already promised to a client, and the instruments they were working with: a spreadsheet, a specification, a budget, a schedule, a scoring matrix.

What is missing

At first, this can look like a failure to identify the conditions people are experiencing.

The night cleaner could tell you which corridor holds the heat in August, and which vent has not ever worked, and roughly what year it stopped. The subcontractor knows exactly the cost of a compressed schedule and who paid for it. Tenants understand the rent changes. Abundant, precise knowledge exists, often having been offered previously to someone who acknowledged it then moved on.

So, what is missing is not always the right information. It is somewhere to put it, and someone with a reason and the authority to act on it.

It is important to remember the difference, because the two problems have different solutions. If the problem were simply a lack of awareness, better communication might be enough. However, more often than not, the knowledge already exists but has no clear route into the decision. In that case, communication still matters, but it cannot do the work alone. The answer has to be structural.

The chapters ahead

- **Chapter 1: What Is Social Value?** explores the boundary of the transaction and introduces a working definition of human impact and social value.
- **Chapter 2: The Missing Thread** examines the five windows of human impact and why our current corporate responsibility languages remain siloed.
- **Chapter 3: How We Learned to Count** traces the origins of our accounting boundaries and what we can learn from the evolution of carbon tracking.
- **Chapter 4: The Omission** looks inside the delivery systems of a real project to see why social commitments can disappear before they reach the budget.
- **Chapter 5: The Cost Comes Back** tracks the accumulation of social debt and how externalized human costs return to the balance sheet under other names.
- **Chapter 6: The People Positive Spectrum** introduces a diagnostic framework for reading what a system actually produces under pressure.

Ship in the Indian Ocean, 1237

Yahya ibn Mahmud al-Wasiti

CHAPTER 1

WHAT IS SOCIAL VALUE?

What does a transaction leave out?

To cross the Arabian Sea in the middle of the eleventh century, a merchant had to accept that his net worth was held together by coconut twine.

When the southwest monsoon caught a trading vessel in the Arabian Sea, the ship did not sail so much as it flexed. This is because, rather than depending on rigid iron nails and fastenings, shipwrights in the western Indian Ocean joined hull planks with coir rope, coconut-fiber wadding, and sealants made from lime, resin, fish oil, or animal fat. As the vessel climbed the rolling waves, the wood worked and groaned against its own stitching. Down in the hold, the cargo was a pitching, highly volatile ecology: spice sacks, textile bales, aromatics, gemstones, and perhaps even the animal heat of elephants, and the rhythmic, wet slap of sailors bailing bilge-water with wooden scoops.

For the men huddled on the salt-slicked deck, listening to the joinery groan, every eventual number on a balance sheet was first a question of whether the cordage, the seam, and the social world behind the voyage would hold.

Twice a year, the Indian Ocean reversed its breath. The southwest monsoon made ocean crossings toward the Indian subcontinent possible, while the northeast monsoon opened the return path toward Arabia, East Africa, and the Red Sea.

At the center of this world was a formally structured merchant guild that originated in the dry, red-earth plateau of Aihole in southern India. They called themselves the Ayyavole 500, also known in Tamil inscriptions as the Five Hundred of the Thousand Directions.

Their commercial presence extended across an economic geography that connected South India with West Asia and Southeast Asia, with evidence of activity in places such as Sumatra, Burma, and China. They moved commodities of wide variety and high value. Beyond the spice sacks, textile bales, and the animal heat of elephants straining in the hold, their manifests listed sapphires, moonstones, rubies, diamonds, cloves, sandalwood, camphor, musk, and saffron, an inventory of high-value goods that depended entirely on a stable network to survive the transit. On paper, if we were to view this network through a modern economic lens, their operations would look like a machine designed to solve a transactional equation: moving physical objects across geographic space to extract a profit margin.

But the objects did not move alone.

Transporting goods across thousands of miles of open water and overland terrain required an infrastructure that nobody could buy or sell at an auction. It required a system that could withstand political upheaval, currency fluctuations, coastal piracy, and the sudden closure of regional markets. In the eleventh century, no modern international arbitration system or global insurance market existed to de-risk an investment. If the social system underpinning a trade route collapsed, the economic value of the cargo vanished.

The Ayyavole did not rely only on distant rulers or imperial protection to secure their paths. They built their own relational infrastructure. The guild drew its membership from different regions, languages, and religious traditions, creating an internal code of conduct that bound competitive merchants to shared rules and mutual defense. Stone inscriptions left by the guild, discovered centuries later in remote coastal towns including Lobu Tua in Sumatra and across the ports of Sri Lanka, record a continuous practice of long-distance contract enforcement based on collective reputation.*

To manage risk, the guild operated through semi-autonomous mercantile communities known as nagara or nagaram, along with diaspora networks abroad. Their inscriptions and later scholarship point to a corporate merchant world with shared law, financial capacity, military power, religious patronage, and relationships with political authorities. When a caravan of the

* *We do need to acknowledge that the guild operated inside, and profited from, an order that came with its own disparities which decided who could trade, who could enter which temple, and who could do neither. What we can learn from them is about relational infrastructure.*

Five Hundred arrived at a foreign trading node, the exchange was not just financial. The merchants operated through local institutions, establishing permanent ties with regional assemblies and making substantial endowments to local temples.

In the medieval Indian Ocean, these temples not only served as spiritual centers; they also served as formal financial institutions where merchants deposited and borrowed funds. By funding these civic nodes, and tying wealth to trusted local institutions, the guild hard-wired its commercial survival into the stability of the communities it entered.

An inscription dated to 1055 CE describes these merchants reaching remote lands by land routes and water routes, filling the emperor's treasury with gold while their presence left a durable mark on the towns where they traded. The fabrics, spices, and gemstones they carried held an objective market price, but it was the living human framework surrounding those goods, the networks of trust, obligation, protection, and shared rules, that created the conditions for exchange to occur at all. Goods moved because social systems held.

Modern industrial markets are skilled at pricing the isolated object. We can calculate the material cost, transport tariff, and margin of a product with flawless precision. Yet we remain far less practiced at accounting for the human syntax that makes exchange possible.

Beyond the transaction

A financial transaction is clean and contained. It isolates an exchange into a single moment, recording price, cost, margin, and legal ownership. But a transaction is a selective map of reality, recording the exchange while leaving out the human conditions that made it possible.

When we limit our definition of performance to the purchase, we filter out a larger set of questions:

- Who made the product?
- Who carried the risk when a deadline was compressed?
- Who gained access, and who was excluded from it?
- Who was made safer, and who was left vulnerable?
- Who benefited beyond the immediate buyer and seller?

The transaction tells us what changed hands, but not always what changed for people. Social value lives in the human conditions that surround a decision.

A working definition

To bring that human consequence into view, we need to move past vague phrases and toward a definition we can all use:

> ***Human impact is the benefit or burden a decision creates in the life of a single person: their health, safety, time, skill, dignity, and agency.***

> ***Social value is the human benefit or burden created by a decision, product, building, policy, service, investment, or organization.***

The two terms are related but not interchangeable. Human impact is what is at stake for a single person. Social value is the pattern that impact forms when a decision reaches many lives at once: who benefits, who carries burden, and what changes for people across the full boundary of the choice.

Human impact is what social value is made of, and social value is how that impact is distributed.

Who was the assumed user?

It is a joke in nearly every office I have worked in, in any city and any climate. It would be 40 degrees outside, or 104, depending on where you are reading this from, and the women are in blazers. Cardigans on the backs of chairs in August. A few have run heaters under their desks, against the rules, but nobody bats an eye.

Every standard, specification, and product is built around an assumed person, whether or not that person is named. That assumed person is the reference case. The building's specification likely details the reference case the room was designed for. He is of average height and build, in good health, and working daylight hours. He is on the payroll. He is comfortable at that temperature. All other people remain variations, pending future budget allocations. The cardigan, the desk heater, and the daily workaround are the private costs of being different from the person the room assumed.

The people who are not him fall into a pattern, not a random assortment: gender, race, caste, class, disability, migration status, age. Where they overlap, they compound one another. This is called intersectionality.

There is one more pattern to add to that list: how a person is linked to the organization. Are they on a payroll, on an agency's book, or in a subcontract?

The question, then, is not simply whether a place is accessible or compliant. It is who the design assumes, who is asked to adapt, and how much time, effort, discomfort, or dependence that adaptation requires of them. A woman who is also an agency worker carries two burdens, not one. If something goes wrong, being easy to replace leaves her with the least protection and the fewest people obliged to help.

What makes this pattern different from the others is that it is written down. A contract, a timesheet, a subcontract agreement all record it plainly, even when it isn't always read that way. That is why the first thing we cover in this book is not a score, but a breakdown of who a decision helps, who it costs, and where the cost surfaces.

The words we use

We often try to map these consequences using a toolkit of specialized concepts: equity, human rights, public health, well-being, ESG, and social impact.

Our enterprise systems have been built to optimize each field in isolation. Social value is the connecting syntax between them. It is the recognition that whether we are evaluating an eleventh-century teak vessel held together by coconut twine or 40 floors of value-engineered synthetic flooring, the transactional machine cannot function unless the underlying human network holds.

The byproduct

Whether tracked or not, hospitals, manufactured products, city streets, and corporate workplaces all create social value daily. Social value is an unavoidable byproduct of organizational choices, whether or not a program or steering committee ever names it.

Each contract term, design line, and daily routine leaves a tangible impact on human lives, spreading either positive support or hidden strain throughout a network of people. Social value is never truly absent from our world; the difficulty is seeing it clearly enough to act on it. Because our spreadsheets are engineered to register upfront cost, speed, and delivery margins, the real human consequences are left to accumulate as a shadow behind the numbers.

The hidden costs of a choice

To grasp how this blind spot works under live commercial pressure, consider a typical procurement decision.

A project team delivering a mid-rise corporate headquarters is reviewing the interior flooring specification for 40 floors of office space.

The plan originally called for a bio-based linoleum flooring solution. The material is non-toxic, highly durable, and leaves a clean indoor environment. However, during a late-stage review, the estimating team identifies a synthetic vinyl alternative that cuts the upfront material cost by $120,000. Linoleum's non-toxic status received more rigorous examination than vinyl's emissions profile.

The project is facing intense budget pressure. The general contractor is holding a tight completion deadline, and the linoleum option requires a significantly longer manufacturing lead time that threatens the critical path, the sequence of critical tasks that determines whether construction finishes on time. The project manager is neither careless nor ill-intentioned, but is making a rational, defensive choice under genuine commercial constraints. They sign off on the cheaper vinyl specification to clear the checkpoint.

The project spreadsheet records the decision as a straightforward example of cost cutting. But if we expand our boundary of attention, a hidden ledger of consequences begins to unspool:

The Chosen Ledger: Upfront cost reduced by $120,000, the budget clears the immediate checkpoint, and project speed is preserved.

The Hidden Ledger:

- It starts on the raw concrete. To hit the compressed Friday handover, a subcontracted flooring installer spends 12 consecutive days working low to the slab, knees bent, back rounded, pulling a notched trowel through adhesive across 6,000 square feet of floor. The ventilation system is not yet online. Temporary ventilation is thin. Solvent-based adhesives release volatile organic compounds during application and cure, and concentrations rise when a slab is worked before mechanical ventilation is running. The documented effects of that exposure include headache, dizziness, eye irritation, and central nervous system depression. The installer works the slab for 12 days under those conditions. Ventilation information from installation is absent from specifications, with no form field accommodating his account.
- Six months later, it has settled into the air. The tenant moves in, greeted by the much-celebrated scent of new construction. In reality, the cheaper vinyl is off-gassing volatile organic compounds into the air. Desk 4B's occupant experiences gritty eyes daily near 4:15 PM. Unsure of the cause, she purchases eye drops, concluding she requires updated medication.
- By year three, it becomes a late-night ritual. The downtown lobby is dark except for the amber glow of exit signs and the high whine of a commercial floor buffer. To keep the tile performing the part of high-end terrazzo, a

night-shift custodian pours alkaline stripper into a yellow bucket. Cleaning chemicals of this class are documented respiratory hazards, and the hazard is compounded when the work is done without adequate ventilation. He cannot prop the exterior glass doors open without triggering the building's after-hours security protocol. So, he drops his chin, leans his weight into the buffer handle, finishes the corridor, and pushes the bucket toward the service elevator to repeat the process on the floor below.

- This is what a value-engineered material substitution can look like once it moves from virtual documents to a physical building. A flooring system selected for the lowest upfront cost, rather than verified low emissions, can continue releasing volatile compounds into the indoor environment long after the ribbon has been cut, and can require stronger chemicals for maintenance.

What failed here was the field of view around the decision, not the decision itself: only some of its consequences were visible when the choice was made. The transaction recorded a saving, while the human system absorbed an unmeasured tax.

Buildings as the lens

This trade-off is the reason the built environment is our chief lens for social value in this book. In a world where most of our interactions, our mail, our meetings, our data, have evaporated into the digital sphere, a building refuses to be an abstract concept. It is the physical crystallization of a long sequence of human choices. It takes dry line items from a specification document on a screen and turns them into permanent conditions in the physical world. A value statement hardens into concrete walls, ceiling heights, ventilation rates, and contract boundaries.

When we examine a structure, we are looking at a permanent bundle of decisions. Every phase of a building's lifecycle holds land, labor, material, and community consequence. The methods by which a project is funded and the site is selected determine which neighborhoods receive critical investment and which communities face displacement or economic hardship. The choices made by architects and interior designers dictate whether a space removes physical strain for a diverse workforce or installs a permanent deficit that occupants must adapt to over decades of use.

The purchasing terms established with suppliers determine whether the raw extraction of stone, timber, and metal across global supply chains honors basic labor standards or forces lower-tier partners to compress margins at the expense of worker safety. The physical layouts designed into the back-of-house areas, including service corridors, loading areas, mechanical rooms, and staff workspaces, govern the daily safety, comfort, and dignity of the maintenance and facilities teams who must keep the complex system running.

A structure creates social value through the materials it specifies, the labor it relies upon, the people it shelters, the neighborhood it alters, and the public systems it touches. It is a continuous set of instructions that decides whose time is protected and whose is routinely wasted; whose health is insulated and whose is compromised.

So what?

Social value is already present in every decision we make.

The challenge is that we have developed many different ways of describing it, measuring it, and acting on it. Understanding why it disappears starts with the languages we use to talk about it.

Social value exists whether or not we measure it; the real question is whether our systems are built to see it.

Sagrada Família, Nativity facade, begun 1894, Antoni Gaudí

Photographed in 2023, still under construction

CHAPTER 2

THE MISSING THREAD

What if our data is sound, and the real trouble is that it sits disconnected?

When I was doing my master's in design, one of our first assignments required us to walk into different spaces of worship and observe how light travels within a room. It is a practice I have never really stopped. Whenever I walk into a building, my eye automatically looks for the invisible shorthand of light exposure, how a space handles daylight, who it privileges, and what it leaves in the dark.

The place that stays with me above all others is the Sagrada Familia, Antoni Gaudí's basilica in Barcelona, known for its branching stone columns, stained glass, and a construction story that once seemed impossible. If we stand in the central nave as the sun moves across the sky, we are looking at a building that can be spoken about in entirely different professional dialects. If we talk to the structural engineers, they will describe the building through complex geometry, catenary arches, and how much weight those stone columns can actually hold. If we talk to the biophilic architect, they will describe the space as a living canopy, tracking how the stone pillars branch out like trees to manage airflow and heat. And if we talk to a lighting professional, the language changes entirely to lux levels, refraction, and the deliberate orchestration of the solar path, letting the cold blues and greens of the stained glass in the morning wake up the occupants, before transitioning into the fiery, high-contrast oranges of the afternoon western sun.

Each of these perspectives is accurate, and each is partial. The engineers, the biologists, and the lighting designers are not arguing with each other. They are simply standing at different points, using the distinct vocabularies of their specific disciplines to create a single, deeply moving human experience.

When we join a late-stage project review for a building today, we encounter a team of professionals who are just as highly specialized and deeply committed. The design lead brings user experience to the table. The mechanical engineer brings ventilation and indoor air quality modeling. Corporate legal counsel manages deep-tier labor compliance. The finance team delivers investment risk analysis, and the community relations director provides feedback from neighbor consultations.

The challenge in these meetings comes less from expertise or willingness to cooperate than from enterprise structures designed to optimize each discipline in isolation. We find ourselves balancing an array of sophisticated, specialized tools, from equity scores and environmental, social, and governance (ESG) metrics to well-being standards, without an integrated system to map how they interact.

We have the data already; what we lack is a shared frame that shows how those maps connect.

The waves of corporate responsibility

The language of corporate responsibility has been expanding for roughly a century, each wave asking a slightly larger version of the same question. The first wave asked whether the organization had done something good. Later waves asked whether the good had been reported and verified. The most recent asks whether it was intentional and whether it holds under pressure.

Wave	Core question
Philanthropy	Did we do something good?
Corporate Social Responsibility (CSR)	Did we give back responsibly?
ESG / Sustainability	What are our environmental and social impacts, risks, and disclosures?
Human Rights Due Diligence (HRDD)	Who might we harm, contribute to harming, or benefit from harming?

Table 1. The expanding scope of corporate responsibility

Each expansion happened because the previous question turned out to be insufficient, not wrong exactly, but too small to capture what was actually happening to people.

The table earlier traces how the language of corporate responsibility has expanded over time. Each approach adds a wider set of questions to those that came before.

In the built environment, we can see the strain of this expansion by looking at the trajectory of the adoption of responsible buildings. For years, a "responsible" building was defined almost entirely by its utility bills: how much power it saved, how much water it captured, and how little waste it sent to the dump.

But eventually, the industry collided with an uncomfortable reality. It realized that we could build a celebrated, net-zero masterpiece using solar panels assembled by forced labor, set on a piece of land that pushes rising rents and trapped summer heat onto the neighborhood next door.

The building itself could be green, but the process of getting it there was extractive.

Standard sustainability tools failed to catch this because they were built to count units of energy, not human dignity. A spreadsheet could track the exact heat loss of a windowpane, but it had no way to register the person who carried it. The push toward social value happened because that gap became too glaring to defend.

Yet the moment these new frameworks threaten a project's budget, organizations often stop discussing the underlying human issue and start negotiating the language instead, which is how a field ends up with six overlapping vocabularies for roughly the same concern.

The temporal silo

The problem runs deeper than language. These disciplines are separated by expertise and, just as much, by time.

These languages dominate entirely different phases of a building's lifecycle, meaning the people speaking them are often separated by years.

- **Pre-Planning and Development:** This phase is dominated by community development and equity language. Teams talk to neighbors, negotiate zoning, and make commitments about local impact to get the project approved.
- **Design and Engineering:** Once the project is greenlit, the language shifts to public health and well-being. Engineers and architects take over, optimizing heating, ventilation, and air-conditioning (HVAC) systems, light levels, and spatial dimensions.
- **Procurement and Construction:** Next, supply chain managers take the wheel. The language becomes contractual, focused heavily on logistics, cost engineering, and labor and human-rights risks several layers down the supply chain.
- **Operations and Asset Management:** Finally, years after the first conversation, the building is occupied and handed over to asset managers. Here, the language shifts to ESG reporting for institutional investors.

Because the building industry often operates like a relay race, handing off the baton from developer to architect to contractor to operator, the data gets dropped between the handoffs. The asset manager optimizing an ESG score in Year 6 has no structural way of linking their data back to the commitments the development team made to the community in Year 0. The challenge goes beyond translating across different departments; it forces practitioners to whisper across decades.

Five ways of seeing human impact

It is helpful to think of these different disciplines as adjacent windows looking into the very same room, each accurate and each partial as a view of the human impact inside it. When we strip away the corporate buzzwords, each window is built on a specific field of research designed to measure a distinct aspect of human experience.

1. Physiology

The physiological window is the oldest of the five, and the most literal. It looks at what an environment is doing to the people inside it: the air, the light, the sound, the temperature, and the chemistry of all four. It comes from public health and occupational medicine, and it works in thresholds and exposure limits: parts per million, decibels, lux, degrees. It can tell us with extraordinary precision that something in the room is causing harm. It can tell us nothing about who decided to put it there.

Sitting in a sealed conference room, people begin to lose their edge. Their posture slumps, their words slow, and they reach for a second cup of coffee. We treat this as a personal failing, the result of a bad night's sleep or a heavy lunch. In reality, it is a basic chemistry problem: the room's carbon dioxide has just ticked past 1,000 parts per million. Outdoor air runs at about 430 parts per million, and it is at roughly that point that people get drowsy, lose concentration, and make measurably worse decisions.

We tend to imagine the human body as a closed loop, but after 40 minutes in an unventilated room, the space is no longer simply an environment. It has become an extension of our circulatory system. The physiological window measures this literal exchange.

At its baseline, public health establishes the floor, setting the strict, non-negotiable thresholds required to keep a building from slowly poisoning its occupants over a 20-year lease. Well-being establishes the ceiling. It looks beyond mere non-toxicity to ask how the deliberate orchestration of circadian light, acoustic dampening, thermal conditions, and biophilic geometry might actively lower daytime cortisol, support nocturnal melatonin, and use the building as an instrument of biological recovery.

The window describes the human body's response to a room with great skill while remaining silent about the chain of decisions that made the room that way.

2. Equity

The equity window comes from planning and social policy. It asks: Who benefits? Who pays? Who was in the room when the decision was made?

Consider a modern, certified downtown high-rise. Its floor-to-ceiling glass windows, specially coated to reflect solar heat, keep the interior at a crisp, carefully controlled 20°C (68°F). But step outside the rendering and stand across the street at 3:00 PM in August. To achieve that interior perfection, the glass acts as a sheer mirror, bouncing the fierce afternoon sun down toward the unshaded public bus stop on the corner and substantially raising the temperature at street level.

The building is a triumph of environmental engineering inside the glass. Outside it, the same design has created a solar oven. Equity is the deeper audit of this exact irony. It moves beyond demographic headcounts to examine the invisible structure of a project's trade-offs. It forces the design team to look at the bus stop and answer three unsparing questions: Who is carrying the immediate physical burden of this design? Who is capturing its long-term commercial upside? And when the decision to use reflective glass was approved, whose voice was allowed in the room?

Through the equity window, the arithmetic of the trade-off becomes legible with remarkable clarity. What the window cannot supply on its own is a price. In the corporate world, a question with no price attached can be answered eloquently, at length, in a glossy report, while leaving the reality on the street exactly as it was.

3. *Human rights*

Human rights establishes the absolute, non-negotiable thresholds of human dignity, and human rights due diligence is the forensic engine that keeps those thresholds from being laundered across supply-chain tiers. The window faces in a different direction from the first two. It looks past the people who use the building and toward the people who made it.

If we walk into the lobby of that same high-rise and look at the floor, it is broad, honey-colored sandstone, cut and honed to a surface so even it reads as machine-made. It feels timeless, quarried, permanent.

The stone has a journey, like everything else in the building. It was finished and installed by the contractor. It arrived on manifests that record the shipment but not the hands that worked on it. If we look further back, the slab was cut from a quarry, much of it worked by hand. India is one of the world's major sandstone producers, and roughly 90% of Indian sandstone comes from Rajasthan. Every surface in the finished tower was shaped by someone, somewhere, and passed through dozens of hands before arriving underfoot.

A human rights lens is a deep-tier periscope, refusing to let the final polish of a surface blind us to the chain of custody between the person who walks across the stone in Year 10 and the people who cut it from the earth in Year 0. Some of those hands, the American Bar Association has documented, belong to bonded and child laborers. The window exists so their dignity travels with the stone, all the way to the floor.

The limit with the human rights window is distance. Today, a project's first-tier suppliers are usually visible. The second tier may be reasonably legible. By the fourth, the view has often blurred almost completely because of the way these systems are set up.

4. *Civic life*

The civic window comes from economic and community development.

We can learn almost everything we need to know about a building's civic posture by looking at how its ground floor meets the sidewalk. Some buildings meet the street with a handshake. Others meet it with crossed arms.

When a corporate headquarters presents the neighborhood with a sterile plaza, keycard-only turnstiles, and three private security guards behind a monolithic desk, it is communicating a very clear spatial message: We are here, but you are not welcome.

Large, place-based organizations such as hospitals and universities shape the economies around them through whom they hire, what they buy, and how they use land and buildings.

The analysis looks outward from the property line. It asks whether money spent on operations, catering, janitorial contracts, repairs, landscaping, and facility maintenance is circulating through the surrounding community and building local wealth, or whether the property is an extraction pump, drawing value from the neighborhood and siphoning it upward into a distant parent company.

This window allows a team to see whether a neighborhood is becoming richer or poorer because the building is there. The complication is time. A meaningful civic reading may take a decade to develop, which is roughly nine years longer than most investment decisions allow.

5. *Financial risk*

The financial window is trained on the other four, or more, on what their failures are likely to cost. It comes from risk management and the capital markets, and its units are probability and exposure.

There is a specific, private panic that passes through a corporate boardroom when a financial model breaks. It usually occurs when a supposedly soft human issue suddenly manifests as hard, expensive physics: a flood that overwhelms a ground-floor server room, a preventable health condition that drives absenteeism across an entire workforce, or a labor stoppage at a third-tier supplier, a vendor three sub-contracts deep down the chain, that freezes a $400 million development site for months.

ESG is often discussed in the warm dialect of corporate virtue, but its actual mechanical function is colder. It translates social and environmental conditions into the language of risk, capital, and institutional resilience.

The market has become reasonably comfortable with the environmental and governance parts of ESG. Carbon can be priced, and governance structures can be audited. The part we are most interested in here is the social component.

For years, the "S" was treated as the unquantifiable sibling, a collection of vague sentiments about employee wellness and community goodwill. It does not look that way from the financial window anymore. In an interconnected economy, the "S" is where the hidden liabilities hide. It is the metric that tracks the volatility of human choices: the cost of attrition when an office environment burns out its staff, the litigation risk of systemic safety shortcuts, or the sudden, catastrophic disruption of a deep supply chain because the hands at the bottom simply stopped working.

It takes the biology of the physiological window, the distributional analysis of the equity window, the law of the human rights window, and the geography of the civic window, then reformats them into questions a risk assessor can read: How likely is this harm? How exposed are we? What will it cost if the system fails?

ESG works to make the human condition financially legible, a task quite separate from repairing it. Its central question is whether an enterprise is behaving in a manner so extractive, brittle, or detached from the real world that the real world will eventually strike back and destabilize it.

The financial window is the only one of the five that a board is routinely required to look through. That makes it the most powerful. It also makes it the easiest to satisfy, because once a human consequence has been converted into a line on a risk register, the organization can claim to have seen it without necessarily having changed it.

Case study

In 2013, people walking past the nearly complete 38-story office tower at 20 Fenchurch Street in London began noticing something strange. Parts of parked cars were melting. The paint was blistering. A storefront carpet reportedly started to burn.

The building, quickly nicknamed the "Walkie-Talkie," had a curved facade covered in highly reflective glass. On paper, the shape created more floor space and gave the tower its distinctive profile. On the street, the curve acted like a giant magnifying glass, concentrating sunlight onto the pavement and pushing temperatures above 60°C (140°F). Let's look at the building through the five windows we discussed above:

Through the physiological window, the building may have performed well for the people inside. Its climate-controlled offices were likely comfortable, even as the facade concentrated intense heat onto the street below. The indoor environment could therefore appear successful while the physical burden fell outside the glass.

Through the equity window, the question is who gained and who paid. The building's owners gained additional floor space and a distinctive design. The heat, property damage, and disruption fell on people outside the project boundary, who had no role in approving the facade.

Through the civic window, the pavement across the street becomes part of the story. In the design model, it appears to have been treated as empty space. In real life, it was somebody's workplace, storefront, commute, and daily route. A decision made for a private building changed the conditions of a shared public street.

Through the human-rights window, the case opens up questions the facade alone cannot answer. Who made and installed the glass, and under what conditions? Which workers spent the most time in the reflected heat? Could they report the danger safely, and did they have a route to remedy? We do not have answers to this, but this window tells us where further investigation is needed.

Through the financial window, the consequences became impossible for the project to ignore. The owners installed a permanent louver system to absorb and diffuse the sunlight, reportedly at a cost of under £10 million. The human and civic effects became financially visible only after the building was complete.

The connective tissue

We need a unifying frame because human experience rarely fits neatly inside one reporting line. A building may be designed by one team, delivered by another, operated by a third, and evaluated years later by people who were not present when the earliest trade-offs were made. Each team may be tracking something real. The difficulty is that the relationship between those signals is often hard to see.

Consider a building six years after completion. People are using the space less than expected, reporting more discomfort, or avoiding certain areas altogether. Maintenance turnover is higher than expected. Quality defects are creating rework and frustration.

Sometimes the pattern is connected. Low engagement may point to working conditions or spatial decisions that people have adapted to for years. Maintenance turnover may reveal that the building asks too much of the teams keeping it running. Quality defects may trace back to a compressed schedule, a procurement substitution, or a handoff that looked efficient at the time.

> ***Social value gives us a way to ask the connective question: what human conditions did this decision create, and where did those conditions show up over time?***

The point is that human consequences often travel across departments, budgets, and years before they become visible, and they seldom trace back to a single hidden cause. Without a shared frame, organizations can end up treating related symptoms as separate problems and missing the conditions that produced them.

Bridging to action

Social value gives equity, HRDD, public health, well-being, community development, and ESG, a shared frame. It helps us see these fields as different ways of reading the human consequences of the same decisions rather than as separate obligations competing for space on a dashboard. Social impact and operating performance are more connected than our systems admit.

We already generate or degrade social value every day in ordinary decisions: what specifications we write, which communities we consult, which raw materials we choose to specify, and which risks we decide to ignore. Asking our systems to measure social value means first recognizing the languages in which it already appears. Because these professional dialects remain deeply siloed, the underlying human cost is continuously translated out of the core execution rooms. To change how we act, the next step is understanding how some forms of value historically became important enough to count, while others remained outside the frame.

A Cotton Office in New Orleans, 1873

Edgar Degas

CHAPTER 3

HOW WE LEARNED TO COUNT

Who decided what counts, and what got left outside the frame?

During the mid-nineteenth century, British economists grappled with a puzzle that defied numerical explanation. Britain was a relatively small island with a population pressing against the limits of its own land's capacity to support. And yet it was producing enough wealth to shape the global economy. On paper, the country did not have enough soil to feed its workers, much less enough productive land to supply the mills and industries generating that wealth. By any straightforward reading of the ledger, the system should have run into its own physical limits.

The economists' oversight was that numerous acres outside Britain, specifically in the Caribbean, India, and the American South, were compensating for each cultivated acre within Britain. In the American South, this went beyond land outside the frame. Enslaved human labor was converted into cotton, and cotton converted into industrial output. The mills of Manchester depended on distant acreage and, beyond that, on a violent system that turned human beings into productive capacity while allowing the profits to appear elsewhere as trade, manufacturing, and national growth.

The explanation was outside the scope of the accounting. Historians coined the term ghost acreage for productive land outside the official frame. This also pushes us to name the human beings made ghostlike by the accounting boundary itself. Their work sustained the British economy, but they were kept invisible inside the columns of local metrics. The scale is worth naming. Around 1830, the land Britain would have needed to grow domestically what it was importing, principally the cotton, sugar, and timber that fed its industry, amounted to somewhere between 25 and 30 million acres of crop and pasture land, more than Britain's entire cultivated and grazed area combined. It was visible in the wealth it made possible, but absent from the columns used to account for it.

The ledgers in London were orderly enough to be persuasive. The structure of the record itself seemed to prove that the system was sound. What the columns did not show was the land, labor, and exhaustion elsewhere that made those numbers possible.

We look back at those nineteenth-century economists and wonder how they could have been so blind to the very foundations of their own wealth. It is tempting to read this as a story about a different century, about ledgers that no longer exist, and about a kind of blindness we have outgrown.

What the system could not see

Today, the same pitfall appears in a different form.

It is not my intention to flatten the violence of empire, slavery, or colonial extraction into a convenient metaphor. Coming from a country that was colonized, I know firsthand how devastatingly that extraction continues to echo across generations. And I have seen the impact of what happens when an entire culture is treated as an externalized asset to line a far-off ledger. The point I want to make here is narrower and colder: our modern corporate ledger descends directly from those early instruments of extraction. Both rely on the same accounting flaw: they treat human labor and the natural world as free, endless resources, and draw their success from extracting from both.

Current organizational systems are exceptionally well-equipped to measure immediate output, but far less equipped to understand the human impact of that output.

> ***Measurement systems do not simply record an existing reality; they define what counts as reality inside our decision-making. When we construct a spreadsheet, a project budget, or a national balance sheet, we are drawing a boundary line. Everything inside that line is treated as a hard reality with real commercial consequences. Everything outside that line is dismissed as an externality, a cost or benefit pushed onto someone outside the transaction, a footnote that can be safely ignored.***
>
> ***Once a boundary is established, what falls outside it loses protection.***

When something is left out of the financial tools that guide decisions, it becomes easy to treat as free. A company can use it, deplete it, or pass the cost elsewhere without ever recording the loss.

What measurement leaves out

"The Gross National Product measures everything, in short, except that which makes life worthwhile."

Robert F. Kennedy, University of Kansas, March 18, 1968

To understand how deeply this exclusion is wired into our global systems, we have to look at the rules that govern the wealth of nations. In 1988, the New Zealand politician and scholar Marilyn Waring published a critique of the United Nations System of National Accounts, the universal blueprint used to calculate global GDP. She exposed a paradox built directly into the international rules of accounting. Under the global GDP framework, if an oil tanker runs aground and spills millions of gallons of crude oil into a marine ecosystem, the disaster registers as an economic windfall. The money spent on salvage crews, litigation, chemical dispersants, and medical treatment for cleanup workers all counts as positive market production. GDP rises.

Conversely, if a parent stays home to raise a child, if clean drinking water flows naturally through an unpolluted watershed, or if neighbors organize an unpaid network to keep the elderly safe during a heatwave, the accounting system values that contribution at exactly zero. No cash changed hands through a formal market transaction, so the system registers the activity as non-production.

Waring's argument was that the boundaries were deliberate. They had been drawn with intent. The support systems that sustain human life and make market commerce possible have been categorized as economically invisible by design.

The boundary line

The same logic does not stop at national accounting. It reappears anywhere we draw a boundary around value.

A site plan can show the property line, the road access, the setbacks, and the footprint of the building. It cannot show the quarry where the stone was cut, the factory where the glass was made, the workers who carried the schedule, or the neighborhood that absorbed the disruption.

We tend to evaluate a real estate asset based entirely on the physical territory described in its legal deed. When we pretend that the asset ends at the property line, we become blind to the full footprint required to construct and operate it. By drawing the accounting boundary strictly around the physical asset, a project can capture the immediate financial upside of a cheap material choice or a compressed schedule, while passing the compounding, long-term human cost entirely onto people outside the frame.

Carbon becomes visible

The challenge of capturing these hidden impacts can feel overwhelming, and it is tempting to conclude that human impact is simply too intangible and too unquantifiable to ever enter the formal ledger. But we have already seen a version of this boundary problem solved in our lifetimes through the evolution of carbon accounting.

Thirty years ago, greenhouse gas emissions were treated by the real estate and finance industries much as social value is treated today: as a vague, unmeasurable environmental externality. Tracking emissions was an abstract concern that belonged to activists and climate scientists, not to chief financial officers or structural engineers.

That changed with the publication of the Greenhouse Gas (GHG) Protocol Corporate Accounting and Reporting Standard in 2001. The protocol took a complex, invisible planetary problem and translated it into a standardized way for organizations to measure and report their emissions by dividing them into Scope 1, Scope 2, and Scope 3. Scope 1 covers direct emissions from sources an organization owns or controls. Scope 2 covers emissions from purchased energy. Scope 3 covers the wider value chain, including emissions from extracting, manufacturing, transporting, installing, using, and disposing of products and materials.

We need to be clear about one key difference: carbon can be reduced to a tradable unit, but human experience cannot.

A person's life, dignity, or exhaustion cannot be flattened into a metric similar to a ton of carbon dioxide. But we can measure the conditions that lead to that exhaustion, the compressed timelines, the unfeasible procurement margins, and the safety shortcuts before they become an active corporate liability.

Social value needs a ledger strong enough to reflect relationships and to hold them as more than a single shorthand number. The Greenhouse Gas Protocol offers a useful model because it expands the boundaries of what an organization must examine. Applied to social value, that same logic pushes an enterprise beyond property lines and legal ownership to trace how its decisions affect people across the full chain of impact.

What the boundary passed on

The real problem is that our tools were built around a narrow definition of value, which makes social impact look harder to count than it is. Once a boundary is accepted, everything beyond it becomes easier to overlook.

An economic model can appear extraordinarily productive for generations, as long as it books the depletion of the natural and social systems it depends on as income and never as the loss it is. The deeper problem is what our accounting leaves out. When a company excludes the human cost of delivering its work from the main ledger, that cost simply moves off the books.

We are seeing chronic burnout, a deficit in institutional knowledge, poor mental health outcomes, and a diminishing capacity of the teams. We praise a lean balance sheet as efficient, while ignoring that its margin may be subsidized by the unrecorded exhaustion of the people holding the organization together.

Fixing this requires first looking at how these omissions respond to pressure. The gap between theory and practice becomes visible when accounting boundaries shape real projects and supply chains. To understand how a rational, defensive decision can impose an unmeasured cost on human lives, we have to look inside the room where that decision is made.

The Courtyard of the Hospital at Arles, 1889

Vincent van Gogh

CHAPTER 4

THE OMISSION

Why do social commitments disappear before they reach the budget?

A building under construction has a raw, skeletal honesty to it before the finishes go up to hide all the choices. Long before writing this book, I was a junior designer on a large healthcare campus, one of my first major hospital projects. I spent my days navigating the construction dust, trying to reconcile the elegant design principles I had learned in university with the chaotic reality of a live job site. On the day I want to tell you about, the window frames were set, but there was no glass yet, just dark, open rectangles. The air was heavy that day, and I could feel it pushing through the concrete shell in slow currents. I remember thinking that the rooms were breathing.

Walking from room to room, I noticed that the corner wards had two windows while the standard wards had one. I stood in one of those corner rooms longer than I needed to and thought about the patients who would recover there. Because of the double windows, I assumed they were the VIP wards.

Windows in hospital rooms are not decorative. A landmark study found that surgical patients whose rooms overlooked trees recovered faster and needed fewer strong painkillers than similar patients whose windows faced a brick wall. Since then, daylight, views, and quieter spaces have been linked to lower stress, better sleep, and shorter hospital stays.

In the review that followed the walk-through, the second window ran up against the project's standards manual, a binder of pre-approved components that allowed no custom variations. Removing the window would bring the corner rooms back into the standard procurement module, with the identical dimensions that kept manufacturing costs down and budgets predictable. I was waiting for someone to bring up the research. The brief had described the hospital as patient-centered, and there was an entire body of clinical evidence connecting the physical environment to the recovery outcomes the brief claimed to prioritize. But the decision was taking place inside a different matrix of professional accountability.

The delivery team had a non-negotiable deadline with financial penalties, and the commercial team's funding arrangements meant that design alterations were costly to revisit.

No one spoke for 10 or 15 seconds. There was no hostility in it, only the pause of people trying to keep a budget together. Then the room agreed the standard schedule should stand, or words to that effect, the log was initiated, and the meeting moved to the next item.

I remained silent. My voice carried no contractual weight in the room, so I wrote the decision down and turned the page.

That meeting stayed with me because it named a problem I did not yet have the language for. I was still early in my career, but I could feel the gap between what the research said, what the project promised, and what the delivery system was built to protect. Years later, that gap is the reason I applied to work at the International WELL Building Institute, the organization behind the WELL Building Standard, a global framework for designing and operating buildings to support human health and well-being. I wanted to understand how health, well-being, and human experience could move from evidence into standards, from standards into decisions, and from decisions into the physical realities people live with every day.

The hospital opened a few years later, described publicly, as projects of this kind usually are, in the language of well-being and patient recovery. The corner windows were never mentioned, and there was no reason they would be. The disappearance of that glass was the system working exactly as intended. Care had little to do with it. There was no single villain, but there was a definitive outcome. It is a clear illustration of how social value disappears: through a run of sensible decisions made inside a structure that was never built to hold the value, with nothing in it that looks like open rejection.

A promise is not a process

A commitment starts small, with a passing line in a leader's speech during an internal town hall. From there, it is stitched into internal newsletters, repeated in company-wide emails, and eventually woven into a formal press release. Before long, the commitment finds a shiny, permanent home on the corporate website.

After that, the phrase hardens into official company lore. It is written into corporate strategies, executive speeches, annual sustainability reports, and glossy brochures featuring photographs of people looking thoughtfully out of large windows.

The words are often excellent, and the desire to be more equitable, inclusive, or socially responsible may be entirely genuine. But organizations are often much better at adopting a commitment than they are at operationalizing it. They change what they say, formalize, and display long before they change the systems that produce day-to-day outcomes.

This gap has a name in organizational theory: decoupling, the formal adoption of policies that satisfy external expectations while day-to-day operations remain unchanged. An organization can create a separate, highly visible department to produce a 200-page sustainability report, while the core procurement team continues to use the same spreadsheet where the social value column is left blank. This is how a hospital can market itself as well-being-focused in public strategy documents, even as the actual decision to eliminate a patient window is made deep within the siloed systems of standard procurement.

Until a commitment enters the boring, everyday documents that govern daily choices, it remains vulnerable to the first meeting where something cheaper, faster, or more familiar is already waiting.

The budget is the test

> ***The fastest way to test the strength of a social commitment is to see what remains protected when money becomes tight. The real hierarchy rarely appears in an annual report or keynote speech. It appears in the budget meeting, when people decide what is essential and what can be cut. Often, those making the decision do not see themselves as responsible for setting that priority.***

The well-being program, the supplier audit, the community engagement process, the additional hire, the material with the stronger labor story, some of them survive in name, but they are reduced in scope, deferred to the next cycle, and left in the project plan merely as placeholders.

Economists call this phenomenon revealed preference: what we choose under constraint shows what we truly prioritize. If a value can be removed from a project without disrupting the core operating model, it has not yet been operationalized. It was adjacent to the operation, tolerated during periods of abundance, and treated as disposable when difficulty arrived.

The hospital meeting I described earlier is an example of this pattern. The cost of the second window was discussed in detail; alongside the maintenance complexity it would introduce and the procurement variance it would create against the standard ward specification. The clinical value of the view from the bed sat in the room as well, present in the medical literature, visible in the building's physical architecture, and entirely absent from the ledger that determined what was built.

The system is working as planned

When a company fails to live up to its values, our hardwired human instinct is to look for someone to blame. We look for a project manager who lacked resolve, a procurement officer who missed a metric, or a team lead who failed to make a persuasive case.

While personal choices matter, treating a system-wide failure as a people problem is just a convenient shield. It suggests that a more ruthless manager or a better dashboard would have saved the day, allowing us to ignore the broken system underneath.

This is why replacing one manager rarely changes the outcome. The system can override individual judgment because our incentive structures are explicitly engineered to reward short-term margin above all else. If you put a deeply empathetic manager into a system where their performance review and career advancement depend strictly on meeting compressed project timelines, the corporate mandate will usually win. The spreadsheet reflects the priorities set above it. Executive directives and shareholder demands shape what it is allowed to count, often filtering out anything that threatens immediate cash flow. A system's design can force outcomes that no one working inside it would ever choose for themselves. Across industries, a chronic gap runs between what an organization says it cares about and what its daily operations actually produce.

We reach for the story of a human failing to follow through because admitting that the system followed through perfectly on the wrong thing is far harder to sit with.

The uncomfortable reality is that the system did exactly what it was built to do. It protected the only variables it was built to recognize: cost, schedule, risk, liability, consistency, speed, and margin. Everything else became invisible.

It may be admired. It may be repeated in the press release.

> ***A value that has no place in the procurement form, no weight in the scoring matrix, no owner in the operating plan, and no consequence in the budget review is not a value the system can reliably carry.***

But unfortunately, admiration is not infrastructure. A system does not need to actively oppose a value to erase it. It only needs to be incapable of measuring it.

What has no owner disappears

Anything without a clear owner is easy to lose. Social value routinely vanishes from day-to-day operations because it lacks the protections that financial values take for granted. It is treated as everyone's shared aspiration, which functionally means it becomes nobody's specific job.

Consider a project that commits to local economic benefit by aiming to source 10% of its construction labor from the surrounding neighborhood. It is a compelling slide for a presentation. But if that target is not mapped to a specific procurement manager's performance metrics, if there is no unique budget code to fund local job fairs, and if the general contractor faces no contractual penalty for missing the mark, the commitment dissolves during the first week of site mobilization, when the crew arrives on site and construction operations begin.

To survive the pressures of project delivery, a priority requires a system of defense. When a technical constraint or a cost overrun threatens a project, structural components survive because they have engineers legally liable for their performance, procurement codes tied to their sourcing, and review gates that prevent the project from advancing if they are compromised. Social priorities rarely have this protection. If a metric has no accountable owner to defend it, no unique budget code to fund it, no dedicated review gate to verify it, and no material consequence for its erasure, it cannot withstand the pressure of a delivery cycle. The system does not need to declare war on human outcomes; it simply drops them through the holes left in the operating plan.

The question taken offline

There is a specific kind of silence that occurs in meetings when a question about human consequence comes up without accompanying paperwork. It is a polite, understated, bureaucratic kind of silence. The room pauses for a moment while the people in it work out where, administratively speaking, the question is meant to go.

The questions are usually surface-level. They sound standard, even mundane:

- *Do we know why Vendor B's pricing is so much lower than the others?*

- *Are we confident the construction team can hit this new milestone date?*
- *Management is asking if we can fast-track the design phase. Can we pull this off without increasing our headcount?*

The room registers the question. Laptops stay open. People look down at their notes. No one argues, but no one answers either. Then someone says, "Let's *take that offline*." And the meeting continues.

The phrase is effective because it sounds collaborative. It implies that the issue deserves dedicated attention, just not here, not now, not inside the workings of the decision currently on the table. The question has not been rejected; it has been moved somewhere soft enough that it can no longer interrupt the process. The minutes will record that the item passed without amendment.

People learn the boundaries of a room quickly. Researchers call this organizational silence: people hold back what they know when raising it would cost them, or when they sense the room is not listening. The junior designer learns not to ask about the user experience unless it is pre-coded into the brief. The procurement officer learns to ignore a suspiciously low bid unless it triggers a specific compliance risk code.

Failing to measure is sometimes how the system protects itself, and it only looks like an oversight. Not knowing keeps the project moving on schedule. At least for a while.

What gets spent first

When a boardroom announces a budget cut, a reduced staffing model, or a compressed timeline as a victory of efficiency, the work has usually just moved to the next available place in the system.

In a project schedule, this can look almost harmless. A deadline moves forward by two weeks. The milestone still appears achievable. No one writes “sleep loss” or “safety compression” into the project plan. But somewhere downstream, the missing time is absorbed by a subcontractor working longer shifts, a junior team member redrawing details late at night, or a facilities team inheriting a handover package that was never properly completed. The system records speed. People absorb the missing slack.

Every organization depends on reserves that rarely appear in the formal ledger: sleep, health, care, trust, attention, and endurance. These reserves make output possible. When the accounting boundary excludes them, their depletion can look like productivity.

The second window in the hospital project stayed with me because it taught me something I have seen again and again since: evidence is not enough if the system has no way to carry it. And when the system leaves human impact behind, the cost does not disappear. It travels.

The next chapter follows what happens when those reserves are spent down long enough to return as visible cost.

Netherlandish Proverbs, 1559

Pieter Bruegel the Elder

CHAPTER 5

THE COST COMES BACK

What costs return later when a decision appears cheaper today?

Once I looked beyond individual projects, I began to see the same pattern writing itself across global headlines, most vividly in the collapse of the British infrastructure firm Carillion. Here was a multi-billion-pound company whose footprint touched millions of daily lives, laying motorway asphalt, cleaning school corridors, and managing public hospital wards under long-term government contracts. For years, it sat at the center of a vast network of subcontractors, fabricators, suppliers, and smaller construction firms whose own commercial survival depended on Carillion paying its bills on time.

Carillion did not pay its bills on time. For years it stretched its payment terms further and further, requiring many suppliers to wait 120 days or more for payment on work already completed, while continuing to bid aggressively for new contracts on margins it could not deliver. When the company collapsed in January 2018, it owed roughly two billion pounds to some 30,000 suppliers, subcontractors, and short-term creditors, most of whom had been carrying the company's stretched payment terms for years on the assumption that the relationship would eventually recover. The British government provided around £150 million in funding to keep essential public services running through the liquidation, and the company's pension schemes were left with a shortfall estimated at roughly £800 million to £900 million. None of this appeared on the savings ledger of any single procurement decision. It appeared as the cumulative return of a thousand decisions to push margin and risk outward, recorded under different categories until the categories themselves stopped holding.

Not every complex executive decision can be reduced to a single corporate misstep; what makes the case relevant here is how an organization protects the appearance of its internal performance by moving risk outward. For years the central ledger looked lean because everyone around it was carrying the weight it had pushed off. When the collapse caught up with the spreadsheet, the physical work did not vanish. Hospitals still had to be cleaned and managed, schools still had to function, and roads, prisons, and public infrastructure still required daily maintenance.

The work does not disappear

An executive directive to slash expenses often means that managers are left to close the gap, often by asking their teams to carry more. Squeezing a supplier's margin to satisfy immediate shareholder pressure looks efficient during a quarterly earnings call, but a physical asset or a human workforce cannot reconfigure itself at the speed of a corporate decree. The near-term financial target is met on paper, but the real-world demand travels down the chain until it finds a human shock absorber.

This means that the financial model balances perfectly, but the work itself does not move with it. Relocating a cost only moves it, and the cost itself remains.

This dynamic can be understood through structural engineering. Remove a column from a building to save money or create more space, and the weight of the roof does not disappear. It shifts to the surrounding beams and columns. If they have spare capacity, the structure may hold. If they are already near their limits, stress accumulates in places not designed to carry it, creating deformation long before a visible crack appears.

The cost returns

Omitted human and operating costs rarely return to the original budget wearing their original name. They convert into separate, seemingly disconnected liabilities that arrive through different administrative doors, and executives routinely treat them as entirely novel crises when they are really the predictable return of historical trade-offs.

When a team is pushed past its capacity to meet a short-term target, the initial data entry records a minor labor efficiency. But the design eventually runs the other way: modern corporate accounting is built to push human costs off the balance sheet without tracking them. This gap, between what organizations record and what they actually consume from their people, is where liability silently accumulates.

The numbers show this, particularly when it comes to employee turnover:

- **The Hidden Cost Of Replacement:** Replacing an employee costs far more than the salary line suggests. The Center for American Progress estimates replacement costs range from 16% of annual salary for lower-wage roles to 213% for the most senior and specialized positions.
- **The Industry Average:** For most positions, the Work Institute places the real cost of losing an employee at roughly one-third of their base salary.

The cumulative toll of this extraction creates an enormous liability across the global system. Gallup estimates that low engagement costs the global economy $10 trillion in lost productivity, roughly 9% of global GDP.

This extraction draws down on three specific hidden reserves that exist entirely outside the reporting boundaries of the firm:

- **The Sleep Subsidy:** We have built an economy that values constant availability, rewards the response sent at 11 at night, and treats exhaustion as a sign of seriousness. The cost accumulates in the people producing the output and eventually reaches the wider economy. A study of the United States, United Kingdom, Canada, Germany, and Japan estimated that insufficient sleep costs their economies up to a combined $680 billion a year in lost output, including as much as $411 billion in the United States alone.
- **The Health Externalization:** The high-intensity sprint, the heroic launch, the quarter where the team gave everything,

all of these produce visible results. They also produce a bill, and the bill is paid somewhere else. Researchers estimate that workplace stressors account for between $125 billion and $190 billion of annual healthcare spending in the United States, or 5% to 8% of the national total, much of it borne by public systems and private families while the employers whose conditions produced the stress bear little of it. For enterprises using self-insured health programs, this bill routes directly back to the originating company, landing on the balance sheet the following fiscal year in the form of increased premiums. The cost is never truly avoided; it waits in the system, gains interest, and re-enters the balance sheet disguised as an attrition premium, a quality defect tax, or a project write-down.

- **The Care Gap:** The workforce that an organization counts as its own is held in place by a second workforce that an organization does not count at all. Meals prepared, children raised, parents tended to, households kept functional. Oxfam calculated that the unpaid care work performed by women aged 15 and over is worth at least $10.8 trillion a year, valued conservatively at minimum wage, and noted that this is almost certainly an underestimate.

Much of this care is unpaid. And when it is paid, domestic work has also long been treated as informal and invisible, even though households and formal economies depend on it. Domestic workers organized to change that. Myrtle Witbooi, a South African domestic worker who became a global labor leader, helped campaign for ILO Convention 189, adopted in 2011 as the first international standard extending basic labor protections to domestic workers. She insisted that domestic work be recognized as work, and that the people doing it receive the same protections as other workers.

How much of the wider care burden is absorbed collectively varies by country. In Sweden, parental leave, sick pay, and a safe working environment are statutory, funded and enforced by the state, with parental benefit payable for 480 days per child. In the United Kingdom a worker can take up to 52 weeks of maternity leave, 39 weeks of it paid by law. But these protections attach to the employment contract, and enterprises have spent decades moving work outside that contract, into subcontracts, agencies, and supply chains where the floor thins with every tier. When Carillion collapsed, that same law still protected the people it directly employed; the 30,000 suppliers and subcontractors who had carried its payment terms had no such contract and absorbed the loss.

Borrowing from human capacity

Software engineers have a name for this: technical debt. The term emerged in 1992 to describe the long-term penalty an organization pays when it ships a quick, imperfect solution today that defers the more complete one that would have taken longer. The temporary fix helps the team meet an immediate release milestone, but it leaves behind a compromised architecture. When not planned well, over time, the software becomes brittle, bugs multiply, and future development slows because every new feature must navigate a web of unstable code. The organization pays compound interest on the debt until the core system is refactored. The metaphor has since been extended to other domains. It has been applied to machine-learning systems, where debt accumulates through data dependencies and feedback loops rather than code alone.

> ***Social debt works the same way, applied to people. Where financial debt borrows money from the future and technical debt borrows engineering capacity, social debt borrows human capacity, and like both of its predecessors, it accrues interest.***

Because financial reports don't usually track the people underneath, the asset looks productive right up until it fails.

Who can refuse?

The simplest way to see where pressure will land is to ask who has the power to refuse it. Pressure rarely spreads evenly across an organization or supply chain. It moves downward until it reaches someone who cannot pass it on.

For much of the last century, unions have provided a collective answer to that problem. At their strongest, they do more than negotiate benefits for members. They are a counterweight in systems that might otherwise treat labor only as a cost to reduce. By organizing workers collectively, unions make wages, safety, scheduling, and worker voice harder to exclude from the calculation. A worker at the bottom of a supply chain may have little power to say no alone. Organized workers have more, because the refusal is shared and the cost of ignoring it is greater.

But that protection is uneven. Many contractors, agency staff, migrant workers, and people further down supply chains have no union and may not even be employed by the company setting the terms of their work.

This gap has widened with the rise of the fissured workplace, a system in which large institutions move core functions, including manufacturing, logistics, maintenance, and janitorial services, outside direct employment and into layers of subcontractors and suppliers.

When a supply chain becomes lopsided, power is measured by who gets to pass the pain down the line. The lead company sets an impossible date; the supplier accepts it because they cannot afford to lose the contract; the warehouse manager pushes the night shift to work longer hours to hit it. The burden moves down like water, settling at the very bottom of the chain where people lack the power to push back.

A symmetrical system behaves in the opposite direction. It is defined by three characteristics:

- **A Shared Speed Limit:** The schedule is set by the real capacity of the people doing the work, not by the urgency of the person at the top. If the lead company wants to move faster, it must fund additional capacity, reduce the scope, or renegotiate the timeline rather than simply passing the pressure down.
- **Visible Margins:** There are no information silos. The lead company doesn't negotiate in the dark to squeeze the supplier's thin slice of profit. Both sides look at the same math, ensuring that a spike in raw material costs or a local crisis doesn't bankrupt the smallest player while the parent company maintains its pristine dividend.

- **Protected Friction:** A ground-level worker or a small supplier can flag a safety risk or an impossible workload without fearing the termination of their contract. The truth does not get you fired; it pauses the machine so both parties can fix the breakdown together.

Symmetry is a matter of mutual exposure, and it does not depend on corporate kindness. A supply chain becomes safe when the lead company's spreadsheet is tied to the subcontractor's ground-level reality, so that if the bottom of the chain is forced to bleed, the top of the chain loses its margin.

When responsibility crosses a boundary

In 2005, Boeing sold its Wichita fuselage operation, creating Spirit AeroSystems and moving a major part of aircraft production outside the company. That decision alone does not explain what happened years later. Aviation safety is far too complex for that. But it did create a new boundary between the company designing and assembling the aircraft and the supplier building much of the fuselage.

On January 5, 2024, an Alaska Airlines Boeing 737 MAX 9 took off from Portland. At about 16,000 feet, a door plug, a fixed panel installed where an optional exit door could have been placed, tore away from the side of the aircraft. The cabin rapidly decompressed, and loose objects were pulled through the opening. The crew returned safely to Portland. No one was killed, and the two seats beside the plug happened to be empty.

The National Transportation Safety Board (NTSB) found that the four bolts meant to secure the plug had not been installed when the aircraft left the factory. The plug had been opened at Boeing's facility so that rivet work completed by Spirit could be repaired. It was then closed without the bolts being replaced. The work was also not properly documented. The NTSB linked the failure to weaknesses in Boeing's manufacturing process, training, and coordination with Spirit.

The mistake moved through several layers of the system without anyone catching it. Responsibility was divided across companies, teams, and processes. At each handoff, the risk of missed information grew.

When an industrial operation is under constant pressure to move faster and cut costs, experienced mechanics and inspectors may leave. Training can weaken. More work may be passed to contractors. Important knowledge becomes scattered, and documentation gaps begin to appear.

A failure in a complex system rarely begins at the moment something breaks. It often starts years earlier, through decisions that weaken coordination, oversight, and resilience. The risk may remain hidden for a long time. Then one day, it becomes visible.

Trust runs out

Trust is one of the primary human reserves organizations routinely spend long before they realize they are spending it. Because trust is a baseline condition and does not appear as a line item, its depletion is gradual and difficult to capture on a standard risk dashboard. For long periods, the system appears entirely stable:

- Employees keep stretching their hours to cover staffing gaps.
- Suppliers keep absorbing unfavorable contract terms to protect long-term relationships.
- Communities keep participating in standard consultation processes.
- Customers keep accepting the organization's public sustainability claims.
- Workers keep raising internal quality and safety concerns through standard channels.

Then the reserve runs out. The shift is rarely gradual. People stop sharing important context in meetings because they know the room will not act on it. Suppliers stop absorbing last-minute changes and begin enforcing contracts strictly. Communities organize against projects. Experienced employees leave, taking years of unwritten knowledge with them. Customers go elsewhere.

Trust is treated as free until its absence becomes a business risk.

Social debt

By the time social debt returns to the organization that created it, it usually appears under a different name. Leaders see a write-down, supply-chain disruption, quality failure, lawsuit, protest, or retention crisis and describe it as unexpected.

Sometimes it is. More often, it is the delayed cost of a decision that was once praised as efficient. It arrives in a later fiscal year, under a new leadership team, and in a form that makes the original cause harder to see.

The missing hospital window and the costs Carillion passed on to its smallest suppliers reflect the same structural problem. When social value is left out of a decision, the cost moves through the system until it returns as something the business can no longer ignore.

Identifying the problem, though, is only a beginning.

The next chapter introduces the People Positive Spectrum, a practical framework for understanding what operations produce under pressure and for spotting the warning signs before the system begins to fail.

The 5 classical orders, 1762

Encyclopédie of Diderot and d'Alembert

CHAPTER 6

THE PEOPLE POSITIVE SPECTRUM

What do our decisions produce under pressure?

Over the past 30 years, those of us working across the built environment have become much more disciplined about asking *the question: what does this decision mean for the planet*? That question has reshaped our products, specifications, rating systems, building codes, investor expectations, and the decisions we can defend in front of a chief financial officer.

But it is not the only question. Beside it sits another that matters just as much: *what does this decision do to people*? If we measure carbon while leaving human impact scattered across systems that cannot easily carry it, the data that travels will continue to shape the decision.

That is where the risk begins. The problem is not the climate transition, which is urgent and necessary. The risk is that we deliver it through systems that can see environmental impact clearly but recognize human impact only in fragments.

The climate transition is driving the largest deployment of capital into the physical world in living memory. The systems built through that investment will determine who carries its costs for decades.

When the measurement of human impact remains fragmented, people make up the difference. Workers absorb compressed schedules. Installers carry the risks of unfamiliar materials without enough training. Maintenance teams inherit systems that weren't properly resourced. Suppliers are expected to meet new environmental requirements without the commercial margin to do so well. Communities absorb disruption in the name of progress without always receiving the benefits they were promised.

What can we do differently? We can build human impact into the decisions that shape everyday work, so that stable and equitable conditions count as part of performance, settled while the work is being planned and not held over as an outcome to weigh later.

The People Positive Spectrum is a framework for doing that. It offers a practical way to examine who benefits from a decision, who carries its burdens, and what those patterns reveal about the system producing them. It is designed to make human impact easier to see across projects, operations, and supply chains, especially in places where it is often dispersed across technical documents, budgets, contracts, and performance data.

The Spectrum tracks movement, not a fixed position. The aim is to see whether a decision is becoming more extractive, holding steady, or moving in a more people-positive direction. A single score would settle the matter as a static verdict, when what we care about is the direction an organization is traveling. Human outcomes can change as budgets tighten, timelines shift, and new evidence emerges.

The practical question is: what would make this decision more people-positive? A spectrum also acknowledges a basic reality of living systems: the work is never fully done. There is no static endpoint called success that lets us close the book and walk away. What matters is the direction of the trend and the willingness to self-correct. The Spectrum is intuitive, meaning no special background is needed; anyone on a project team can quickly see whether a live choice is drawing down human capacity or building it up.

The missing axis

Carbon accounting gave sustainability a shared way to measure environmental performance. At the bottom of the scale are high emissions, waste, and ecological damage. At the top are efficient design, circular systems, and low-carbon performance. Its influence comes from making environmental impact easier to count, compare, and carry into decisions.

But environmental performance is only one part of the picture. To understand the full impact of a major decision, we also need a horizontal axis for human impact. This axis asks whether a project or operation depletes human capacity or strengthens it.

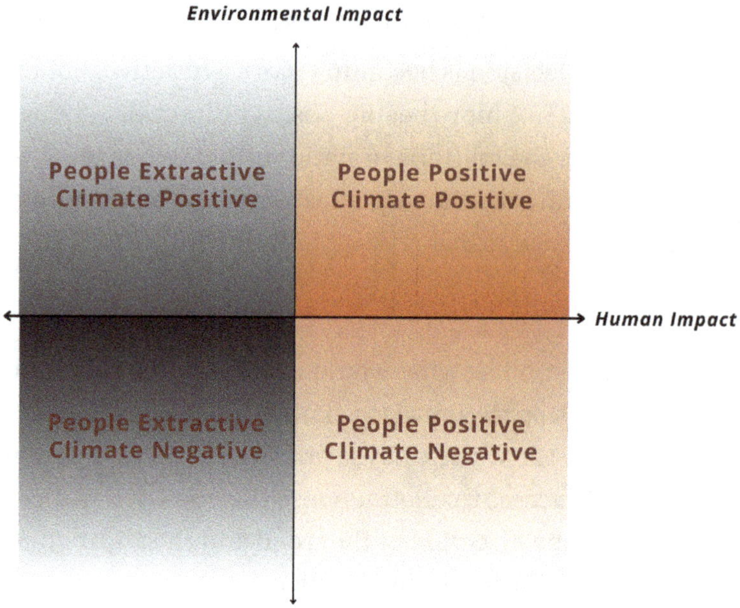

Together, the two axes create four quadrants:

- **Lower Left—Extractive On Both Fronts:** High environmental harm is combined with weak labor protections, unsafe conditions, and accelerated timelines.
- **Lower Right—Socially Supportive But Environmentally Incomplete:** People benefit from stable work, fair wages, or strong protections, while the operation remains tied to high emissions or ecological damage.
- **Upper Left—Environmentally Positive But Socially Extractive:** Environmental gains are achieved by shifting costs and risks onto workers, suppliers, or communities with limited power to refuse them.
- **Upper Right—A Just Transition:** Environmental progress and human benefit are pursued together, creating a low-carbon economy that is equitable in who bears its costs and who receives its gains.

Elements of this social axis already exist in human-rights due diligence, equity indicators, public-health metrics, and social lifecycle assessments. But they are often separated from the budgets, contracts, and operating decisions that determine what happens in practice.

The World Benchmarking Alliance's 2023 Corporate Human Rights Benchmark found that 85% of assessed companies included human-rights expectations in supplier contracts, while only 39% committed to responsible purchasing practices of their own and 27% engaged affected rights holders in due diligence. The problem is not simply that social data is unavailable. It is that the data often lacks the authority to shape the decision.

Green is not automatically People Positive

Environmental standards matter. The next question is whether the systems used to verify environmental performance also show who can participate and who gets left out.

The use and certification of mass timber shows how the human-impact axis can play out in a real project. The term refers to engineered wood systems that can replace steel or concrete in some buildings. The 2021 International Building Code permitted tall mass timber construction of up to 18 stories, helping make its use more commercially viable. Studies have found that constructing a building with mass timber can generate fewer greenhouse gas emissions than constructing a comparable building with steel or concrete.

Project teams often ask for third-party certification to confirm that the timber was harvested responsibly. That certification costs money, and smaller forest owners tend to pay far more for it.

One study in the Americas found that forests smaller than 4,000 hectares paid median annual certification costs of between $6.45 and $39.31 per hectare. Forests larger than 400,000 hectares paid between $0.07 and $0.49 per hectare. Per hectare, certification could therefore cost a small producer around 100 times more than a large industrial company.

A family-run forest may have cared for the same land responsibly for generations. It can still be shut out of the certified market because it cannot afford to prove its practices in the required format.

The certification system may accurately identify environmental value while making it harder for smaller producers to have their value recognized. The Forest Stewardship Council has introduced group certification to lower the burden. Even so, smaller producers face much higher certification costs per hectare than large industrial companies.

The floor of harm prevention

The practice of human rights due diligence gives this work a necessary floor. Under the UN Guiding Principles on Business and Human Rights, organizations are expected to identify, prevent, mitigate, and account for adverse human rights impacts across their operations and value chains, as a baseline expectation of responsible conduct that applies whether or not an organization chooses to aspire to it.

That floor matters. Without it, any conversation about social value becomes too soft to trust, and the Spectrum itself has no stable ground beneath it.

> ***But social value does not stop at harm prevention. Avoiding harm is the minimum condition of operating responsibly, a different thing from creating durable human benefit. The Spectrum asks the next question: who benefits, who carries the burden, and whether people are left better off because the system exists, not just less harmed than they might have been.***

The pattern beneath the promise

In the 1880s, the industrialist George Pullman built what appeared to be a model future on the American prairie.

The town of Pullman was engineered as a complete, self-contained industrial community. While thousands of manufacturing workers in nearby Chicago lived in crowded tenements defined by soot, noise, and poor sanitation, Pullman's employees moved into brick houses with indoor plumbing, gas lighting, paved streets, and public parks. The town included its own library, a theater, and civic spaces designed to project order and permanence. It drew international visitors who traveled to see what corporate benevolence looked like when an enterprise chose to resource the whole life of its workforce going beyond the hours those workers spent on the factory floor.

From the outside, the town looked advanced. The housing was superior and the streets were clean. The company had built a real-world asset that visibly upgraded the daily environment of its inhabitants.

The ledger shifted, however, when the numbers were read as a single system.

Pullman employed the workers and also controlled much of the life surrounding their work. The town tied housing, utilities, and daily consumption into the same corporate loop. Employees lived in company-owned buildings, paid rent directly back to their employer, and purchased food through a local commercial economy that Pullman managed. A significant portion of the wages paid out by the manufacturing plant flowed back into the financial ledger of the firm.

For a time, this closed loop could be presented as care. It provided a safer physical environment than the urban alternatives available to the workforce. But it also concentrated structural leverage. The same enterprise that determined the wage also determined the rent. The same corporate system that appeared to offer a social benefit captured that value back through the terms attached to its occupancy.

When the economic depression of 1893 arrived, the arrangement broke apart. Pullman cut manufacturing wages sharply to protect the company's cash reserves, but he left the rent rates in the town unchanged. The decision treated the workers as employees when corporate costs needed to fall, and as tenants when corporate revenues needed to remain intact. The two identities were separated administratively on the spreadsheet, even though they belonged to the very same people.

For the families living in the town, that administrative split was a physical fiction. Rent deductions continued to be pulled directly from reduced paychecks before the wages were distributed. Household costs and grocery bills remained fixed. A model community became an economic trap, and what was built to demonstrate corporate stewardship became the exact means of enforcing dependence.

This resulted in a strike in 1894. Wages were documented, rents were filed, deductions were tracked, and prices were clear. Each piece of data could be defended on its own narrow terms. The problem was that the facts lived in isolated moral and administrative columns: wages belonged to the manufacturing division, rent belonged to the real estate division, and housing quality belonged to the public relations narrative of benevolence.

When the United States Strike Commission investigated the conflict, it did not uncover missing ledgers. Instead, it placed the existing ledgers next to one another. Once wages, rents, automatic payroll deductions, and worker testimonies were analyzed as a unified network, the pattern became clear. The extraction had not been hidden. It had been distributed.

The closed loop eventually collapsed under external pressure. In 1898, the Illinois Supreme Court ruled that the company could not lawfully own and operate the town, and ordered Pullman to divest its non-industrial property, a process that took the better part of a decade to complete. The reckoning arrived because the state refused to look at the manufacturing and property divisions as isolated administrative columns.

That distinction is important. The Pullman case illustrates why social value cannot be evaluated by looking at a single, isolated benefit. Better housing, indoor plumbing, and manicured parks mattered to the people who used them. But those physical assets did not erase the underlying distribution of risk, the asymmetries of power, or the direction of the financial return. A system can easily create a real benefit in one dimension while steadily drawing down human capacity in another.

Reading the pattern

The People Positive Spectrum examines what an operational system actually produces under pressure rather than ranking companies morally or measuring corporate virtue or stated intent.

It asks whether a system creates value by depleting human capacity, limits itself to avoiding visible harm, or actively builds durable human benefit.

To apply the Spectrum, we need to know where to look. In the built environment, social value does not sit in one place. It appears across a chain of decisions made by different teams, at different stages, and through different budgets.

In Chapter 2, we looked at five windows for interpreting human impact: physiology, equity, human rights, civic life, and financial risk. Those windows help us understand what an impact means. The five sites that follow show where that impact appears in practice: People, Place, Product, Partners, and Public Good.

- **People** are the workers, occupants, users, caregivers, service teams, and others whose daily lives are shaped by the system.
- **Place** is the physical setting: the building, site, neighborhood, infrastructure, and spatial conditions in which people live and work.
- **Product** is what gets designed, specified, manufactured, installed, used, maintained, and eventually removed.
- **Partners** are the contractors, suppliers, consultants, operators, and other organizations responsible for carrying part of the work.
- **Public Good** is the wider civic effect: what the project contributes to shared life, local resilience, access, trust, and long-term community benefit.

Read these as places to look across a system, each one a vantage point on where value is made and where burden lands. A single decision may create benefit in one area while transferring the burden to another. The Spectrum helps make that pattern visible.

People Extractive

A people-extractive system creates value for one group by drawing down the health, safety, dignity, time, trust, opportunity, or resilience of another.

Performance is achieved by consuming people's effort and capacity faster than they can recover, while treating that capacity as free and uncounted.

This can appear across all five areas:

- **People:** An accelerated construction schedule is carried by subcontractors working extended shifts because the delivery date is treated as fixed. A logistics warehouse operates a night shift with a skeleton crew after a headcount freeze. A hospital cleaning team is expected to cover three floors instead of two after a facilities contract is renegotiated on price alone.
- **Place:** A flagship office tower performs well for tenants and investors while service crews work in poorly ventilated back-of-house spaces. A distribution center is designed for performance, with minimal rest areas, weak lighting, and long walking distances that contribute to physical strain over time. In a large independent survey of Amazon warehouse workers, 41% reported an on-the-job injury, and 69% said they had taken unpaid time off because of pain or exhaustion in the previous month. A school may meet indoor air quality standards while never evaluating the experience of the custodial staff who spend their working day inside it.

- **Product:** A flooring product reduces chemical exposure for occupants while installers absorb the risk through the adhesives used during installation. A recycled material carries a strong environmental story while the labor conditions involved in extracting its feedstock remain undocumented. An automated procurement platform lowers sourcing costs while favoring suppliers that can already afford the cost of compliance, excluding smaller operators that cannot.

- **Partners:** A low-cost bid is possible only because a lower-tier supplier has compressed wages, reduced safety margins, or absorbed unpaid overtime. A garment factory accepts a last-minute order increase at the same unit price because losing the account would be worse. A small timber supplier accepts extended payment terms that protect the buyer's working capital while weakening its own.
- **Public Good:** An infrastructure project improves regional connectivity while pricing out the community that absorbed years of disruption during construction. An urban regeneration scheme delivers new amenities and rising asset values, but the gains flow mainly to incoming residents and institutional investors. A green retrofit improves an asset's environmental rating while passing costs to tenants through higher service charges.

A system can be People Extractive without anyone intending harm. Intent does not determine the category.

A project manager or purchasing officer may be following instructions exactly, reducing risk and meeting every target. But when the reporting boundary allows the human cost of those targets to remain outside the spreadsheet, the system will continue to reward extraction.

People Neutral

A people-neutral system avoids obvious harm and meets expected rules, but it does not yet examine the full human consequences of how value is produced.

It may be compliant, measured, and defensible within its stated scope. But it does not reliably create durable human benefit or track where burdens are being transferred beyond that scope.

This often appears through conventional compliance measures:

- **People:** A well-being program is available to permanent employees and reported in the annual sustainability disclosure, while subcontracted workers on the same site cannot access it.
- **Place:** A certified building performs well within its measured environmental criteria, but its evaluation does not consistently include the experience of maintenance and facilities staff working in service areas.
- **Product:** A product carries credible health and environmental certifications, but no one assesses the conditions under which it is installed or the end-of-life burden transferred to the municipality that must manage it.
- **Partners:** Supplier codes, social audits, and responsible-sourcing clauses are built into contracts, but purchasing terms and pricing models remain unchanged. Procurement continues to reward the lowest upfront cost, while audits fail to identify recruitment debt or illegal placement fees charged before workers reach the factory floor.

- **Public Good:** A community development project produces extensive outreach records, public amenities, and polished engagement reports, but creates little lasting benefit for local residents, businesses, or the wider local economy.

Neutral is where many systems begin: compliant, bounded, and not yet examining what sits outside the frame.

People Positive

A people-positive system is designed so that human benefit is built into how performance is achieved, present in the design of the work well before any harm could appear. In such systems, stable and equitable human conditions are built into the operating model before constraints tighten.

To achieve a people-positive pattern, an organization integrates human conditions directly into its definition of success:

- **People:** Safety, fair compensation, predictable schedules, adequate recovery time, transparent advancement opportunities, and effective management are designed into daily operations and treated as part of the core work, so they do not sit apart as separate human resources initiatives. The subcontracted workforce is included in the same well-being and safety protocols as direct employees, because employment status should not determine whose health and safety count.
- **Place:** A people-positive space includes ways to identify human friction early, treating behavioral workarounds and occupant strain as live signals for improving design or

operations before the burden becomes normalized. Back-of-house areas receive the same design attention as tenant floors, because the people who maintain the building may spend more continuous hours in it than many of the people who occupy it.

- **Product:** A healthier material does not create real-world impact simply because it exists in a catalog. Its value also depends on the safety of the people manufacturing it, the conditions under which it is installed, the burden of maintaining it over its operational life, and the end-of-life obligations it passes to whoever receives it last. The specification includes installation guidance, training requirements, and disposal protocols as standard deliverables, not optional appendices.
- **Partners:** Commercial contracts are structured so that better human conditions are supported by stable purchasing practices, rather than imposed as an administrative demand on lower-tier vendors without the resources to fund them. Payment terms are set to protect supplier liquidity, not simply to improve buyer cash flow.
- **Public Good:** At the community level, a project measures its performance by its capacity to help existing residents remain, strengthen the local economy, and ensure that a long-term share of the physical and financial value stays within the neighborhood. Legacy residents hold a binding governance role, not only a place in the consultation process.

We see this shift when a hospital standard explicitly protects both staff support spaces and patient outcomes within the primary capital budget, acknowledging that caregiver fatigue can affect care quality and patient outcomes. It appears when a procurement contract funds the labor standards it demands, using stable pricing to reduce pressures that might otherwise be passed to the workforce. It takes form when a community-benefit structure gives legacy residents a legally binding role in long-term governance, rather than treating them as an approval step in a public relations exercise.

> ***People Positive does not mean perfect. It means the system has a way to see, respond to, and improve when human burden appears. It means the system has been built to learn from its own strain.***

One system, many coordinates

Our instinct with any framework is to convert it into a static checklist or score. But the Spectrum does not label an organization as good or bad. It reads a pattern. Large enterprises are rarely homogeneous. They are complex, fragmented networks of decisions, which means that different positions on the Spectrum can exist within the same system at the same time.

A multinational corporation can be demonstrably People Positive in its direct employment practices, providing excellent wages and comprehensive health benefits to its corporate staff, while operating a supply chain that remains fundamentally People Extractive.

A flagship corporate headquarters can be People Positive for the tenants who occupy its sunlit office floors, while remaining People Neutral or People Extractive for the subcontracted facilities crews who clean its mechanical bays at midnight. The word "occupant" carries a decision inside it. If the definition of a "user" is drawn so tightly that it excludes maintenance teams, the building's performance depends on a hidden human subsidy.

A building product can be significantly healthier in use, reducing harmful toxins for occupants, while failing to address hazardous working conditions at the raw-material extraction stage or passing burden to a local municipality.

A major municipal transit project can be environmentally positive, reducing regional emissions and improving urban connectivity, while remaining socially extractive if it creates market pressures that price out the working-class community that spent years absorbing the disruption of its construction. The diagnostic value of the Spectrum lies in its capacity to show this multi-layered complexity without flattening it into a generic corporate score.

The People Positive Spectrum gives us a way to diagnose the pattern. The next question is where to use it in practice. Part 2 applies the framework to the five recurring sites where social value becomes visible in the built environment: People, Place, Product, Partners, and Public Good.

The strongest objections

Before applying the People Positive Spectrum, we need to be honest about where a framework like this can fail. Measurement can create the appearance of progress without changing the conditions people experience.

A metric can be collected, published, and displayed on a polished dashboard without changing a single budget, contract, or project decision. The People Positive Spectrum is useful only when the information it produces can influence what gets questioned, funded, approved, changed, or refused.

Five objections matter here. The first three concern how measurement works in practice. The final two objections go deeper. They ask whether a tool operating inside the system can change the incentives that system was designed to protect, and whether access to the tool itself will remain open.

1. The checkbox trap

Anyone who has worked on a major project has seen how fatigue, frustration, and operational strain are cleaned up as information moves through a reporting chain. For example, consider a construction crew that describes exhaustion, rushed work, and repeated safety workarounds. The site report records a capacity concern. The quarterly dashboard turns that concern into a percentage. By the time the finding reaches leadership, the daily reality that produced it has largely disappeared.

A clean metric can sit on top of a deeply strained system.

Moving beyond passive reporting means giving human-impact data authority inside the decisions that shape the work. A serious concern should be able to trigger a review, change the weighting of a bid, or delay an approval until the risk has been addressed.

That means the question is: *what information is allowed to change?*

2. The cost of proof

The cost of proving responsible practice is rarely distributed evenly.

As the certification example earlier in this chapter showed, a small family forest may pay far more per hectare for verification than a large industrial operator. The same standard applies to both, while the cost of entering the system can be dramatically different.

A local supplier may have years of strong practice, trusted relationships, and deep knowledge of its region. It can still remain invisible to a buyer because it cannot afford to translate that work into the required forms, audits, and certifications. The buyer is then left with a narrower pool of larger companies that already have compliance teams and reporting systems.

When an organization asks suppliers to produce additional evidence, it should also ask what that evidence costs to create. In some cases, the buyer may need to fund or share the cost of verification. Otherwise, a standard designed to recognize good practice may exclude some of the people already doing the work well.

3. The limits of the tools

A supplier code or vendor questionnaire cannot repair a contract whose economics make responsible delivery impossible.

Global supply chains run through layers of contractors, subcontractors, factories, labor brokers, and temporary workers.

Most standard audits reach only part of that chain. A signed compliance form offers limited protection when the purchasing team continues to demand prices and lead times that leave no room to meet the conditions written on the page.

Safe work, fair wages, careful documentation, and rapid delivery all cost something. A budget that funds none of them still expects the supplier to produce all four.

The buyer's daily decisions shape the human conditions downstream. Price, payment speed, forecasting, lead times, and late changes determine how much room a supplier has to protect its workforce. When those choices contradict the standards in the contract, the contract becomes a promise the supplier is expected to fund alone. Sourcing tools can drive change when the commercial agreement pays for the conditions it requires.

4. The incentive objection

The strongest objection to this book is that it may be operating at the wrong level of the problem.

A social-value question can be written into a bid package, weighted, and scored, and the cheapest bid may still win, because price accounts for 60% of the score and the social question is worth two. The process produces a paragraph in the file confirming that human impact was considered. The project proceeds in exactly the same way. The form changed. The results remained the same.

The field was left off the form by design. Passing costs on to other people is where much of the profit comes from in many industries. For example, a firm that pays honestly for a subcontractor's night shift will often lose the bid to one that does not. The pressure to cut costs comes first, and the form only reacts to it. Adding a new field changes nothing; it just gives that same pressure more paperwork to move through. This is not a fault in the system. It is the way the system is meant to work, because squeezing subcontractors, holding wages down, and ignoring the cost of chemical exposure are what pay the profit.

When we feel entirely powerless to change these terms, we are reading the system's design accurately. The power is concentrated at the top so that the people in the middle cannot easily say no.

Economist Milton Friedman gave this arrangement one of its clearest arguments in a 1970 essay for The New York Times Magazine. A business executive, he wrote, is responsible for increasing profit on behalf of the owners. Spending company resources on wider social goals amounted, in his framing, to imposing a tax without democratic authority.

That argument shaped generations of management thinking. It entered business education, executive targets, incentive plans, and the daily definition of a defensible decision. Over time, it became possible for a manager to leave a human cost outside the calculation while believing, correctly, that they were following the rules of the institution.

In 2019, 181 chief executives in the US Business Roundtable, an association of major corporate leaders, signed a statement declaring that corporations should serve all stakeholders. Researchers later examined what the signatories had changed inside their companies. In most cases, the statement had not reached the board, the governance documents, or the operating practices that determined how decisions were made. This is the decoupling argument arriving at the highest level of corporate leadership.

The objection is right about one thing: measurement alone cannot repair an economic model that rewards the transfer of human cost. The People Positive Spectrum cannot substitute for labor protections, collective bargaining, responsible purchasing, regulation, or changes in corporate governance. Its role is narrower: it makes the transfer visible early enough for someone to question it, price it, govern it, or refuse it.

I have three responses to the objection, although none fully resolves it:

- **Weighting Is Where the Real Impact Takes Place:** A social-value question is worth 2% of a scoring matrix because someone decided it was worth 2%, in a meeting, inside a document. That number can change. Carbon once carried no weight in most building procurement decisions. Today, it appears in specifications, investor requirements, rating systems, and bid evaluations because it became legible enough to argue for. Visibility does not guarantee funding, but it provides a starting point.
- **The Reality of Authority:** Few people working on a project can redefine what a company is permitted to record as profit. Many can change what the brief, contract, procurement form, specification, or scoring matrix leaves out this week. The document may already be open on their desk. Telling them to wait for a different economic

settlement would leave the current decision untouched, along with the people already carrying its consequences.

- **Understanding the Limits of Impact:** If the questions in this book improve the forms while leaving every transferred cost in place, the framework has failed. Visibility should lead toward responsibility, funding, and correction. When an impact becomes visible and no consequence follows, the result is a more polished description of the same injury.

5. The access test

The final objection is about my own stake in this work.

I developed the framework through Liveable, the company I founded, and I may benefit professionally if its use leads organizations to work with us. That could reasonably be perceived as a conflict of interest.

The question here is whether readers can use the frameworks without paying me. They can. Readers are free to use, teach, adapt, and challenge the frameworks in this book within their own work, with attribution. They do not require a license, certification, permission, or paid relationship with Liveable.

If people have to pay before their impact can be seen, this book has missed the point.

Recap of Part 1

We spend our professional careers trying to manage what we can see. In the climate conversation, that visibility improved by translating a complex environmental problem into a standardized ledger for carbon. The translation has its critics and its flaws, but it brought the conversation into the room, forced finance to listen to physics, and made climate change legible, trackable, and expensive to ignore in a boardroom.

That visibility remains incomplete. Human consequences that fall outside the main ledger may still be carried by workers, suppliers, occupants, households, and communities.

Part 1 traced that hidden debt. Diagnosis alone cannot change our daily work, so to close the gap between corporate intent and daily reality we need a tool that can map human capacity under live commercial pressure. That is the role of the People Positive Spectrum: a compass for reading what an enterprise is actually producing, choice by choice, before the budget locks.

Four points to carry forward

- **Every Decision Has an Impact.** Every line in a specification and every clause in a contract leaves a direct mark on human lives. Those consequences are present whether or not the project formally names them.
- **Compressing a Budget Or a Timeline Shifts the Load.** Changing a cell on a spreadsheet moves the work onto someone else; it does not make the work go away. When you cut margins, compress schedules, or freeze headcounts, the weight transfers to whoever is working with the least

room to refuse it. Hidden reserves like the sleep subsidy, the health externalization, and the care gap are the off-ledger accounts that fund the appearance of corporate efficiency.

- **Omissions Return As a Delayed Invoice.** When a system leaves human consequence out of its accounts, the cost changes its address. It waits in the system, accrues interest as social debt, and returns to the originating ledger wearing a different name: an attrition premium, a quality defect, a lawsuit, a project write-down, a community that stops cooperating.
- **The People Positive Spectrum Reads Patterns, Not Intentions.** It evaluates what a system is actually producing under pressure, not what it claims to value and not what it reports in the annual disclosure. A single organization can be People Positive for its corporate tenants and People Extractive for the overnight cleaning crew. The Spectrum holds both truths at once without flattening either into a score.

It helps to be clear about where that cost comes from. It is not the work of careless or cynical people. Most of the people inside these systems are competent and well-intentioned, working under real deadlines and real budgets, with tools that were never built to hold the human part. The omission is structural, which is the discouraging news and also the hopeful part, because a structure can be changed.

Authority is often fragmented across budgets, codes, contracts, schedules, and prior commitments. Even senior decision-makers may not be able to reopen all of them at once. Change becomes more possible when a question reaches the right person, at a point where the decision is still movable, with evidence that can be recorded and acted upon.

The People Positive Decision Check, set out in the Bonus Section at the end of the book, gathers the questions that the chapters in Part 2 apply across People, Place, Product, Partners, and Public Good:

- What does this decision do to the people who will use it?
- Who is making it, and what risks do they carry?
- What are we assuming and have not verified?
- Who absorbs the risk when the budget or timeline moves?
- Who should have a say before we decide?
- Could we defend the decision to occupants, the client, and the community?

Part 2: Assess applies those questions to the five recurring places where human impact becomes visible.

The People Positive Spectrum

Coordinate	Operating pattern	What may appear in practice
People Extractive	Achieves performance by consuming human capacity faster than it can recover	Unmeasured exhaustion, uncompensated risk, and high turnover
People Neutral	Meets defined legal and compliance requirements within a bounded scope	Important conditions outside that scope may remain unclear
People Positive	Integrates human conditions directly into its primary definition of operational success	Shared risk, protected capacity limits, and structural self-correction

Table 2. The People Positive Spectrum

PART 2

ASSESS

The first part of this book focused on diagnosis, tracing hidden reserves many organizations rely on: sleep deprivation, externalized health costs, and compressed procurement timelines.

We examined how human consequences can disappear from view when a budget tightens or a schedule slips.

Part 2 moves the focus from diagnosis to location: shifting from the broad theory of social debt to the specific places where choices harden into buildings, products, and contracts.

Dignity and human experience cannot be measured or reduced to a number. But the conditions that protect or erode them can be assessed, specified, funded, and changed. Leaving those conditions unexamined does not protect human dignity. It leaves important consequences outside the decision.

We are going to look at five sites where human consequence becomes tangible: **People, Place, Product, Partners, and Public Good.**

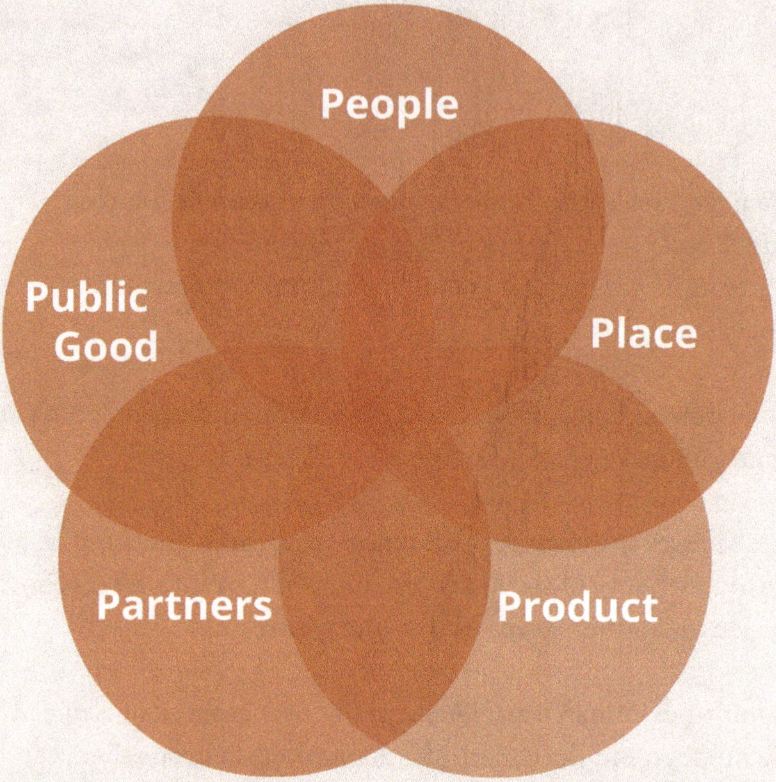

How to read the chapters that follow

To keep this field guide practical under real commercial pressure, every upcoming chapter runs through the two shared tools. Some chapters also introduce a tool specific to that site of impact. Think of them as a compass to diagnose the project, and a map to locate where you can act.

Tool 1: The People Positive Spectrum

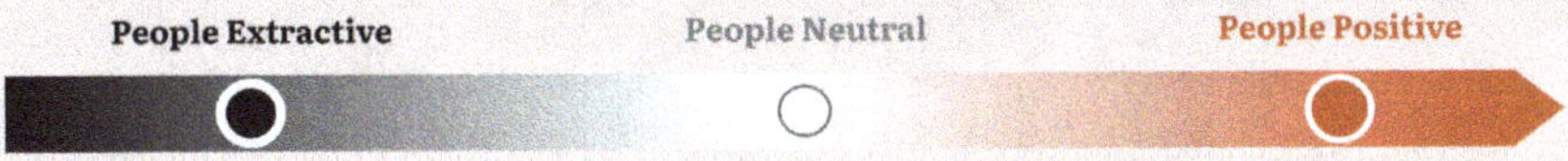

This tool asks what a decision is producing for people in practice.

- **People Extractive:** The project succeeds because people absorb the hidden cost. They work longer, take on more risk, or give up health, time, or stability so the budget or schedule can hold.
- **People Neutral:** The project meets the rules and avoids obvious harm but stops at compliance. It does not yet ask who else is affected or where the burden has been shifted.
- **People Positive:** The project is designed to succeed without depending on people to absorb hidden costs. Safe, fair, and stable conditions are planned, funded, and protected from the start.

Tool 2: The Circles of Responsibility

This tool helps locate responsibility in relation to the decision being examined:

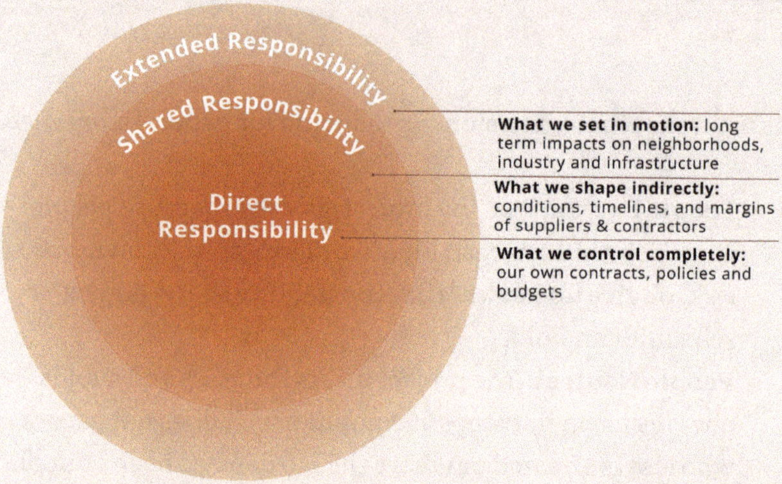

Circle of responsibility	What it covers
Direct responsibility	What we control completely: our own design criteria, project budgets, and master contract terms
Shared responsibility	What we shape indirectly: the daily conditions, timelines, and margins of our direct suppliers and contractors
Extended responsibility	What we set in motion: the long-term impacts on local neighborhoods, industry, and infrastructure

Table 3. *The Circles of Responsibility*

Scales of application

Each chapter applies these tools at three scales:

- **A building** creates human conditions in a physical place.
- **A product** carries those conditions across its lifecycle, from extraction and manufacturing to use and disposal.
- **An organization** embeds them in its policies, purchasing practices, project briefs, and everyday decisions.

The goal is to make the responsible choice easier to protect before the pressure arrives. By embedding human data directly into our baseline tools, we can make the socially valuable choice the built-in default, so it no longer has to be defended as an additional concern each time.

One decision at a time

Set out on the page like this, the tools look like something that has to be adopted, with a steering group and a rollout and a name. Formal programs can be useful, but they are not the only way to begin.

They work the other way round. One decision, one site, one person who already has the file open and a reason to look at it harder than usual. A procurement officer staring at a bid that came in 20% under everyone else needs one good question, not a complex framework. A designer being asked to approve a substitution needs to know what the substitution would be compromising.

You will rarely assess all five sites at once. The point of naming them is that when the burden lands somewhere you were not looking, you will have a name for where it went, and some idea of who is carrying it.

So, each chapter starts somewhere specific, with a real place and a decision already underway, and lets the tools do their work there. They make more sense in use than on the page.

The chapters ahead

- **Chapter 7: People** examines the three human networks supporting any system, the workforce, the users, and the transients, and asks who we are actually designing for.
- **Chapter 8: Place** looks at the physical settings where decisions become conditions and assesses the spatial dimensions of access, exposure, and agency.
- **Chapter 9: Product** traces the lifecycle of what we put into the world and follows its human footprint from raw extraction through manufacturing and use to final disposal.
- **Chapter 10: Partners** examines the commercial agreements that shape our supply chains and asks whether our contracts fund responsibility or mandate extraction.
- **Chapter 11: Public Good** examines what a project leaves beyond its immediate boundary and asks whether communities can remain, participate, govern, and share in the value created.

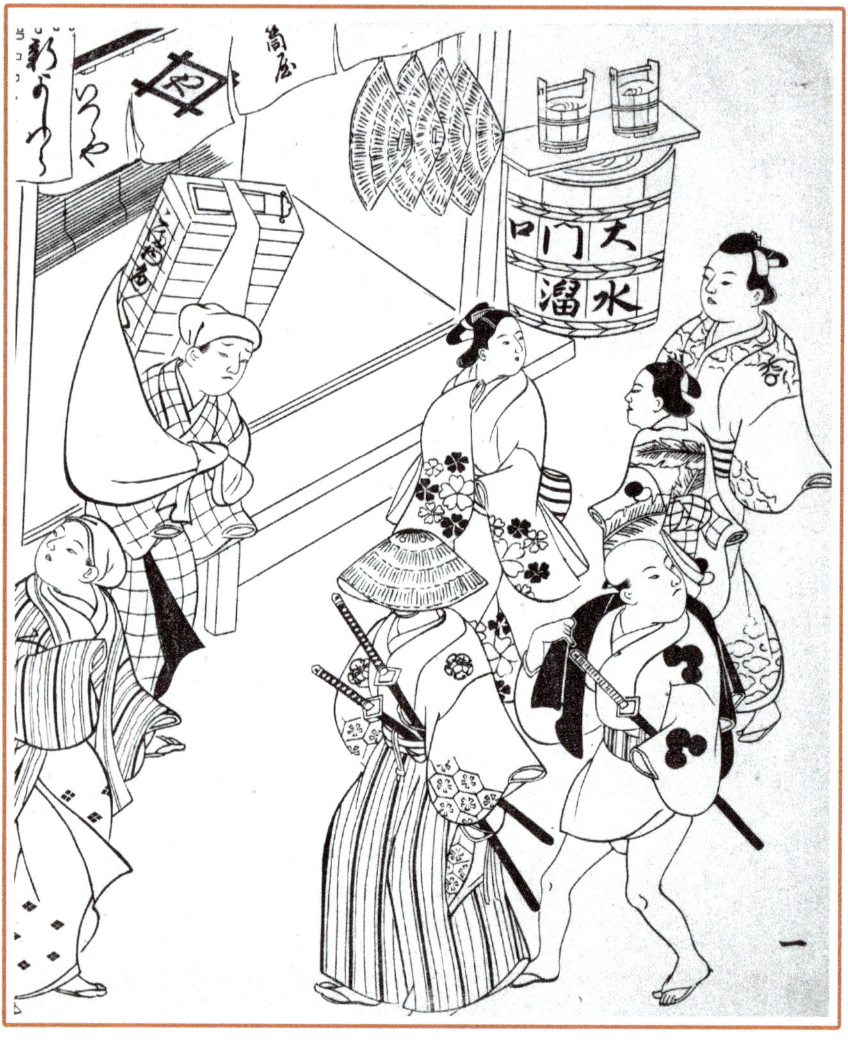

Street life in Japan, 1868–1912

Woodblock print based on an early eighteenth-century design by Okumura Masanobu

CHAPTER 7

PEOPLE

Who is counted, who is missed, and who keeps the system working?

Years before I would spend a career on the other side of these decisions, advising the teams that make them, I was a design student in Stockholm, exhausted from days of study, nights without sleep, and a brief that had started to feel impossible.

The computer had crashed multiple times, as computers tend to do before a deadline. At three in the morning, staring at a frozen rendering screen and a file that refused to open, we were ready to throw in the towel. We had spent the last two days arguing over a structural column that blocked the daylight and a layout that felt more like a maze than a fluid pathway. Every time we fixed a spatial bottleneck for our imagined visitors, we accidentally broke a building code rule somewhere else. It felt like trying to solve a Rubik's cube where every turn ruined the work we had just finished.

But somehow, through a mix of desperation and eleventh-hour redrafting, the pieces finally clicked. The design worked. We had managed to meet the brief. My group members and I were haggard, running on coffee, but proud.

The day of the design evaluation was cold and snowy outside, warm and cozy in the classroom. If you have never been through a design critique, lucky you. It is a session where professors and designers that you respect sit around and vocally criticize your work. Yes, it makes you a better designer. No, it does not mean you will not cry.

We presented our design and talked about how the light changed the space during the day, how people would move through it, and how the experience would feel almost magical. It was a multipurpose space, so we walked the room through different scenarios and scenes. Knowing that we were running on fumes, and perhaps to buffer the emotional experience of the critique, our professors had brought homemade apple pie. We promptly started eating it after we presented.

Our professor was silent for a beat. Then he took a breath and asked: "This all sounds great. But how is it going to be maintained? Have you thought about the safety of the janitors who will be cleaning this late at night?"

The apple pie gave us something to do for a few seconds. But the honest answer was no: we had not. And suddenly, our beautiful, intentional design proposal felt like a house of cards.

The capacity choice

That classroom realization showed me that "occupant" is not a neutral word: it decides who counts. My group had fallen into a classic design trap: we designed entirely for the high-profile user out front while treating the late-night maintenance crew as an invisible background function.

As Chapter 1 established, every system carries assumptions about the person it was built to serve. The task here is to see how those assumptions determine who appears in the data, whose conditions are examined, and whose capacity is treated as available to absorb the strain.

This is how corporate systems handle project execution today. When we evaluate this first site of impact, People, we are looking at visibility. It is a close look at how project briefs, budgets, and contracts decide whether human time and energy are treated as real limits on a project, or just as free resources that can be stretched indefinitely.

Every project team makes a foundational choice before any other:

Is human capacity a fixed constraint, or a flexible variable?

Treated as a flexible variable, human capacity is what stretches when the schedule cannot. When timelines get tight or budgets drop, the pressure is directly absorbed by the team through longer hours, stressful deadlines, and extended shifts.

Because standard tracking tools focus strictly on whether the final milestone is met, they log these choices as clean efficiency gains on paper. On the surface, the delivery metrics look strong, but the downstream teams are simply left to resolve the underlying execution constraints.

The trouble is structural. No project can operate under peak, urgent timelines indefinitely. Without built-in recovery cycles, a schedule stops being efficient and simply begins drawing down on reserves no one has priced.

Origins

The question of whether a person is visible to the system that houses or employs them is an old one, and the instruments we have for answering it were built slowly, usually by people the system had already failed. We have designed an industrial economy that is brilliantly suited for production but profoundly unsuited for life.

The worker came first. In 1700, the Italian physician Bernardino Ramazzini published a study of the diseases of tradesmen, having spent years walking into workshops to see what the work itself was doing to their bodies. His practical contribution was a single, subversive question. To the list of things, a physician was expected to ask a patient, Ramazzini added the patient's occupation. That single line made the workplace a legitimate object of medical attention, shifting it from a private matter between a man and his employer into a shared ecological reality.

The state followed a century and a half later. The British Factory Act of 1833 appointed just four factory inspectors for the entire country and gave them a statutory power of entry, which meant that for the first time someone could walk into a mill and look. A condition that no one is permitted to inspect is a condition that will not be recorded, and a condition that is not recorded will always be treated as a free externalized cost.

The occupant became visible along a separate line, and much later. In 1842, Edwin Chadwick published his report on the sanitary condition of the laboring population, which set mortality data alongside housing conditions and made the relationship between the two difficult for Parliament to avoid. Nearly 50 years after that, Jacob Riis photographed the raw interiors of New York tenements and published the images. The public reaction contributed directly to the Tenement House Act of 1901, which mandated that new tenements provide light, ventilation, and indoor sanitation. In both cases, the conditions themselves were not new. What was new was that they had been made visible to people who had never been required to look at them before.

Between these two lines sits the study most often cited when the subject comes up. Between 1924 and 1932, engineers at Western Electric's Hawthorne plant outside Chicago ran a series of experiments on the factory floor. They raised the lighting at the workstations, and output went up. They lowered the lighting, and output went up again. The result was taken to mean that workers respond less to their physical conditions than to the experience of being observed and attended to, and the "Hawthorne effect" passed into management teaching on that basis.

Careful reanalysis of the original data has since found very little support for it. The study is still used to argue that culture matters more than conditions, which is a claim its own data does not sustain. What it does establish is narrower: a large industrial employer had turned its measuring instruments around and pointed them at its own workforce, and having done that, it did not stop.

Later research made the relationship between work, control, and health much clearer. In 1979, workplace sociologist Robert Karasek proposed that pressure becomes most damaging when high demands are paired with little control. The same workload can affect two people very differently depending on whether they have the authority to decide how the work gets done.

A similar pattern emerged from the Whitehall studies, a long-running research program that began in the late 1960s and followed thousands of British civil servants working at different levels of the government hierarchy. Researchers found a clear gradient: the lower a person's position, the greater their risk of illness and early death. Smoking, diet, and income did not fully explain the difference. Limited control over work and working conditions accounted for a substantial part of it. The people with the least authority over their conditions were carrying the greatest share of the harm.

A third group, the transients, were never given an instrument. By transients, I mean people who pass briefly through a system without formally belonging to it. There is no inspectorate for the person who is briefly inside a system without belonging to it, and no equivalent of Ramazzini's question for the delivery driver, the visiting care worker, the agency cleaner, or the family member doing the caring. Their conditions are set by decisions taken about somebody else, and they are recorded nowhere.

An affordable housing scheme shows exactly what that inheritance produces. The project will be assessed on units delivered, code compliance, cost per unit, and increasingly on carbon performance. Each of those instruments describes the physical asset accurately. But the resident enters the accounts as an occupancy metric rather than as a household with a rent she may or may not be able to afford in five years. The maintenance worker who services the plant room, where the building's major mechanical equipment is housed, does not appear at all, and his route through the building is drawn only after the unit count has been fixed. The home care worker who visits three times a week has no line in the project's accounts, no allocated parking, and nowhere to wash her hands.

Three separate populations depend on the building, and the instruments that govern its delivery were built for only one of them. We have optimized the math of the structure, but we have completely omitted the biology of the community inside it.

The People Positive Spectrum

To manage these variables under live commercial pressure, we run our choices through the three coordinates of the People Positive Spectrum:

- **People Extractive:** Cost or schedule targets are met by drawing on human capacity that has not been funded. Deadlines tighten, crews work longer, inspections are shortened, and experienced people leave. The savings appear in one budget. Turnover, lost knowledge, and rework surface later in others.

- **People Neutral:** Legal obligations are met for direct employees, but the boundary stops at payroll. Staff may be paid, trained, and surveyed, while subcontractors, agency workers, and night crews remain outside the data. The project has no clear record of what its own decisions required of them.
- **People Positive:** Workforce stability and field knowledge are treated as part of successful delivery. Capacity is assessed and funded before work begins, everyone doing the work is counted regardless of employer, and the schedule reflects what the team can deliver safely and well.

The problem sits in the documents themselves, whatever the intentions behind them. When a leadership team filters out the practical knowledge of the people closest to the daily work, such as the subcontractor installing an unfamiliar material, or the cleaning crew dealing with a bad layout, they lose the exact information needed to keep a project from failing. Ground-floor feedback is the early warning system that protects your project from hitting a hidden bottleneck.

A single project decision does not affect every group the same way. To build a picture that reflects reality, we cannot just track one big average. We have to break those numbers down and look at the workforce, the users, and the transients separately.

Who the system relies on

Building an accurate project model requires looking at specific populations. If we look back at our design failure in Stockholm, the blind spot was an incomplete mapping of the people our project relied on to function. Every commercial project operates across three distinct human networks:

- **The workforce** (*the people who make it run*): The people whose daily labor makes the system function. In a building, this means construction teams, facilities staff, cleaners, security guards, maintenance crews, installers, operators, and service workers. In a product, it includes the people who make, install, handle, maintain, repair, or dispose of it. In an organization, it includes employees, contractors, shift workers, vendors, and the people whose labor keeps the enterprise running.
- **The users** (*the people it was built for*): The people the system is formally designed to serve. In a building, this includes patients, students, residents, office workers, tenants, customers, and guests. In a product, it is the person expected to buy, use, wear, sit on, operate, or rely on it. In an organization, it includes customers, clients, members, employees, or service users.
- **The transients** (*the people who pass through*): The people who interact with the system briefly, indirectly, or without being formally recognized. In a building, this includes visitors, caregivers, delivery drivers, event staff, gig workers, families, and people passing through. In a product, it includes repair workers, cleaners, recyclers, waste handlers, and people exposed through use or disposal. In an organization, it includes applicants, families, former workers, neighboring communities, and people affected by policies without being named as stakeholders.

The point is that the same individual shifts between these categories depending entirely on where you draw your data boundary. For example: An office worker is the workforce of their employer, the occupant of their building, and, to the night-shift cleaning contractor, unindexed background.

The Thrive Pyramid

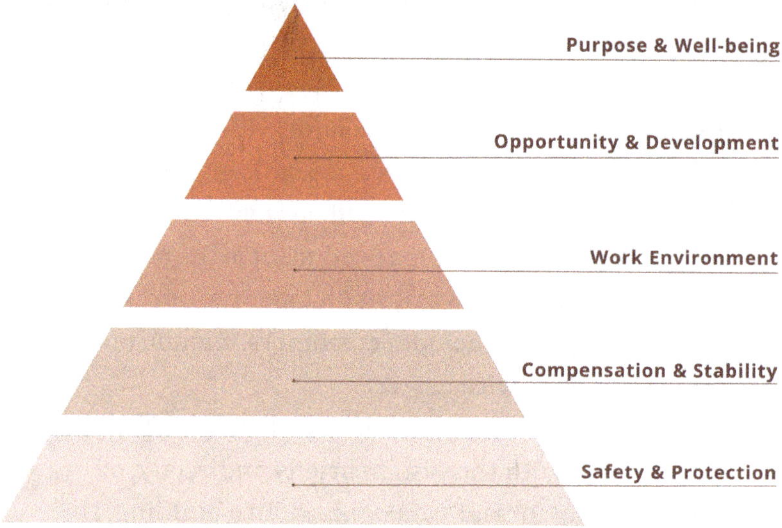

The visible signals of a thriving culture depend on the conditions beneath them. The Thrive Pyramid is a tool we developed for asking whether the people keeping a system running are supported by real conditions. It is built as a pyramid because the upper levels cannot compensate for a broken base.

- **Level 1 Safety and Protection:** Can people get through a day of work without being harmed, silenced, or penalized for raising a real risk?

- **Level 2 Compensation and Stability:** Do wages and benefits meet a credible local living-wage benchmark to establish a predictable household floor?
- **Level 3 Work Environment:** Are daily workloads, schedules, and manager relationships sustainable without requiring heroic individual endurance?
- **Level 4 Opportunity and Development:** Does the system provide transparent pathways to build skillsets, expertise, and future economic choices?
- **Level 5 Purpose and Well-Being:** Can people sustain a meaningful working life without their health or relationships becoming the hidden cost?

The height a system reaches on this pyramid determines its coordinate on the People Positive Spectrum.

A mental health benefit or meditation app (level 5) offered to a workforce that cannot safely question an unrealistic deadline or a safety hazard with a manager (level 1) is simply a high-level gesture resting on a broken base.

In practice

People Extractive: The textile mills of Lowell

In the 1830s, the textile mills of Lowell, Massachusetts, were celebrated as a marvel of early industrial efficiency. The owners recruited young women from nearby farms, promising decent wages and supervised boarding houses. For two decades, output soared.

But the workers understood that they were more than inputs in a machine. They organized early and repeatedly, striking in 1834 and 1836, and forming the Lowell Female Labor Reform Association in 1845, widely regarded as the first union of working women in the United States.

They also insisted on keeping their own record, creating a sharp divide in the media of the time:

- **The Lowell Offering:** A company-sponsored literary magazine written by the mill women. It was a corporate-tolerated showcase, sympathetic to the owners.
- **The Voice of Industry:** A genuinely independent labor paper taken over by the Female Labor Reform Association, turning it into a workers' instrument to campaign fiercely for the ten-hour workday.

When new market competition arrived, the owners reacted with standard industrial logic. They cut piece rates, accelerated machine speeds, and increased the number of looms each woman had to tend. The farm women walked away. The owners replaced them with a lower-cost immigrant workforce, principally arriving from Ireland.

The productivity decline that followed had a documented cause: a deskilling of the work, a collapse in wages, and the degradation of the community the mills had originally marketed. The owners treated wages as a line-item expense to be minimized, completely blind to the value of skill retention or the cost of losing an experienced, organized workforce.

The model did not fail because the machines broke down. It failed because the social contract dissolved, and the contract was the only thing that made it sustainable in the first place.

Toward People Positive: The Mondragon Corporation

Mondragon began in the Basque region of Spain in 1956, when a small group of students founded a single cooperative to manufacture paraffin heaters and stoves. Today, it has grown into a massive federation of roughly 100 worker cooperatives employing nearly 70,000 people.

Its architecture pulls the workforce entirely inside the boundary that traditional enterprises draw around ownership:

- **Democratic Capital:** Worker-members hold a direct financial stake in the enterprise.
- **One Person, One Vote:** Governing bodies are elected democratically, bypassing the influence of outside capital wealth.
- **Capped Disparity:** Pay ratios between the highest and lowest earners are set by vote. This ratio is typically capped around six-to-one, whereas traditional corporate firms routinely run into the hundreds.

We also need to acknowledge the limits of this model. When a subsidiary of the Mondragon Corporation, Fagor Electrodomésticos, filed for bankruptcy in 2013, it employed roughly 5,600 people globally. The federation scrambled to protect its own, redeploying or retiring the large majority of the 1,900 Basque cooperative members into other healthy cooperatives. In contrast, thousands of non-member employees, including 1,800 workers at the French subsidiary, received no such safety net.

The reality gap

What a system does not know about its people eventually shows up somewhere else. If a project team only measures the people already named in its software, the strain carried by everyone outside that frame does not disappear. It returns through turnover, deferred maintenance, safety shortcuts, delivery breakdowns, and avoidable cost.

- **Operational Risk:** In a building or facility, ignoring the teams who maintain the systems creates immediate vulnerability. If a mechanical access path is blocked, if the cleaning route requires unventilated work, or if service areas are treated as leftover space, the asset becomes harder to operate. The cost shows up later as higher turnover, missed maintenance, workarounds, and equipment that fails sooner than expected.
- **Financial Risk:** Workforce strain has a measurable cost. The Work Institute estimates that replacing an employee can cost roughly one-third of that worker's annual salary once direct and indirect costs are included. When the conditions driving turnover are not measured, the organization simply receives the bill under another name:

recruitment, training, lost productivity, overtime, or service disruption.

- **Delivery Risk:** The same pattern appears beyond the formal workplace. When external workers are treated as background, basic operating needs become project risks. Delivery drivers, couriers, contractors, caregivers, and service workers still need bathrooms, waiting areas, safe access, and clear routes. When those needs are ignored, the strain returns through delays, retention problems, safety risks, and unstable service. The bipartisan Trucker Bathroom Access Act emerged from exactly this kind of gap: workers essential to the supply chain were being denied access to basic facilities while expected to keep goods moving.

The point is, if the people a system depends on are missing from the data, the system is already carrying risk it cannot see.

In 2023, Deloitte and Workplace Intelligence surveyed executives and employees on how the workforce was really doing. More than three out of four executives believed their employees' well-being had improved over the past year. Only about a third of employees agreed, and roughly a quarter said their well-being had worsened.

This gap reflects a disconnect between executive tracking and frontline reality. By the time it reaches the executive dashboard, the workforce's actual condition has been replaced by the organization's preferred version of it.

The Circles of Responsibility

A diagnosis on its own can be paralyzing, because a system can be extractive in ways that reach far beyond anything one team can plausibly fix. The Circles of Responsibility sort the diagnosis by proximity to our own decisions, which is how a problem that feels boundless becomes a set of choices we can actually make.

The same consequence can sit in the direct circle of one system and the extended circle of another, because what places it is not the role of the people affected but the boundary drawn around the system we are examining.

- **Direct responsibility** covers the people whose working conditions we set ourselves, through what we design, specify, fund, contract, operate, or measure.
- **Shared responsibility** covers the people whose daily conditions we shape through our commercial relationships: the suppliers, installers, contractors, and facilities team whose payroll we do not sign but whose working conditions our commercial terms govern.
- **Extended responsibility** covers the people our choices reach beyond traditional boundaries, and whose strain traditional financial tools treat as invisible.

Circle of Responsibility	Product	Building	Organization
Direct Responsibility	The people directly involved in making, installing, handling, maintaining, repairing, or disposing of the product	The workforce directly involved in building, operating, cleaning, securing, maintaining, repairing, and servicing the asset	Employees, managers, direct contractors, and workers whose conditions are governed by policies, budgets, schedules, and systems
Shared Responsibility	The intended users and regular handlers whose experience is shaped by the product's design, instructions, and maintenance metrics	Occupants and regular users: tenants, residents, patients, students, customers, and staff whose daily experience is shaped by the building	Customers, clients, service users, vendors, and regular partners whose experience is shaped by organizational decisions
Extended Responsibility	People affected beyond the point of sale: repair workers, recyclers, waste handlers, production communities, and end-of-life lines	Transients and affected users: caregivers, delivery workers, event staff, gig workers, neighbors, and people briefly depending on the place	Families, applicants, former workers, informal workers, supply-chain workers, communities, and people affected by market behavior

Table 4. People: The Circles of Responsibility

The goal is to widen our field of vision, so that across product, building, and organization the question stays the same: whose experience is counted, whose experience is shaped, and whose experience is altered without being formally recognized?

The work of this chapter is to move from occupant to people, shifting from a single counted user to the full set of workforce, users, and transients a system actually relies on to function. In practice, run the three tools in order over the decision in front of you:

1. **The Thrive Pyramid** asks whether the basics hold: can people work safely, are they paid enough to live, is the workload survivable.

2. **The Spectrum** shows the direction of travel: whether the decision draws people down, holds steady, or leaves them better off.

3. **The Circles of Responsibility** locate where you can act: what you control directly, what you shape through others, and what reaches beyond your walls.

Applied to your own work, this is a discipline of attention. It means asking who your data already holds and who it has never named, checking whether the satisfaction score that looks stable in the aggregate was gathered only from the people in your premier zones, and looking for the strain that broad averages are built to hide.

The reason this requires structural discipline goes beyond moral bookkeeping. As Lowell demonstrated, a workforce recorded strictly as a line-item expense looks cheap on an immediate spreadsheet, but the social contract it rests on is not free, and when that contract breaks, what the owners lose is not only labor but the thing they had been selling.

A table of frameworks that follows shows what already exists, and what may be needed to complement their blind spots. This can help us use existing organizational disclosures as a baseline, and pair them with indicators to surface the data that might be hidden.

Current Framework or Standard	What It Clarifies	What to Pair It With
Engagement and satisfaction surveys (*Gallup, Peakon, internal tools*)	Aggregate sentiment and engagement trends across the counted workforce	Disaggregation by role, shift, contract type, and site, to surface the strain that averages hide
Labor and wage standards (*Living-wage benchmarks, ILO conventions*)	Baseline pay floors and statutory protections for directly employed workers	Subcontractor and agency conditions; checking whether the standard reaches people not on the payroll
Health and safety systems (ISO 45001, OSHA *reporting*)	Recorded incidents, hazards, and compliance within the direct workforce	Near-miss and workaround data from facilities, maintenance, and night crews; checking whether raising a risk carries a cost
Workforce disclosures (ISO 30414:2025, GRI 401–418)	Reportable human-capital metrics for investors and corporate governance	The lived condition behind the metric; checking whether contractors and service workers appear in the numbers at all

Table 5. People: Existing frameworks and what to pair them with

Basic human needs and workforce protections travel across regions, but enforcement and reporting vary widely. In environments where labor protections are loosely policed, an absence of formal complaints reveals very little about the quality of the workplace; it usually reflects the professional cost of speaking up.

This variance means that regional data requires local context to remain accurate. Lived performance cannot be validated solely by reviewing a signed certificate. It must be evaluated against local realities of power, contract structure, and the concrete consequences an individual faces when they become visible to management.

Applying a people-positive lens

Engagement surveys, safety systems, and workforce disclosures give an organization a real starting point, and a generation ago most of this was not asked at all. What they capture well is the population the system already counts. What they capture less well is everyone else, and the conditions that produced the number in the first place.

Here are some ways to assess against these operational lenses:

- **Who Is the Assumed User?** Who was the building primarily designed to serve? What assumptions were made about ability, age, schedule, income, culture, language, sensory needs, job type, and control over the space?

- **Who Else Depends On the Building?** Does the assessment include cleaners, security staff, maintenance teams, food-service workers, delivery workers, contractors, visitors, neighbors, and night-shift staff, as well as primary occupants?

- **What Conditions Does Each Group Experience?** What are the air, water, daylight, temperature, acoustics, safety, privacy, rest, and access conditions in the specific places where each group spends time? Are building-wide averages hiding poorer conditions in particular zones?

- **How Are Benefits and Burdens Distributed?** Does the building perform equally well for front-of-house and back-of-house spaces, office and service workers, permanent employees and contracted staff, and day and night shifts?

- **Who Has Agency?** Who can adjust light, temperature, seating, privacy, breaks, schedules, or reporting pathways, and who is expected to adapt to conditions they cannot control?

- **How Easy Is It to Request an Accommodation?** Does the building work for a broad range of abilities, needs, and circumstances? Are adjustments easy to request, clearly communicated, and reliably delivered?

- **Who Remains Accountable After Handover?** Is there a named person responsible for tracking conditions, responding to feedback, and making corrections during occupancy?

- **Can Feedback Change Conditions?** Is there a clear way for people to report what is working and what is not? Who reviews that information, and what decisions can it influence?

- **What Happens Next?** How will the findings lead to design changes, operational improvements, procurement requirements, maintenance protocols, tenant guidance, contractor standards, or reporting metrics?

The ultimate purpose of the exercise is to understand whether our operating model is performing because its underlying conditions are genuinely stable, or because vulnerable people are spending their own physical capacity to work around the design.

The Colosseum, eighteenth century

Giovanni Battista Piranesi

CHAPTER 8

PLACE

How can places work better for everyone who uses, maintains, and moves through them?

Nearly 2,000 years ago, a person entering the Colosseum in Rome did not simply choose a seat. The building had already assigned one.

Closest to the arena floor sat the emperor, vestal virgins, and senators, their positions established on wide marble tiers. Above them sat the equestrian class. Higher still were ordinary citizens, with different sections strictly segregated by social status, citizenship, and gender. Those with the least civic power, the poor, foreigners, and enslaved people, were pushed farthest from the center of public life, directed into the upper wooden galleries beneath the colonnade.

The Colosseum was an engineering marvel, but it was also a social diagram built in stone. Its entrances, corridors, stairs, and tiers did more than move tens of thousands of people efficiently. They translated Roman hierarchy into daily physical experience. The building taught each person how close they could come to the center, how easily they could move, how much shadow they were granted, and how visible they were allowed to be.

2,000 years later, our buildings make many of the same assignments, without carving the hierarchy into the stone where everyone can read it.

Where decisions become conditions

A place begins shaping our experience before we have settled into it. It gives some people a direct path and sends others around the side. It offers shade, a view, clean air, and a place to rest, while asking others to climb farther, wait longer, endure more noise, or adapt on their own.

Place, in this chapter, means the physical space people move through and work inside. It is the room and the office floor, the factory and the warehouse, the corridor and the stairwell behind the lobby, the loading dock and the home. It is wherever a decision made in a drawing or a budget becomes a condition somebody has to live with.

Modern buildings rarely announce hierarchy as openly as the Colosseum did. Instead, the hierarchy is embedded directly into the fabric of the environment. It appears in the route someone is expected to take, the temperature they are expected to tolerate, the chair they are expected to sit in, the light they are expected to work under, or the distance they are expected to walk before anyone considers it a problem.

A place assigns routes, exposure, effort, comfort, and belonging before a user ever walks through the front entrance.

I have felt this asymmetry during my most mundane days. On days when the weather outside was brutally hot or freezing cold, I would often use the service entrance simply because it was the faster route. I had the luxury of choice for convenience, but I could feel the difference the moment I stepped inside. The public path had been designed as an experience, while the service path had been designed as a function. Behind that heavy door, the air grew harsher, the overhead fluorescents hummed and flickered, and the furniture looked like an afterthought.

But the deepest difference was not the temperature or the lighting. It was the agency. I was using that corridor as a temporary shortcut, a choice I was free to make or abandon. For the people who spent their shifts there, the guards, the cleaners, the facilities technicians, that same environment was a boundary. The building did not ask their permission; it imposed its conditions, and they did not have the luxury of another door.

None of this means every back corridor needs the same finish palette as the main lobby. The realities are different, and those differences are not neutral. They tell us whose experience has been studied, funded, and maintained, and whose has been treated as background. One building can contain several human realities at once.

A place is never neutral

The experience in a space impacts the people inside it whether or not anyone intends it to, which is why it cannot be treated as neutral. The moment a route is drawn, a temperature is set, or a rest area is located, the environment begins deciding who is able to move easily and who is taxed, and it goes on deciding long after the project team has left.

Once we accept that a place is always acting on people, the question is no longer whether it does so but in which direction, toward supporting the people who pass through it or toward depleting them.

Origins

The idea that a place is designed for the people who inhabit it is thousands of years old.

In India, Vastu Shastra draws on ancient texts that explored the relationship between a home, the sun, the wind, and water. In China, Feng Shui emerged with a similar premise: that placement, orientation, light, and flow shape the life inside a place long before the walls are finished. Across Asia, these principles shaped design for centuries. Vernacular traditions carried the same intelligence into the local climate. Mediterranean and North African courtyards turned homes inward around shaded, cooler spaces. Wind towers in Persia and the Arabian Peninsula used vertical shafts to pull hot air out and draw cooler air in.

In other words, the human body has always been part of the brief.

Modern professional practice has extended that inheritance in more explicit ways. In 1963, Selwyn Goldsmith wrote Designing for the Disabled after polio left him paralysed down one side of his body. His manual was one of the first serious attempts to write access into the discipline itself. The independent living movement, born in Berkeley, California in the early 1970s and carried across Europe by disabled activists who refused to be placed out of sight in institutions, moved that argument from design guidance into policy. The UN Convention on the Rights of Persons with Disabilities was adopted in 2006 and entered into force in 2008, carrying the principle into international law.

At the same time, another body of work was making the invisible effects of buildings measurable. Industrial hygienists, public health researchers, and building scientists began documenting what indoor air, temperature, ventilation, and light do to the human body. In 1983, a World Health Organization working group gave a name to sick building syndrome. In the same period, Ole Fanger's thermal comfort model, first published in 1970, was being written into the international standards that still govern how we size a heating system, and after the SARS outbreak of 2003 and again after COVID-19, ventilation researchers reshaped how the field understood air movement and airborne infection risk.

Access, exposure, agency

Three dimensions hold true whether we are looking at a building, a production setting, or a workplace:

- **Access Above Code:** Code asks whether access is technically provided to clear a legal checkmark. Social value asks whether it is dignified, intuitive, and equal in practice. Minimum compliance can easily pass a legal audit while still leaving specific users with routes that are longer, obscured, or harder to navigate. True access tracks the everyday journey of entrances, routes, elevators, bathrooms, and wayfinding, accounting for temporary injuries, caregiving, strollers, older adults, and neurodivergent processing. When a system relies only on statutory checklists, it imposes a hidden time and effort tax on the users forced to spend extra physical and social energy simply to move through the space.
- **Exposure Accumulates:** An environment is a continuous series of physical inputs the human body has to process, so a healthy place does not merely avoid harm, it minimizes the daily physiological cost of being inside it. Place governs the day-to-day exposures of the occupied setting: air quality, daylight, thermal comfort, acoustics, water, and sensory load. When these are poorly designed, the consequences are rarely immediate; they accumulate as a gradual strain on the body, attention, and capacity to recover. This exposure is unevenly distributed, heaviest for the workforce in back-of-house zones and transients at the perimeter. Averages hide this strain; property dashboards typically report a clean building-wide average while masking the localized pockets where the load actually falls.

- **Agency and Adaptation:** A place becomes extractive when people have to spend their own energy compensating for conditions the design could have addressed, so agency measures how much control a person has over their immediate experience. Can an occupant adjust light, temperature, and privacy, or are they locked into a centralized profile? Where an environment offers no way to sit, pause, or report discomfort and expect remediation, people adapt privately, inventing workarounds and avoiding whole wings of a building at the cost of their own focus and health.

The people most taxed by this are often the ones a building or a place was never designed for, and we find that all the users are impacted in different ways:

- Occupants absorb a constant background hum, solar glare, or poor circulation as a steady drag that shows up over months as fatigue, slower processing, and elevated stress hormones.
- The workforce of facilities staff, overnight cleaners, and security guards is routinely assigned to the back-of-house areas and windowless hubs where exposure to noise, heat, and poor air is highest. Commercial cleaners are among the most consistently under-studied occupational groups in the built environment, despite documented rates of musculoskeletal injury and chemical exposure. They also know the building in a way its own reports do not: which corridors hold heat, which vents never worked, which room has to be aired for an hour before anyone can use it. That knowledge is available for the asking, and it is almost never asked for.

- Transients such as delivery drivers, couriers, and visitors absorb high wayfinding stress and a lack of basic amenities while trying to service the asset.

The temperature of the room

The thermostat is the clearest place to watch an industry standard work exactly as designed and still produce an unequal result.

Offices are often too cold. They are colder for women, and the reason is not the one usually given.

The usual story is that the model underneath the office temperature setting was built for men. It was not. Ole Fanger ran his comfort experiments on roughly 1,400 people, equal numbers of men and women, and found that both groups preferred much the same temperature. The American Society of Heating, Refrigerating and Air-Conditioning Engineers (ASHRAE), whose standards guide ventilation and thermal comfort in many buildings around the world, has said so, publicly, and on that point they are right.

What is true is narrower. The reference metabolic rate in the standard's tables, the number the model actually runs on, comes from a standardized average male. Kingma and van Marken Lichtenbelt argued in 2015 that it overestimates women's metabolic rate by as much as 35%.

In 2021, a team at the University of California, Berkeley stopped arguing about the model and went to look at the buildings themselves. In the field, across a large sample of working offices, they found that offices are systematically overcooled well past what anyone in them wants, that energy is being spent to achieve it, and that the conditions this produces are measurably less comfortable for women.

So, the standard is sound and the room is still cold. It is the same gap as the certificate on the wall of a sick building, valid the entire time, while the people inside went home with headaches. A standard can be honestly derived, properly validated, correctly applied, and the room can still have been designed around somebody who is not you.

The People Positive Spectrum

People Extractive: A place is **People Extractive** when one group's comfort or performance depends on another group tolerating unsafe, inaccessible, or degrading conditions. A commercial tower may remove courier waiting areas to increase leasable space, leaving drivers outside without shelter. A factory may expose workers to extreme heat, poor ventilation, or excessive noise that the finished product never reveals. An organization may depend on working conditions that steadily deplete the people doing the work while leaving that strain unrecorded.

People Neutral: A place is **People Neutral** when it meets expected standards for the people it formally counts but does not look beyond that boundary. A headquarters may certify its office floors while leaving cleaning and facilities teams in poorly ventilated service areas. A manufacturer may monitor conditions in its own assembly plant while knowing little about raw-material sites operated by suppliers. An organization may collect environmental and accessibility data for employees while excluding contractors and service workers who use the same spaces.

People Positive: A place is **People Positive** when access, exposure, and control are treated as part of how it performs. Conditions are assessed across different groups and spaces, and problems can be corrected before people are forced to adapt around them. In a building, back-of-house areas meet the same basic standards for air, light, temperature, acoustics, and safety as public-facing spaces. In a production setting, factories and warehouses are held to the same expectations as corporate offices. In an organization, people can adjust their surroundings, report problems safely, and expect those problems to be addressed.

The diagnosis is a reading of economics over time rather than a moral verdict. An extractive place tends to look cheapest at handover, because the exposure it transfers does not appear as a cost until it returns as healthcare claims, turnover, or a slow erosion of performance, while a positive place carries a visible cost up front and a lower one across the life of the asset.

In practice

People Extractive: Sick Building Syndrome

When the energy crisis of the 1970s pushed builders to seal offices against outside air and cut heating and cooling loads, the result was a generation of buildings that met every code and still made the people inside them ill. The pattern was consistent enough to earn a name. A World Health Organization working group described sick building syndrome in 1983, cataloguing the headaches, fatigue, irritation, and respiratory symptoms that eased when workers left the building and returned when they came back. The harm was not incidental. The cost of running the building cheaply was transferred onto the people who worked in it, and the certificates on the wall stayed valid the whole time. The gap between the certificate and the person has not closed with greener buildings, since post-occupancy studies of certified offices still find measured performance and lived experience diverging.

People Neutral: Larkin Administration Building

A neutral environment meets or even exceeds the regulatory minimums of its era, but it treats human well-being strictly as an instrument to optimize corporate output. When Frank Lloyd Wright's Larkin Administration Building was completed in Buffalo in 1906, it was heralded as a brilliant masterpiece of industrial care. The structure was fully air-conditioned and sealed tightly against the heavy soot of the surrounding rail yards to protect the health of its workforce. It featured advanced amenities for its 1,800 clerks, including a top-lit central court, custom built-in furniture, a company dining room, employee lounges, classrooms, and even a pipe organ. However, this physical care operated alongside intense spatial surveillance. The architecture was explicitly designed to watch. The 1,800 clerks worked in a massive, open central court directly under the gaze of managers seated on the floor with them, while the walls featured corporate mottoes like Cooperation and Industry. This means that the building delivered light and clean air, but it used those exact elements to enforce discipline and the company's idea of itself. The building was demolished in 1950.

People Positive: Saitex denim factory

A people-positive environment integrates human dignity straight into the physical and economic design of the operation before constraints arrive. The Saitex denim factory outside Ho Chi Minh City is a modern blueprint for this shift by treating a production plant as a space built well for the people who work in it. Mechanically, the facilities are LEED certified, run largely on renewable energy, and utilize a closed-loop system that recycles roughly 98% of manufacturing water. The critical differentiator, however, is how this design philosophy extends to the inside. Through a dedicated initiative called Rekut, Saitex built and trained a specialized production line for workers managing physical and developmental disabilities. The company set a public target to scale this initiative to 1,000 workers, which would comprise roughly one-fifth of its total workforce. To keep our focus honest, we must note that current employment on the line stands in the tens rather than the hundreds, meaning it remains a goal the company is still working toward. Yet, the underlying architecture is fundamentally positive. Saitex did not stop at lowering its environmental footprint. By pairing its infrastructure with Fair Trade certification, the factory explicitly binds the environmental performance of the building to a sustainable wage and working-condition standard for the people who run it.

Tracing the costs

1. Access risk and the retrofit premium

When we rely on statutory checklists, we hide the real strain our users face. If our compliant accessible path runs twice the distance of the standard route, we create widespread underuse and a widening gap between our stated corporate values and the actual experience of the asset.

- **Designing Access In:** The United Nations has estimated that incorporating accessibility from the initial planning stages of a building adds almost nothing, or around 1%, to construction cost, while retrofitting an inaccessible building later can cost up to 20% of the original construction cost. The earliest empirical study of the question, conducted for the U.S. Department of Housing and Urban Development, put the premium for designing access at between 0.12% and 0.5% of construction cost.
- **The Market Exclusion Tax:** When a layout excludes disabled users, it forecloses a substantial market. Working-age adults with disabilities in the United States held an

estimated $490 billion in after-tax disposable income as of 2018, a figure later revised sharply upward. Globally, the disability market including friends and family has been estimated at more than $18 trillion. The access question comes first, and the market follows it.

2. Exposure risk and the productivity drag

Property management systems track environmental data as building-wide averages. These look flawless on an executive dashboard, but they mask localized pockets near loading bays, intake thresholds, and sub-levels. Over time, cumulative exposure surfaces on the ledger as higher healthcare claims and reduced capacity.

- **The Value Per Seat:** In a controlled, double-blind chamber study, cognitive function scores were 61% higher on days when participants worked in a simulated green building environment and 101% higher on days with enhanced ventilation, compared with a conventional building environment. A companion analysis estimated the productivity benefit of doubling ventilation rates at roughly $6,500 per person per year, against an energy cost of between $14 and $40 per person per year across the climate zones studied. These are chamber-study figures with a small sample, not a field result, and they should be cited as what they are: a strong signal that the economics of ventilation are lopsided in favor of the people in the room.

3. Adaptation risk and supply chain drag

When a workforce must constantly spend its own energy fighting an environment that rejects their physical needs, the strain builds silently. We see it return as deferred maintenance, as zone avoidance, and as delays.

- **The Logistics Penalty:** According to the U.S. Department of Transportation's Office of Inspector General, driver detention, the unpaid time drivers spend waiting to load and unload, may reduce their annual earnings by roughly $1.1 billion to $1.3 billion.
- **The Crash-Risk Point:** The delay is more than administrative. The same analysis found that a 15-minute increase in average dwell time is associated with a 6.2% increase in the average expected crash rate.

The Circles of Responsibility

Finding a solution can feel overwhelming, because a place impacts people in ways that reach past any single team's control, so the circles categorize the solutions by proximity to our own decisions.

The direct circle covers the conditions we set through what we design, fund, and specify. The shared circle covers the conditions we shape through the workforce, occupants, and transients who use the place daily. The extended circle covers the people our choices reach beyond the property line. The same exposure can sit in the direct circle of one system and the extended circle of another, because what places it is the boundary drawn around the system, not the role of the people affected. The table that follows maps these three circles across the product, the building, and the organization.

Circle of Responsibility	Product (Production Setting)	Building (Physical Setting)	Organization (Operational Environment)
Direct Responsibility	The physical conditions where the product is made, assembled, finished, stored, or processed: air, heat, noise, light, ventilation, crowding, safety, rest access, and ergonomic strain	Entry points, routes, air, light, heat, acoustics, seating, bathrooms, service areas, waiting spaces, and back-of-house zones	Workplaces, service environments, digital or physical access points, policies, support systems, and operational settings
Shared Responsibility	How workers experience the production environment through daily tasks, pace, exposure, posture, equipment, breaks, and the ability to raise concerns	How the workforce, occupants, and transients experience the physical place through daily use	How employees, contractors, customers, partners, and service users experience the organization's environments and processes
Extended Responsibility	People and communities affected by conditions around production: factory-adjacent exposure, unsafe storage, waste handling, transport yards, and outsourced processing sites	People affected by routes, crowding, access friction, waiting conditions, security, neighborhood interface, or off-hour use	People excluded or burdened by organizational norms, locations, service channels, physical or digital access, or assumptions about the assumed user

Table 6. Place: The Circles of Responsibility

Standards and signals

Most of us already rely on standard compliance tools and environmental scorecards. Those frameworks stay; the goal is to recognize where their visibility stops, and to identify the ground-truth data we have to carry alongside them.

Framework or Standard	What We Measure Now	What We Need to Pair It With
Healthy Building Standards (WELL, Fitwel, RESET, UL Verified)	Global thresholds for interior air, light, acoustics, and baseline occupant well-being	Zone-by-zone exposure, back-of-house service loop conditions, and localized environmental control
Accessibility Codes (ADA Standards, UK Part M, ISO 21542)	Statutory physical minimums required to clear a legal property audit	Lived-route friction, wayfinding clarity, and navigation layout for temporary injuries or caregiving
Workplace Health & Safety (OSHA, ISO 45001, ILO Guidelines)	Regulatory baseline protections for physical safety, ventilation, and ergonomic strain	Task-level contractor conditions, near-miss reporting, and whether protections hold across off-hour shifts
Post-Occupancy Evaluations (Leesman Index, CBE Survey)	Macro satisfaction data reported across the primary corporate floor plan	Disaggregated sentiment by role, shift schedule, and employment type to isolate pockets of hidden strain

Table 7. Place: existing frameworks and what to pair them with

Every standard, code, and framework named in the table is cited in full in the appendix.

Applying a people-positive lens

The impact of a physical space on people does not change when crossing a geographic border, but the institutional systems that enforce and report on those needs vary. In regions where building layouts or accessibility codes are loosely policed, a lack of formal legal complaints tells us nothing about the actual quality of the environment.

Building certifications like the WELL Building Standard, Fitwel, and LEED are strong foundations to work from. WELL and Fitwel focus on health and well-being, while LEED covers a broader range of environmental performance. WELL has been credited with moving health and well-being from a soft aspiration into a structured, measurable part of building practice. It gave teams a shared language for air, water, light, thermal comfort, acoustics, materials, movement, nourishment, mind, and community.

A social value lens builds on that work. The next step is to understand not only whether a building meets a threshold, but who experiences the benefit, who carries the burden, and where the building's impact is unevenly distributed.

To take a people-positive approach, we need to examine:

- **Assumed User**: who was the building primarily designed around? What were the assumptions about ability, age, schedule, income, culture, language, sensory needs, job type, and level of control over the space? Does it align with the expected user?

- **Population Beyond Assumed User:** Who does the asset actually rely on to function day-to-day? Does the assessment look beyond primary tenants or leaseholders to explicitly include cleaners, security guards, facilities teams, food service workers, and delivery drivers across all shifts?

- **Lived Conditions:** Are variables like air, water, daylight, temperature, acoustics, safety, and rest options assessed in the specific zones where people spend time, or are they masked by clean, building-wide averages?

- **Distribution of Benefit:** How does the physical and social experience compare across different groups and spatial zones? Are there significant performance gaps separating high-profile, sunlit front-of-house spaces from the back-of-house service loops or night shifts?

- **Level of Control:** Who has the authority to adjust their immediate environment and who is forced to privately adapt? Do workers have agency over environmental elements like light, temperature, seating layout, operational breaks, and non-punitive reporting pathways?

- **Access and Accommodation:** Does the layout practically function for a wide range of people, life circumstances, and neurodivergent needs? Are spatial modifications straightforward to request, clearly communicated, and actively implemented on the floor rather than left as passive paperwork promises?

- **Ongoing Accountability:** Who owns the human impact of the asset after handover and occupancy? Is there a named, accountable internal owner responsible for tracking conditions, handling frontline feedback, and executing corrections over time?

- **Feedback Loop:** Is there a functional, transparent channel for occupants and service teams to report operational failures? Does frontline data directly trigger a formal administrative response and physical adjustments, or does it stop at passive data collection?

What it adds up to

Place makes the abstract idea of social value physical, because a decision made in a specification hardens into a route someone walks and the air they breathe.

Too Early, 1873

James Tissot

CHAPTER 9

PRODUCT

How does a product impact people through its lifecycle?

In the winter of 1775, the Swedish chemist Carl Wilhelm Scheele created a color that rapidly took over European high society. It was an emerald green of a vividness the market had never seen before. Until then, green vegetable dyes were dull and unstable, fading quickly to a drab olive or brown. But under the gaslight of Victorian drawing rooms, this new dye did not lose its depth; Scheele's Green glowed with a brilliant, almost magical intensity.

The color became an instant commercial obsession. It was spun into silk ballgowns, printed onto wallpapers for nurseries and parlors, crafted into artificial green leaves woven into hair, and used to color sweets given to children. It was celebrated as a triumph of stability, cost-efficiency, and market trend.

It was also made of copper arsenite, a highly toxic arsenic compound.

Scheele monitored the parameters his work was evaluated against: vibrancy, permanence, and profit margin. The chemist had solved for color and permanence, manufacturers solved for speed and demand, and households solved for taste and status. The market rewarded exactly what it had been trained to see. What the evaluation system did not register was the child sleeping beside wallpaper releasing arsenic into the room, or the factory workforce breathing the dust of a product that looked harmless, because no one had been required to ask what it was doing to the people around it.

A product can succeed by every visible commercial measure and still be a social failure.

What "Product" means here

A product is the tangible or intangible output of an organization's work, the materials, systems, services, and technologies it creates, specifies, purchases, or sells. A product impacts the people who make, use, maintain, and dispose of it.

To understand these effects, we have to look across three distinct scales:

- **At the Object Scale:** This is the literal, physical item, the pigment, countertop, flooring, adhesive, coating, chair, light fixture, or digital tool created by a product company.
- **At the Building Scale:** This is the goal of a building project. Here, the "product" is not just the envelope and the concrete, but the social and economic function the building is organized to perform.

- **At the Organization Scale:** This is the organizational output, the software, the report, standard, services, policy, program, or procurement requirement.

Bridging the scale gap

Admittedly, defining a PDF report, a policy, or a certification standard as a "product" can feel like a conceptual stretch compared to a physical object like a chair or a brick. A physical material's impact is immediate, tactile, and chemical. An organizational deliverable's impact is systemic and administrative.

Yet both function as products. Both are designed, packaged, distributed, and used to produce a specific outcome. Purpose is what a system says it is trying to do. The product, whether a material, a space, or a policy, is what people actually receive, use, navigate, depend on, or are excluded from.

Today, the challenge is rarely that products are obviously or intentionally harmful. Often, the opposite is true. A product may be lower carbon, healthier in use, more efficient, or more beautiful than conventional alternatives, yet still fail to create social value if its full human story is lost. A healthier material does not create impact simply by existing; it has to survive the journey from the manufacturer's technical file to the architect's specification, the developer's budget, the contractor's bid, the installer's hands, the facilities team's routine, and the tenant's daily life.

Origins

The practice of judging an object by more than its finished appearance has a deep lineage. It runs through the industrial hygienists who first traced disease back to the substances workers handled, pioneered by Alice Hamilton's early twentieth-century investigations into lead and industrial poisons. In the 1960s and 1970s came Life Cycle Assessment, later written into the ISO 14040 standards, which taught us to look past the finished object to what making it, using it, and dumping it really cost. William McDonough and Michael Braungart pushed further with Cradle to Cradle, asking whether materials could be designed to be reused for good rather than thrown away. More recently, Social Life Cycle Assessment carried that same discipline from the environment to the people along the supply chain. This work builds on all of it, and on the generations of workers whose injuries made the case for looking past the surface.

Understanding Social Life Cycle Assessment (S-LCA)

The S-LCA is an assessment gaining popularity. Where traditional environmental LCA measures physical footprints like carbon emissions and water use, S-LCA assesses the positive and negative socio-economic impacts of a product. Formalized under United Nations Environment Programme (UNEP) guidelines, S-LCA operates on the premise that a product's social footprint is made of human stories.

To move S-LCA from an academic exercise to an actionable tool, the framework organizes human impact around five core stakeholder categories:

- **Workers:** Evaluates fair salaries, working hours, forced labor, gender equity, and workplace health and safety.
- **Local Communities:** Assesses how extraction and manufacturing impact nearby populations, including community engagement, local employment, and impacts on cultural heritage.
- **Consumers:** Looks at product safety, privacy protection, and accessibility during the active use phase.
- **Value Chain Actors:** Examines fair competition, intellectual property integrity, and ethical procurement practices among suppliers.
- **Society:** Gauges broader macroeconomic contributions, public health impacts, and the prevention of corruption.

It is relevant to our conversation here because it provides a methodology to identify "social hotspots": areas in the global supply chain where human rights violations or exploitative labor are most likely to occur. This methodology serves as the conceptual foundation for our work: it teaches us to evaluate our outputs across the full arc of their existence, well beyond the moment they look clean, efficient, or high performing once installed.

Following the product lifecycle

To understand the human impact of a product, we must follow it across its life.

Design and production

Long before a product, building, policy, or service reaches the people it is meant to serve, its human consequences are already taking shape. For a material, this begins in mines, farms, factories, and assembly lines. For a building, it begins in the site, structure, construction schedule, and labor model. For an organizational output, it begins in the assumptions, rules, and administrative demands written into the tool. What appears finished at delivery has already asked something of the people who made it.

Delivery, use, and operation

Once it enters use, the burden shifts to the people expected to install, occupy, operate, clean, maintain, administer, or comply with it. A material may require hazardous cutting or specialist cleaning. A building may create difficult maintenance routes or daily physical workarounds. A policy, platform, or standard may generate reporting burdens, compliance work, or new risks for the teams expected to carry it. The question is not only whether it works, but what it requires from people to keep working.

Removal, transition, and legacy

The formal end of a product, building, or organizational initiative does not end its impact. Materials leave waste, demolition hazards, and disposal costs. Buildings leave stranded infrastructure, displaced uses, and long-term effects on the surrounding community. Policies, standards, and services can leave behind paperwork, dependencies, exclusions, or obligations that outlive the team that created them. When there is no clear path for repair, reuse, handover, or closure, the final cost passes to whoever inherits the system.

We rarely acknowledge the expertise that disposal and end-of-life demand, but it is real, and in much of the world it belongs to informal waste pickers. By one modeling estimate, the informal sector accounted for around 58% of the post-consumer plastic collected for recycling worldwide. In Bogotá, Colombia, an association of recyclers led by Nohra Padilla, who began working as a waste picker in childhood, took the city to court and won in December 2011. Colombia's Constitutional Court ordered Bogotá to recognize recyclers as public service providers and pay them for the material they recovered. Formal contract payments began in 2013. What had been treated as scavenging on sufferance became waged, credentialed work. A product's afterlife is a question about the material, and about the people who handle it, who hold more expertise than the system usually admits.

The People Positive Spectrum

The People Positive Spectrum tracks the direction of a product's impact across every phase of its lifecycle.

People Extractive

A product is People Extractive when its commercial success depends on shifting a physical, financial, or cognitive burden onto people with less visibility or less power to refuse it. This model cuts costs at the top by squeezing the bottom.

- **In a Product:** A quartz countertop enters the home as a premium choice, while its human story begins earlier with the fabricators cutting it.
- **In a Building:** A former manufacturing plant is converted into high-end office suites, replacing accessible industrial jobs with high-income knowledge work and shifting the demographics of who is served and who is excluded.
- **In an Organization:** The core deliverables, platforms, or services created by the enterprise bring measurable harm to its end-users or the larger society, even if the organization itself remains highly profitable.

People Neutral

The system is compliant but incurious. It meets a narrow brief, satisfies standard check-the-box certificates, and protects the immediate buyer or end-user, but remains blind to the wider human environment it sets in motion.

- **In a Product:** A certified material performs well on carbon or emissions but doesn't examine installer exposure, maintenance burden, or end-of-life handling.
- **In a Building:** A code-compliant conversion improves energy performance without upskilling or training the existing workforce.
- **In an Organization:** The enterprise declines overtly harmful or unethical projects to protect its reputation yet remains structurally blind to its own operations, completely failing to measure, track, or follow up on

the harmful approaches and negative societal impacts embedded in its day-to-day business model.

People Positive

A product is People Positive when human safety, capability, and dignity are built into the design of the product and into its path to real adoption.

- **In a Product:** A material is designed for safer chemistry, safer manufacture and installation, easier maintenance, clear disclosure, and responsible removal.
- **In a Building:** The project creates accessible jobs and dignified conditions for new occupants, community and service workers alike.
- **In an Organization:** All services and deliverables are in service of social well-being. Pre-approved procurement terms and contract language are applied across all initiatives and cannot be easily bypassed.

In practice

People Extractive: Engineered Stone

Engineered stone is a factory-made material used for kitchen and bathroom counters. It became popular because it is strong, consistent in color, and often cheaper than natural stone.

But making it can be dangerous. Engineered stone can contain more than 90% silica, a mineral also found in sand and rock. When workers cut or grind the slabs, they can breathe in very fine silica dust. Over time, this dust can cause silicosis, a serious lung disease that cannot be cured but can be prevented. The U.S. Occupational Safety and Health Administration estimates that about 100,000 workers in the country may be at risk.

The workers cutting the stone have testified to what it did to them. In July 2023, Leobardo Segura Meza, 27 years old and breathing through an oxygen tank after ten years at the saw, asked California's occupational safety board to act so that others might be spared. Nearly three years later, as the same board moved toward a ban on fabricating the material, another fabricator, Jose Francisco Andrade Peña, who had cut slabs for more than three decades before his diagnosis, told the board that the makers had lied to him and to his employers.

The product performs well after application in the kitchens it is installed in while the harm concentrates in the workshop, invisible to the buyer and to most of the supply chain above the person holding the grinder. Today, the extractive conditions are being balanced. In August 2024, a Los Angeles jury awarded $52.4 million to a young fabricator, Gustavo Reyes-Gonzalez, in the first U.S. engineered-stone silicosis case to reach a jury, years after the slabs were sold.

People Neutral: Healthier Flooring

Some bamboo and engineered-wood floors are tested to make sure they release only small amounts of harmful chemicals into the air after installation. This can make the finished room safer for the people who live or work there.

That is a real improvement. But the test usually looks only at the air inside the completed space. It may not examine the conditions in the factory, the workers who install the floor and handle glues or finishes, or what happens when the flooring is removed and thrown away.

The product has not failed the test. The test is simply designed to answer one question: how much pollution does the finished floor release into the room? It does not tell us the full story of how the flooring affected people from production through disposal. That makes it a fair example of a people-neutral product.

Toward People Positive: Product and Facility Labels

The Declare label works like a nutrition label for building materials. It tells buyers what a product contains and checks those ingredients against a list of chemicals known to harm people or the environment. This wider view matters because a chemical can affect more than the person using the finished building. It can also harm factory workers who make the product and installers who handle it on a construction site.

The JUST label looks at the company behind the product. It shares information about how the organization treats its workers, including pay and benefits, safety, fairness, diversity, purchasing practices, and community involvement*.

SA8000 works at the level of the facility rather than the product. Published by Social Accountability International since 1997 and revised in 2026, it draws its requirements from the Universal Declaration of Human Rights and the ILO conventions. It audits a site against seven decent work principles supported by a management system the site has to keep running between audits.

Cradle to Cradle Certified assesses the product across six categories covering material health, circularity, air and climate, water and soil, environmental management and social fairness. Social Fairness examines conditions inside the facilities where the product is made and aligns with the UN Guiding Principles on Business and Human Rights.

None of these labels guarantee that a product or company is people-positive since participation remains voluntary across the board and disclosure is not synonymous with good practice. Yet together, these frameworks shift the baseline and nudge us toward a people-positive frame.

* *Full disclosure: My firm, Liveable, serves as Social Sustainability Partner to the International Living Future Institute for Declare Equity, and I advise on the JUST label. Both belong to ILFI, but my perspective is shaped by having worked on them."*

The Circles of Responsibility

To act on these scales, organizations must map their influence. The table below outlines how responsibility is structured across companies, projects, and organizations.

Circle of Responsibility	Product companies	Building projects	Organizations
Direct Responsibility	Chemical formulations, ingredient choices, material safety parameters, and product instructions	Project specifications, substitution constraints, approved product lists, and installation requirements	What the organization directly designs, funds, approves, standardizes, offers, or requires
Shared Responsibility	How factory workers, trade installers, cleaners, and repair teams interact with the product's handling complexity	How the specified product affects the workloads, safety margins, and physical exertion of installers and facilities crews	How employees, contractors, suppliers, and customers experience and execute the deliverable
Extended Responsibility	Multi-tier extraction, manufacturing-community exposures, deep value-chain labor, and end-of-life pathways	Upstream component sourcing, downstream construction waste, replacement cycles, and public-system burdens	Market effects, administrative burden, exclusion, access barriers, and long-term waste

Table 8. Product: The Circles of Responsibility

Standards and signals

Current framework or standard	What it clarifies	What to pair it with
Product and material: HPDs, EPDs, LCAs, Social LCA, Declare, GREENGUARD, FSC, Living Product Challenge.	Ingredients, chemical emissions, carbon metrics, sourcing lines, and end-of-life material profiles	Trade-installer exposure, long-term maintenance burdens, end-of-life responsibility, and certified affordability
Building and project: sustainable product libraries, approved product lists, LEED/ WELL material credits, Living Building Challenge.	What gets specified, substituted, documented, and carried into the project boundary	Value-engineering logs, real installation conditions, facilities maintenance budgets, and live operational feedback
Organization: GRI, SASB/ISSB disclosures, human rights due diligence, B Corp, JUST, ISO 45001, ISO 30414:2025.	Reported workforce conditions, governance signals, investor-relevant risk, and outward social footprint	Internal product design and research, regional service-delivery methods, baseline purchasing terms, and customer administrative burden

Table 9. Product: existing frameworks and what to pair them with

Every standard, code, and framework named in the table is cited in full in the appendix.

Applying a people-positive lens

To take a people-positive approach to a product, and to keep its value from being engineered out, assess:

- **The Assumed User:** How do we look past the end user to trace the experiences of those who make, transport, install, maintain, repair, and eventually remove it, knowing that the vast majority of the human story sits with an invisible workforce the primary buyer never sees?

- **The Sourcing, Installation, and Maintenance Burden:** Are the ingredients, coatings, binders, and additives transparently disclosed, or are hidden hazards being passed down to a workforce left unable to manage the exposure? What explicit physical toll, in weight, cutting requirements, curing times, toxic dust, volatile fumes, or specialized training, does installation demand from trade crews, and are these liabilities being designed down or simply offloaded? Furthermore, what recurring operational burdens does the asset create after completion through specialized cleaning cycles, frequent replacement, harsh chemical exposures, or complex maintenance routines?

- **The End-of-Life Burden:** Who ultimately inherits the material or asset once its active working life is over? Can it be safely repaired, reused, taken back, or recycled, or does it mutate into a toxic, expensive liability for demolition crews, waste handlers, local communities, and future owners?

- **The Substitution Test and Specification Language:** What specific human, environmental, or operational values would be lost if this item were replaced by a cheaper alternative? How do we lock these human outcomes directly into the legally binding specification document rather than leaving them in a design narrative, ensuring that if a value-engineered substitution request cannot meet identical health, labor, durability, and disclosure thresholds, it is rejected as unequal?

- **Accountability and the Improvement Pathway:** Who explicitly owns the human impact of this selection after the specification is signed and the asset is occupied? If no named internal role, whether manufacturer, architect, contractor, or facility operator, is held responsible for tracking these conditions, how will we prevent the value from being engineered out? Finally, how do we translate real-world operational feedback into tougher specifications, reduced worker exposures, and better field conditions so the progress becomes a repeatable baseline?

A better product could clear every laboratory test but still be extractive if people responsible for making, buying, installing, and maintaining are in conditions that strip away their time, resources, and agency.

Catalan Atlas, ca. 1375

Attributed to Cresques Abraham, detail of a caravan crossing Asia

CHAPTER 10

PARTNERS

What becomes possible when contracts make responsible work easier to deliver?

For centuries, China was effectively the world's only large-scale producer of silk, and the techniques were closely held. The knowledge eventually seeped outward over the years, into Korea, Japan, and the oasis kingdoms of Central Asia, long before it ever reached the Mediterranean.

However, for most of that history, everyone else could get silk only by buying the finished cloth. The West wanted it badly enough to build the most sophisticated trade network of the ancient world just to carry it across thousands of miles of desert and mountain.

But a trade route across thousands of miles of hostile terrain cannot run on a product alone; it needs translators, financiers, and protectors. The Silk Road was a relay network running from Chang'an toward the Mediterranean, sustained in large part by Central Asian merchants known as the Sogdians. Because no single empire controlled the entire route, the Sogdians had to build a network out of kinship and shared festivals, held together by letters they mailed to communicate. They translated languages, currencies, and legal systems across borders. In this system, the human relationships were the logistics.

We still have their correspondence. A bag of letters apparently lost or confiscated in transit and recovered from a watchtower west of Dunhuang dates to around 313 CE. In one of them, a woman named Miwnay, abandoned in Dunhuang by her merchant husband, writes that she and her daughter have been left destitute, dependent on charity, and that she has been forced into service. The network held because breaking an obligation held social costs. And when it failed, it failed the people least able to absorb the failure.

In this chapter the Sogdians are an example of how goods move through partnership, a case where human relationships and mutual trust carried a product across vast distances, doing the work that rigid rules imposed from above never could.

By contrast, modern procurement has replaced this relational web with distance. A large company hires a few firms directly, those firms hire smaller ones, and those hire smaller ones again, and the legal paperwork is arranged so that the company at the top never has to see the human cost at the bottom of the chain or feel answerable for it.

The more firms a product passes through, the further its human cost travels from the people who set the terms, until no one along the chain feels responsible for the conditions it was made under. Good design and good intentions can fail the moment the deals underneath them are hollowed out. A company can draft excellent policies, set environmental targets, and expect clean work from its suppliers. Those promises get weakened when the contracts, the prices, and the agreements strip away the time, money, and authority its suppliers need to protect people.

Origins

For most of history, supply chains were short enough that a buyer could see the conditions behind a product or a service. Industrialization and colonial trade changed that, stretching the distance between the person who made or delivered a thing and the person who bought it until the conditions behind it disappeared from view.

Organizing a response took more than a century. The International Labour Organization began setting international labor conventions in 1919, starting with hours of work and, over the following decades, forced labor and freedom of association. That work gave the field a shared language for what a decent condition of work is.

The fair-trade movement built its first certification label, Max Havelaar, in the Netherlands in 1988. A collapse in world coffee prices had led a Dutch development agency and a Mexican farmer cooperative to guarantee growers a price above the market. The anti-sweatshop campaigns of the 1990s carried the same argument into apparel and footwear, forcing brands to answer for factories they did not own. The same logic now reaches the cleaners, guards, installers, and delivery workers who are hired through other firms to provide services a company relies on but does not employ.

More recently, an idea called the 'fissured workplace' traced how the ordinary habit of contracting work out to other companies moves responsibility away from the firms that set the terms.

The people behind a purchase

Partnership responsibility begins with the relationships closest to the decision: the suppliers, vendors, contractors, consultants, manufacturers, service providers, and delivery partners a company hires directly. These are the connections an organization sees most clearly. We choose them and scope their work. We set the price, fix the timeline, write the clauses, approve the results, and decide what counts as success. Because this layer is so visible, it is often where inspections stop.

Supply chains are often described in tiers, which is a way of counting the layers. The first layer, tier 1, is the firm a buyer hires directly. That firm hires the next (tier 2), which hires the one below it (tier 3), and the layers keep going down toward raw material and the workers closest to it. Visibility falls at each step, and the buyer's sense of responsibility tends to fall with it, which is why inspections cluster at the top layer while the harder conditions sit further down.

This plays out differently across the three scales this book has followed:

- **For a product company,** the partners are the mills, farms, and factories that supply and move materials.

- **For a building project,** they are the main contractor and the chain of smaller firms, installers, and hiring agents who put the building up.
- **For an organization,** they are the contractors, including outside firms that run cleaning, security, catering, and deliveries.

In each case, the terms set at the top shape the conditions far below. Partner responsibility does not end at the edge of the first contract. The firms a company hires directly often lean on a wider network of smaller firms, hiring agents, installers, temporary workers, delivery providers, and local suppliers. A buyer may never deal with those firms in person, and the terms set at the top of the chain still shape the conditions of the people working at the bottom.

So, the question is not just: who did we contract with? The deeper question is: what conditions did our contract create for the people who deliver the work?

The role of a contract

Every project and procurement team faces a fundamental choice when structuring a commercial relationship: Is a vendor contract treated as an exercise in shifting risk, or as a way to build shared capacity?

The buyer controls the terms: the price, the deadline, the speed of payment, and the scope of work. Those terms set the conditions the firms below have to survive, and responsibility attaches to the terms the buyer controls.

When a contract is treated as an exercise in shifting risk, the goal is to protect the buyer by pushing costs, swings in price, and delivery pressure onto the supplier. The assumption is that once the deal is signed, the supplier's daily choices, staffing strains, and thin profits are theirs alone to manage. If a supplier cuts corners, loses staff fast, or has a safety failure under a punishing deadline, the buyer often records it as the supplier's failure. The terms of the contract that caused it go unnamed.

When a contract is used to build shared capacity, the team acknowledges that commercial terms drive real conditions on the ground. The buyer understands that an unworkable profit margin, an unpredictable payment window, or an impossible lead time leads directly into human strain downstream.

Designing for social value means ensuring that the terms of the deal make it physically and economically viable for the people tasked with doing the work.

How pressure travels

A supply chain rarely produces strain because one manager decides to be cruel. Strain builds up little by little, out of the ordinary day-to-day running of a normal buying process, moving through a chain of middlemen who each pass the pressure downward because their profits are too thin to absorb it.

The examples that follow are realistic composites. They represent the daily, exhausting math faced by mid-sized firms trying to survive under punishing contracts from the companies above them:

- **The Volume Trap:** A second-tier structural steel fabricator scales up operations based on bulk volume promises, only to face severe margin compression when final purchase orders are chopped into smaller, piece-rate runs to protect the primary buyer's liquidity.
- **Compressed Horizons:** A regional glass-tempering plant in Ohio carries heavy fixed equipment overhead. When a buyer squeezes lead times, the plant needs to have a forced weekend shift to hold the contract.
- **Invisible Overhead:** A local masonry partner handles a tight commercial facade schedule. When a late-stage design change arrives on a Friday afternoon without a timeline extension, the foreman absorbs the shift change as uncompensated overtime to avoid a formal flag on the vendor scorecard stating that the work failed to meet contract requirements.

The buying organization is rarely causing harm directly. Instead, it sets commercial terms that leave strain as the supplier's only rational adaptation if it is to keep the business. The three examples differ in trade and geography, but the way it works is the same in each: a decision made at the top of the chain becomes a cost paid at the bottom.

The three tests

Evaluating whether a commercial relationship protects human impact requires looking beyond basic compliance checks and examining three pressure points.

1. Terms

Can the financial terms and timelines of an agreement support the human standards required by the project? When a buyer insists on top-tier worker protections or careful quality control while squeezing the price to the bone or making the supplier wait months to be paid, the terms do not add up. Fair terms make sure the money and the schedule actually pay for the safety equipment, the living wages, and the reasonable hours the job needs.

2. Capacity

Does a partner have the workforce, equipment and capacity to deliver under real-life conditions? That means checking, before the contract is handed over, whether the supplier has a steady workforce, the right skills, and some slack to spare. If a partner is already stretched to the limit with too few staff, piling on a fast, demanding job without moving the deadline means the safety, health, and dignity of frontline workers can be sacrificed to hit the target.

3. Accountability

Can a problem or strain surface and be corrected without triggering commercial punishment or concealment? Traditionally, admitting a delay, a safety hazard, or a labor shortfall can often result in financial penalties or the loss of a future contract. This means that people are often under tremendous pressure to deliver, even under seemingly impossible conditions. Real accountability relies on open feedback loops, safe escalation channels, and reasonable ways to resolve disputes that let partners flag system-wide strains before they manifest.

The People Positive Spectrum

The Spectrum reads the direction a partnership pushes strain and pressure over the life of the contract.

People Extractive

A partnership is People Extractive when the buyer's savings or speed depend directly on the supplier being left exposed, having its already-thin profit squeezed, or being pushed past what it can handle. Here a company demands strict safety and ethical standards on paper, while pricing, timing, or arranging the work in a way that makes meeting those standards impossible to afford. The strain is passed down to the workers at the base of the chain, who are watched least and have the least power to refuse.

People Neutral

A partnership is People Neutral when it leans on legal cover, formal rulebooks for suppliers, and paperwork passed down the chain claiming the rules are met by the firms it officially counts. The boundary stops where the contract ends. A neutral buyer checks that its direct suppliers meet the legal minimum but stays incurious about how slow payment or a constant stream of extra work with no extra pay might strain the smaller firms further down.

People Positive

A partnership is People Positive when the terms of the deal make responsible work possible at every layer of the chain. The buyer treats the price, the speed of payment, and steady deadlines as core parts of how it delivers social value. That means setting the price to match what sustainable work actually costs, holding deadlines steady, paying fast so smaller firms do not run out of cash, and building open lines of feedback so problems in delivery can be worked out together before they turn into human harm.

Understanding Human Rights Due Diligence (HRDD)

To move past passive inspection, more organizations are turning to Human Rights Due Diligence, or HRDD, which means checking on an ongoing basis where in your supply chain people are most at risk of harm and acting on it. It was set out in the United Nations Guiding Principles on Business and Human Rights.

A traditional social audit is a snapshot of the past. It checks whether a supplier is breaking a rule right now. HRDD is an ongoing, preventive process, built to spot, prevent, and reduce the real and possible harms a company causes across its whole supply chain, and to answer for how it handles them.

The HRDD process is built on four continuous pillars:

1. **Assessing Actual and Potential Impacts:** Actively mapping the entire supply chain to identify "hotspots"

where labor exploitation, unsafe conditions, or community displacement are most likely to occur.

2. **Integrating Findings and Taking Action:** Using this data to reform internal purchasing practices, ensuring that buyer lead times, design changes, and pricing structures do not actively force suppliers to violate labor standards.

3. **Tracking Performance:** Monitoring the effectiveness of mitigation efforts through ongoing worker feedback and direct operational data, rather than relying solely on scheduled, third-party paper audits.

4. **Communicating and Remedying:** Publicly reporting on how impacts are addressed and establishing safe, accessible grievance channels so that when harms do occur, affected workers have a direct, non-punitive path to remediation.

By shifting the focus from corporate liability protection to active risk management, HRDD turns partnership from a policing exercise into a shared system of accountability.

In practice

The same terms can be seen in real contracts and relationships around the world.

People Extractive: Sandstone Suppliers

The sandstone in the lobby of Chapter 2 arrives through a chain that works exactly as designed. India supplies a large share of the world's sandstone, and roughly 90% of India's production comes from Rajasthan, and the American Bar Association has documented that there are instances of bonded labor, child labor, and silicosis across a seasonal workforce of some three million people.

The buyer at the far end does not visit the quarry, does not select the workers, does not set their hours, and in most cases does not know the quarry's name. The chain is arranged so that this is true. A merchant sells to an exporter, an exporter to an importer, an importer to a fabricator, a fabricator to a contractor, and by the time the slab reaches a specification it has passed through enough hands that no single person is answerable for what happened at the first point. Nobody in that sequence has to refuse anything, because nobody in it is being asked.

People Neutral: Supply Chains in Everyday Products

The most common situation falls under People Neutral. Supply chains are notoriously hard to get transparency on. This means that, because of the number of partners involved, organizations are unable to understand who their suppliers are using as suppliers. So, often, we find systems that stop at the first tier. A buyer issues a supplier code of conduct, collects a signed self-assessment, and runs periodic third-party audits, all of it legally sound.

This means that the rulebook can travel down the chain on paper while the muscle to enforce it stays at the top. In practice, inspection reports are widely used and widely criticized, because suppliers can hide breaches and still pass, and rulebooks improve conditions mainly where local law enforcement or an organized workforce already exists to back them up. The signed policy does not do the real work. It certifies the layer the buyer can see and leaves the conditions on the ground to whatever local power happens to hold them.

People Positive: Diaspora Co.

We are seeing examples of what a partner-led organization can look like all around the world. One of the most compelling is Diaspora Co., a single-origin spice company. The historic spice trade was a primary driver of colonization, and that dynamic still echoes through modern market structures. Founded in 2017, the company rebuilt a partnership model for the spice trade. In the conventional spice trade, value routes upward to brokers, exporters, and brands while the operational risk is left at the farm. A spice can change hands dozens of times before it ever reaches a shelf. Diaspora Co. bypassed these commodity auctions to buy directly from agricultural partners across India and Sri Lanka.

The company reports that it works with roughly 150 farms and pays its partners an average of six times the standard market price, far exceeding the typical fair-trade premium of 15%. Since its inception, it has paid several million dollars directly to farmers, underwritten farm infrastructure and equipment, and established a dedicated fund for farmworkers.

The model proves that generations-old supply chain hierarchies can be shifted. This model changed where pricing power sits inside the network, the exact variable most primary buyers treat as entirely fixed. While their retail pricing is higher than conventional alternatives, the case shows us a different way of doing business, one that includes paying suppliers on time, holding deadlines steady, and refusing to add scope without adding compensation.

The reality gap

Organizations are rarely short on procurement metrics. Supply chain systems track unit prices, on-time delivery rates, legal compliance certificates, and supplier audit scores with exceptional precision. The problem is that these corporate systems are built on checklist tracking, and a ticked box can hide deep strain.

A standard inspection of a supplier's rulebook can report that a direct supplier has signed every required labor and human rights statement. That signature on its own misses a lot. The buyer's own production team may have just ordered a huge, last-minute change without moving the deadline or raising the pay. To avoid the fines written into the contract, the supplier can be forced to skip normal procedures, move the work to backup factories no one has checked, order double shifts, or cut the wages of temporary staff. Because the tracking systems watch only for a signed policy, the organization stays blind to the strain its own choices created. Where the terms of the deal give way, the workers at the far edges of the network carry the strain.

When purchasing pressure travels

Buying pressure is often treated as a money matter. The way a company places its orders is itself a labor decision. Buyer decisions about price, deadlines, sales forecasts, payment, and changes to orders shape the conditions suppliers can offer their workers.

- **Price Pressure:** The International Labour Organization's global survey on purchasing practices and working conditions examined responses from 1,454 suppliers across 87 countries. The study identified buyer practices including contract clauses, technical specifications, order placement, prices, lead times, and changes to orders as factors that influence wages and working conditions in global supply chains.

- **Low Prices and Subcontracting Pressure:** Human Rights Watch has argued that poor sourcing and purchasing practices by brands contribute to labor abuses, especially where buyers hold significantly more commercial power than suppliers. Low prices, poor forecasting, and sudden order changes create incentives for suppliers to use excessive overtime, casual labor, or unauthorized subcontracting to meet buyer demands.
- **Audit Burden:** Supplier responsibility systems often rely on a supplier code of conduct as a starting point. These tools can clarify expectations, but they also consume time and resources if they are duplicated, poorly coordinated, or disconnected from the buyer's own pricing and lead-time behavior.
- **Payment Pressure:** Late or extended payment terms create acute cash flow strain for smaller suppliers and subcontractors. In construction and service contracts, that strain affects staffing, payroll timing, safety investment, and the ability to absorb changes without passing pressure along to workers.

The takeaway here is that purchasing terms are not neutral. Price, payment, lead time, forecasting, audit burden, and change order behavior can shape whether partners have the capacity to meet the standards being asked of them.

Acknowledging the limits

To be clear, designing people-positive relationships is not a bulletproof solution to the messy realities of global commerce, nor is it a declaration of perfection. What it actually provides is preparation. Changing the commercial terms makes the deep, blurred layers of a layered supply chain far easier to reach, audit, and support when issues arise or when regulations change.

For example, Apple runs one of the most extensive supplier responsibility programs in the world, conducting hundreds of supplier facility assessments a year, surveying hundreds of thousands of supplier employees, and publishing the results.

Despite that reach, independent monitors have continued to document problems across Apple's supplier network, including excessive overtime and heavy reliance on workers hired through staffing agencies. Even a program this extensive will not find and fix everything at once. That is no reason to avoid looking. The work is to keep finding, responding, and improving.

Circle of Responsibility	Product companies	Building projects	Organizations
Direct responsibility	Supplier selection, vendor requirements, bid scoring, contract terms, pricing models, payment speed, lead times, scope clarity, change orders, penalties, and reporting metrics for first-tier suppliers	Selection and terms for the general contractor and directly contracted trades: price, schedule, scope, and change-order rules	Selection and terms for directly contracted vendors and service providers, including the wage and staffing assumptions built into the contract
Shared responsibility	How first-tier pricing, timelines, and scope changes shape the conditions subcontractors, installers, and factory workers work under	How the general contractor's terms cascade into the workloads, safety margins, and overtime of lower-tier subcontractors	How the vendor's margin and timeline shape conditions for the cleaners, guards, and support workers who deliver the service
Extended responsibility	Deep-tier extraction, manufacturing-community exposure, labor-broker dependence, recruitment debt, and end-of-chain labor risk	Upstream material sourcing, informal labor at the base of the build, and burdens shifted onto local public systems	Deep-tier subcontracting, migrant and informal labor, and community effects of how the service is staffed and priced

Table 10. Partners: The Circles of Responsibility

The core questions stay the same: for the direct circle, do our commercial terms make responsible delivery possible? For the shared circle, what pressure are our partners forced to absorb or pass down? And for the extended circle, what human burdens do our purchasing decisions create beyond the formal contract?

Standards and signals

Current framework or standard	What it clarifies	What to pair it with
Sustainable procurement standards (ISO 20400, EcoVadis guidance)	Frameworks for evaluating vendor sustainability policy, governance structures, and formal environmental commitments	Verification of actual purchasing practices, checking whether buying teams override sustainability criteria during final bid scoring
Responsible sourcing guidelines (OECD Due Diligence Guidance, Better Buying Principles)	Methodologies for identifying and mitigating human rights, labor, and environmental risks in procurement operations	Internal alignment checks, evaluating whether buyer lead times and pricing models conflict with responsible sourcing goals
Social auditing frameworks (Sedex/ SMETA, SA8000)	Visible compliance markers regarding facility working hours, statutory wage minimums, and direct worker headcounts	Disaggregated worker feedback, looking for unauthorized subcontracting, and evaluating deep-tier labor broker dependencies

Table 11. Partners: existing frameworks and what to pair them with

Applying a people-positive lens

Sustainable procurement and responsible-sourcing standards give the field a real starting point. What they capture less well is how a buyer's own behavior, its prices, timelines, and change orders, shapes the conditions further down the chain.

This is where a social value lens extends the reading through a few critical assessment points:

- **Payment Delays:** What is the actual speed and path of payments as it travels down the supply chain? If an enterprise enforces 90-day payment terms at the top, does it recognize how that delay forces lower-tier subcontractors to finance the work or pass the pressure downstream?

- **Lead-Time Compression:** How stable are the delivery deadlines handed down to production partners? When scheduling margins are aggressively squeezed at the top, does management account for how this impacts overtime, workforce exhaustion, and safety protocols?

- **Audit Burden:** How much administrative friction is your procurement strategy placing on the vendor network? Are sourcing teams forcing a supplier to dedicate its finite financial resources to managing compliance checklists instead of funding the safety gear and fair wages those audits are supposed to protect?

- **Scope Drift:** Are uncompensated project changes silently accumulating across the lifecycle? When small design additions pile up without a corresponding, formal adjustment to the purchase price or the execution schedule, is the workforce left to privately absorb the resulting physical and time strain?

The exercise is meant to tell whether a partnership works because the deal underneath it is genuinely stable and fair, or because the workers at the bottom are burning through their own health and hours to survive the way the contract is built.

My family comes from Kerala. The floor of my great-grandmother's house there stays cool in summer. It is laid with red oxide, a paste made from laterite, the iron-rich red rock that sits just below the surface of the soil across much of South India, burnished smooth, the color of the earth it came from. The roof tiles were fired from local clay. There is a jackfruit tree outside and a paddy field behind. Nothing has traveled far to get there. And if something cracked or failed, it was not a mystery where it came from or who had laid it.

I am writing this book from my home in Silicon Valley, where many of the materials in the houses around me have traveled farther than anyone is required to explain and arrived with more prestige than accountability. Fairer supply chains are entirely possible to build. What keeps them from being the norm is a system that rewards whoever can move the cost far enough from the buyer that no one feels responsible for carrying it.

Once we understand how responsibility travels through partner relationships, the next question is what remains beyond the contract itself: local benefit, shared resilience, public systems, and community staying power.

Plaza Mayor de Mexico, 1836

After Carl Nebel, lithographed by P.-F. Lehnert

CHAPTER 11

PUBLIC GOOD

How can a project create value that helps people stay, participate, and benefit over time?

What does this project leave beyond its immediate boundary, and who is still able to live, work, govern, belong, and benefit once the value arrives?

In Mexico City's central square, the Zócalo, the past and present do not sit in a neat sequence. They occupy the same ground. On any ordinary afternoon, street vendors, worshippers, protesters, tourists, and construction workers move among ruins, cathedral stone, state ceremony, and everyday errands all at once, none of it walled off from the rest. You can smell meat roasting on a vertical grill while standing beside the Templo Mayor, the excavated ruins of the Mexica capital, with the heavy stone walls of the metropolitan cathedral rising right next to it.

What stayed with me was the way history and daily life occupied the same ground. The square was also commercial, ceremonial, touristic, and contested, but it continued to function as an ordinary civic space used by residents, vendors, worshippers, protesters, workers, and visitors at once. The people crossing it are residents, vendors, and passersby going about their day, and a place like this holds deep social value only when a community has been able to stay long enough to build shared meaning there.

The trouble with many modern, self-labeled 'community-positive' projects is that they cash in on this very quality while weakening the conditions that let it exist in the first place. We see this clearly in the familiar cycle of gentrification. A development borrows local street art and the texture of a historic community as brand language, and then, as property values climb without tenant protections, the very people who made that culture are priced out. The community is improved out of the place it was consulted about. The mural stays, and the artist has to move further out.

Development always changes a place. The question worth asking is who the place is still for once the development is complete. Public Good asks whether a project builds up the conditions that let people remain, belong, govern themselves, and benefit from it.

Origins

The idea that the people who will live with a decision should have power over it is old, and it has been argued from several sides. Its early forms were usually narrow, granting a real voice to a favored few while leaving most people out.

The principle runs through the community-organizing traditions of the twentieth century, and through the urban criticism of Jane Jacobs, who argued that the people who use a street understand it in ways a planner looking at a map cannot. It took its sharpest modern form in the disability rights movement, and it was carried into international law by the UN Convention on the Rights of Persons with Disabilities. More recently, the environmental justice movement extended the same logic to who bears the environmental burden of a development and who is present when it is planned.

Nothing about us without us

A deceptively simple benchmark sits underneath every valid claim of Public Good: nothing about us without us.

The relevance of this idea extends directly across the planning, design, and development tracks that shape our physical infrastructure. A project cannot structurally strengthen a community while authoring the future of that environment without the active participation of the people who inhabit it.

The phrase comes from the disability rights movement: nothing about us without us. It became a rallying cry against spaces built to shut out the very people who would have to live in them.*

This framework treats consent as a design principle. Every system of measurement shapes a system of protection. What it counts gets defended, and what it leaves out gets spent. A company's balance of accounts works as a design system of its own. When local knowledge is screened out of a project brief, the system carries a design error. Bringing in the voices of the people who

* *The activist and scholar James Charlton recorded the phrase in 1993, after hearing it from the South African disability leaders Michael Masutha and William Rowland.*

inherit the physical and social costs of an asset is a technical need for a building that lasts.

Participation power, not participation volume

Too often, community participation arrives after the important decisions have already been made. The site is selected, the investment capital is ready, major tenants are lined up, and even the story about how the project will serve public space is written. Then residents are invited to respond to a future that has already been largely decided.

That is late-stage validation.

A people-positive approach asks entirely different questions:

- Who was involved before the brief hardened?
- Who was paid for their expertise?
- Who could change the plan?
- Who could challenge the assumptions?
- Who could influence the budget?
- Who could shape the rules for public space after opening?
- Who has a role in governance after the ribbon-cutting?

Public Good depends on these queries because local knowledge is not decorative. Residents know which routes feel unsafe after dark, which small businesses hold the neighborhood together, which public spaces are welcoming only in theory, which services are trusted, which histories are being flattened into branding, and which improvements will raise local costs before they raise the quality of life.

If that knowledge is excluded, the project may still look community-positive from a distance. It may have beautiful murals, cultural events, open plazas, local food options, historical references, and animated public programming. But without the people most affected positioned inside the planning structure, the project risks extracting the image of the community while weakening the community itself.

> ***Participation fills the room; power is what proves Public Good. The test is whether the community's presence changed what was built, how it was funded, who benefited, and who could remain.***

Defining Public Good across scales

Public Good represents the long-term value a project leaves behind beyond its own property lines. To evaluate it accurately, we need to distinguish a process from an outcome.

> ***Community engagement is a process: the act of listening, hosting workshops, and documenting feedback. Public Good is an outcome: it is the measurable reality of whether a project actively strengthens or gradually weakens the wider community around it.***

Because a building is not an island, this outcome cannot be evaluated in isolation. The question takes a different shape at each scale:

- **For a Product Company:** Public Good is the legacy its manufacturing plants and corporate headquarters leave on the civic health of the towns they inhabit. It is the choice between anchoring a town with stable skills and fair employment or treating it as a temporary labor pool to be abandoned when margins shift.
- **For a Building Project:** It is the physical, social, and economic footprint the development leaves in the immediate neighborhood around it. It asks whether the asset integrates into the existing fabric of the street or creates an exclusive enclave that accelerates the displacement of legacy residents.
- **For an Organization:** It is how the entity deploys its hiring pipelines, corporate power, and purchasing decisions to actively anchor and replenish the public systems it depends on.
- **For a City:** It is the long-term equity of the civic floor, the baseline of public infrastructure, services, access, and protection available to everyone. It directs investment zoning protections, and budgets toward historically excluded neighborhoods so that growth does not automatically trigger displacement.

These are some ways to track Public Good:

- The preservation of local housing and commercial affordability.
- Small-business continuity and protection from displacement.
- Local hiring pipelines that lead to durable workforce pathways.

- Genuine public-space access free from exclusionary commercial control or heavy-handed profiling.
- Neighborhood trust and institutional legitimacy.
- The protection of shared cultural memory.
- Shared environmental and resilience infrastructure.
- Local asset ownership, ground leases, or collaborative governance models.

The People Positive Spectrum

The Spectrum reads the direction a project is pushing the community.

- A project is **People Extractive** when it draws value from a community's culture, labor, land, or identity while weakening that community's ability to remain, govern, or benefit.
- A project is **People Neutral** when it provides some local benefit but treats the surrounding community as a static context, not as a party with enduring claims.
- A project is **People Positive** when it increases local staying power, local footing, and the community's share of the value created.

In practice

People Extractive: Atlanta, Georgia

In 1999, Ryan Gravel proposed turning a ring of disused rail corridor around Atlanta into a loop of parks, trails, and transit, stitching 45 neighborhoods back together. The city took the idea seriously, and over the next two decades the BeltLine became one of the most admired urban redevelopment projects in the United States. It also did what good public infrastructure does: it raised the value of everything near it. Home values along the corridor rose as much as 26.6% in the four years to 2015, and developers moved into neighborhoods that had been low-income for generations. The project carried a duty to deliver 5,600 units of affordable housing. It was not close. In September 2016, Gravel resigned from the board of the Atlanta BeltLine Partnership, along with Nathaniel Smith of the Partnership for Southern Equity. Their letter noted that the $7.5 million then committed from tax allocation bonds, public debt repaid from expected increases in local tax revenue, would fund fewer than two hundred affordable units against a target of 5,600 and called it 'a drop in the bucket when compared to the need.' The man who had dreamed up the project walked away from it, on the grounds that a trail meant to bring the city together was pulling it apart. Nothing in that sequence asked anyone to behave badly. The parks were built. The trail is good. The value it created was real, and almost all of it flowed to the people who arrived after it. The people who had lived beside a derelict rail corridor for 30 years, and who took the disruption of its construction, saw very little of it. Affordable housing was a stated promise with a number attached to it, and it lost the way stated promises usually lose, to a land market moving faster than any covenant meant to protect people from it.

People Neutral: Christchurch, New Zealand

The reconstruction of central Christchurch following the 2011 earthquake highlights the threshold where public input meets delivery power. The municipal *Share an Idea* process generated more than 106,000 ideas and helped shape the draft central city plan, and the engagement was substantial and meaningful.

What happened next is our lesson here. The national recovery minister set the council's draft aside and established a central unit, the Christchurch Central Development Unit, within the Canterbury Earthquake Recovery Authority, which produced a delivery blueprint in roughly 100 days and organized the rebuild around 17 large anchor projects, most of which ran years past their original timelines. The case shows the difference between participation at scale and durable authority over capital allocation, delivery economics, and who can remain in the rebuilt center. Many local businesses, priced out by higher-cost commercial development, never returned to the core they had helped imagine.

People Positive: Medellín, Colombia

Medellín shows how public infrastructure can be directed toward historically excluded neighborhoods instead of waiting for private capital to move outward. Through social urbanism and a series of integrated urban projects between roughly 2004 and 2011, the municipality invested in mobility infrastructure, public escalators, Metrocable aerial connections, library-parks, schools, childcare, recreation centers, and public space in low-income peripheral neighborhoods.

The projects were deliberately concentrated in the *comunas* the city had excluded from investment for decades, and which carried the highest homicide rates and the lowest quality-of-life scores as a result. They were funded in large part by transfers from the city-owned utility, Empresas Públicas de Medellín, which is required to pass a substantial share of its annual profits to the municipal budget, rather than by private developers. Residents used participatory budgeting and local planning to press their own investment priorities into the city's decisions.

We do need to acknowledge that Medellín is not a perfect model, and persistent inequality, maintenance challenges, and displacement pressures did not disappear. The honest edge of the case is that the more architectural set-pieces proved less durable than the modest mobility and public-space projects. The Biblioteca España, the most recognizable building of the whole program, developed structural failures within a few years of opening and was closed indefinitely in 2015. The result stopped short of utopia, and it stood as a public-sector choice to build a stronger civic floor where exclusion had been most visible.

Public Good at city scale

The three cases are, in the end, decisions made by cities, and Public Good is the one site in this book where the primary actor is often a public body rather than a private one. A city government assessing the impact of its own equity measures faces the same question the framework asks of any project, whether an intervention strengthens or weakens the capacity of residents to remain, govern, and benefit, but it faces the question at a wider scale and with a longer horizon.

At city scale, the People Positive Spectrum reads civic function rather than a single development:

- An **extractive** civic posture markets a city's culture and affordability to attract investment while allowing the residents who created that character to be priced out, treating displacement as an acceptable byproduct of growth.
- A **neutral** posture delivers real services and consults widely without giving residents durable authority over the decisions that follow, tracking outputs like housing units approved without tracking who can still afford to live there.

- A **positive** posture builds the civic floor first, directs public infrastructure and budget toward the neighborhoods that have been excluded, and gives residents structured, binding channels to shape where investment goes.

Ahmedabad, in western India, offers us another example. Through the Mahila Housing SEWA Trust, grassroots women in informal settlements were trained to run their own climate-risk assessments and to design the responses, from cool roofs to water access, and their findings informed the city's cool-roof program under the Heat Action Plan. The assessment was theirs to run, and the women became the risk assessors and the negotiators with the municipal corporation, which is what it looks like when a city builds its floor together with the people who will stand on it.

The measures a city already produces, equity impact assessments, participatory budgeting, inclusionary zoning, are the right tools, and the same caution applies to them as to any other measurement in this book. An equity assessment that counts consultation numbers tells a city how many people showed up. It does not tell the city whether those people could change anything, or whether the residents most affected can still afford to be there in five years.

The reality gap

Community risk behaves like structural load: it builds slowly and silently beneath the surface, appearing as project risk under another name. It rarely starts as an open failure. Instead, it manifests early as approval delays, unexpected litigation, intense political opposition, public mistrust, construction disruptions, and the steady loss of social license, the continuing public acceptance a project needs in order to operate.

Research found that the most frequent cost of company-community conflict was the cost of lost productivity due to delay, and that a major extractive-sector project with capital expenditure between $3 billion and $5 billion can lose roughly $20 million a week in net present value terms, the current financial value of future income lost to delay.

Neighborhoods are also labor markets. Hospitals, universities, hotels, transit hubs, restaurants, and factories all lean on a frontline workforce that has to live within easy reach of its shifts. If a project helps drive out the very people its own operations rely on, the cost comes back to the business as chronic staffing gaps, wage pressure, long-commute fatigue, and higher turnover.

The Circles of Responsibility

Circle of Responsibility	Product companies	Building projects	Organizations	Cities
Direct Responsibility	Local investment, sourcing, and operational impacts directly funded or governed in the locations of manufacture and sale	Public-realm investments, affordable housing covenants, below-market commercial space, local hiring requirements, and community benefit agreements	Organizational hiring paths, direct procurement terms, living wage standards, and philanthropic or community capacity funding	Inclusionary zoning mandates, community land trust support, participatory budgeting, and long-term public maintenance funds
Shared Responsibility	How the scale and siting of manufacturing operations shape local rents, local employment markets, and public infrastructure	How asset scale, tenant mix, and programming shape surrounding neighborhood rents, small-business survival, and public-space use	What an organizational footprint and remote-work policies exert upward or downward pressure on local housing markets and transit systems	What public infrastructure investments and transportation planning set economic pressures in motion across unmanaged neighborhoods
Extended Responsibility	Long-cycle effects of corporate growth on local community identity, informal care networks, and wealth capture	Long-term neighborhood displacement, cultural thinning, public infrastructure strain, and long-term staying power	Systemic economic exclusion, barriers to institutional access, and the depletion of public resources	Who gains decision-making power, who loses geographical staying power, and who captures generated value over generations

Table 12. Public Good: The Circles of Responsibility

Standards and signals

Current framework or standard	What it clarifies	What to pair it with
Environmental and social impact assessments	Expected project disruptions and regulatory baseline risks identified before municipal approval	Longitudinal tracking of post-occupancy affordability, business survival, and social networks
Community engagement reports	Who was consulted, the headcount of attendees, and the qualitative feedback logged	Evidence of what specific design terms, timelines, or budget items changed because the community spoke
Community benefit agreements	Formal commitments made by a development team to secure local political support and zoning signoffs	Active delivery tracking, checking whether community funds and space allocations hold when project margins tighten
Participatory budgeting frameworks	Public input avenues for the allocation of local municipal funds or community grants	Transparency tracking: who participates, who is missing, and whether inputs affect meaningful capital
Equity impact assessments	The demographic distribution of potential benefits and environmental burdens	Longitudinal tracking of who remains, who loses access, and who captures value five years post-delivery
Municipal planning frameworks	Public priorities, regional density targets, and statutory development constraints of a city	Project-specific financial and legal mechanisms that protect staying power through delivery and operations

Table 13. Public Good: existing frameworks and what to pair them with

Every standard, code, and framework named in the table is cited in full in the appendix.

Applying a people-positive lens

The tools above give us a starting point, but they rarely capture what happens after the ribbon-cutting, whether the community is left with more capacity to remain and benefit or less.

A social value lens extends the reading here, through a few assessment points that apply as readily to a single development as to a city's own equity measures:

- **Affordability Runway:** Who can still afford to live and work near the project five years after completion?

- **Workforce Integration:** Who lands secure jobs that allow them to participate and benefit over time? Track whether local residents find career-track roles or are funneled into low-wage shift work.

- **Public Sphere:** Does the outdoor space truly operate for the community, or does it just perform as a commercial experience? If private guards and heavy surveillance clear out street vendors, teenagers, and unhoused neighbors, it is no longer a public asset.

- **The Expertise Tax:** Are you paying local organizers and legacy leaders for their specialized understanding of the place? The people who use a street understand it in ways a planner looking at a map cannot.

- **Value Capture:** Who captures the wealth when a new development drives up local land values? Follow the money beyond your immediate property boundary.

From public relations to measurable Public Good

To shift these practices from passive compliance into active defaults, we have to look at the structural leverage points that decide who holds the cards:

- **Community Benefit Agreements:** How can the project transform verbal outreach promises into contracts and covenants? Consider tying these commitments directly to zoning approvals, financing terms, or project milestones.
- **Displacement Mitigation:** What mechanisms can the project use to buffer low-margin legacy businesses and families from sudden tax and rent spikes? Establishing targeted project contributions helps protect the local neighborhood from economic pressure. This strategy serves as a structural defense that shields the asset from future political friction and a loss of social license.
- **Affordable Commercial Space Covenants:** How can the project legally protect the independent local shops, like the bookstore, barber, or bakery, that give the street its character? Creating long-term, below-market space

protections keeps legacy businesses in place before the market reprices the neighborhood.

- **Community Trusts:** Can a portion of the property or the underlying land be placed into a community-held trust or classified as open access? This structure allows local residents to maintain a material stake in the financial upside and long-term governance of their area, instead of just absorbing the noise and traffic of construction.
- **Long-Term Shared Governance:** How can the framework give local stakeholders a true voting seat regarding programming, public space rules, and maintenance priorities? Moving past a passive suggestion box helps build active co-governance.
- **Public Benefit Tracking:** How can community commitments be tracked? Tracking public benefit on the main project dashboard ensures these human outcomes are managed with the same professional rigor as the financial budget.
- **Civic Infrastructure Investment:** Does the project actively invest in or support vital local public offerings like schools, libraries, health clinics, or public parks? This requires looking beyond the immediate property line to fund and strengthen the shared civic resources that support neighborhood life.

When community benefit is measured clearly, it stops being a discretionary public-relations expense and becomes a core part of project risk, value, and delivery.

Recap of Part 2

Part 2 moved from naming the omission to locating where it lands.

In the climate conversation, visibility was won through decades of relentless, data-driven alignment. Carbon accounting showed how a complex, distributed impact could become easier to track, compare, and carry into financial and technical decisions. Human impact requires a wider set of measures, but the lesson about visibility still matters.

Part 1 uncovered the human costs our current tools fail to record; Part 2 located where those costs land. Again and again, the pattern appears across five recurring sites: **People, Place, Product, Partners, and Public Good**. These are the literal interfaces where decisions harden into human conditions.

Four points to carry forward

- **Identify All the Occupants:** Every building relies on three overlapping populations to function: the workforce out back, the occupants out front, and the transients passing through.
- **Accessibility Is More Than a Code Checklist:** Meeting minimum accessibility requirements can clear a legal audit while still imposing a tax of time and effort on non-"standard" users. Dignity needs to be designed in from the start; retrofitting it afterward rarely achieves the same result.
- **A Product's Footprint Also Includes Human Lives:** A material can clear every laboratory emissions test while

still poisoning the fabricators who cut it or externalizing toxic disposal risks onto municipal waste handlers. We must look across the entire lifecycle.

- **Contracts Dictate Working Conditions:** Squeezing vendor margins, stretching payment terms, and demanding impossible lead times are not neutral negotiation tactics. They are direct instructions to pass pressure down the chain until it hits someone unable to refuse it.

An honest accounting of social value names what is known, what is estimated, what is assumed, and what still sits outside our immediate field of view. It connects dignity to realities: the schedule, the staffing model, the safety buffer, the payment term, the layout clearway, the maintenance plan, the contract clause, and the way value is shared.

To move from location to integration, we must embed these insights directly into the organizational machinery that approves, funds, and executes our daily work. Part 3: Adopt turns to the specific **gates and levers** that let better conditions take root before the pressure arrives.

Site	Core Question	Operational Metric
People	Whose experience counts, and who disappears from the frame?	Retention, safety, and engagement data separated by role, shift, site, and contract type
Place	What conditions do people inhabit, navigate, maintain, and recover inside?	Localized exposure levels, spatial agency, and access routes
Product	What is the system built to produce, and what does that production ask people to carry?	Material disclosure, installation conditions, maintenance burden, and end-of-life handling
Partners	Do our terms make responsibility possible, or push pressure downstream?	Payment speed, lead-time stability, scope changes, and alignment between pricing and labor requirements
Public Good	What remains beyond the boundary, and who can still live, work, and benefit?	Affordability, local wealth retention, access, staying power, and shared governance

Table 14. The five sites of social value

PART 3

ADOPT

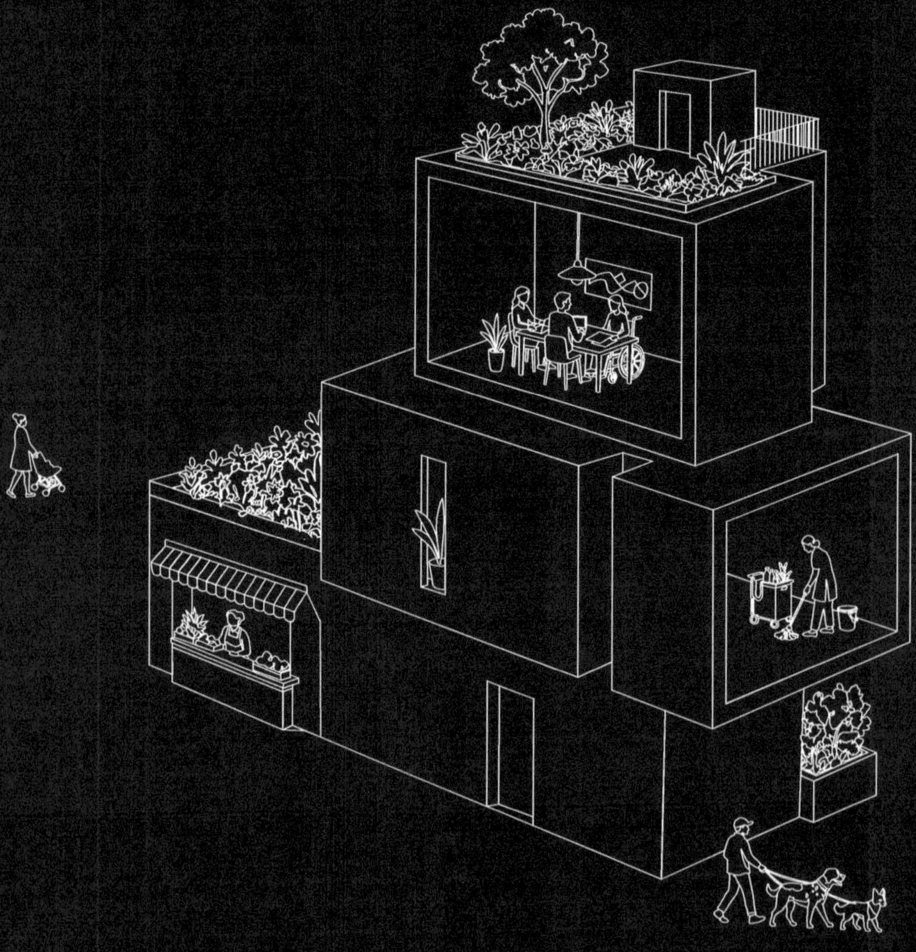

A strong design and a progressive policy are only as strong as the processes that execute them. If our commitments do not enter the unglamorous mechanics of our budgets, specifications, and contracts, they remain vulnerable to the first meeting where a cheaper default is already waiting.

By this point, we have done two things. First, we have named the human evidence that our industrial systems often leave outside their main field of view. Then we mapped exactly where that uncounted burden settles: People, Place, Product, Partners, and Public Good.

That brings us to the most honest threshold in any transformation: **now what?**

Recognizing a pattern does not, by itself, change the system. A committed project team can complete an assessment, identify the risks, and present clear evidence, only to find itself stalled before the same institutional barriers. Part 3 is about building the root system that allows social value to survive under pressure. We do this by updating the everyday administrative channels, the briefs, plans, specifications, and review checkpoints that already decide what gets funded, bought, built, and repeated.

The infrastructure of impact: Gates and levers

To understand how a practice takes root, we have to look at the ordinary tools of a project through two types of mechanisms: gates and levers.

Gates are the conditions and checkpoints at which work is authorized, financed, revised, delayed, or stopped. They include sponsorship, budgets, timelines and feedback. A functioning gate has clear criteria and enough authority to affect what happens next.

Levers are the ordinary documents and decisions that carry intent toward those checkpoints: the brief, the plan, the technical specification, the procurement package, the contract, and the operating procedure.

Because these instruments are already part of daily work, they are often the most practical places to begin. In practice, the two alternate along the workflow. A brief is a lever, and it feeds into the sponsorship gate. The plan is a lever, and it feeds into the budget and funding gate.

Going with the flow

Adoption is not a call to create an entirely new workstream for social value. Most organizations already have enough workstreams, and the people expected to carry this one are often already overloaded.

A project already has a brief. A budget already has review gates. A procurement team already has supplier criteria. A specification already names what can be used and what can be substituted. A contract already defines scope, payment, timing, and recourse. A change order already decides what happens when reality no longer matches the original plan. A report already decides what becomes visible to leadership and the public.

Adoption is about updating the workstreams that already decide what happens. It is the unglamorous work of finding the administrative channels where better conditions can take root, moving the baseline little by little through the choices we already make every day. By updating those existing channels, human impact is no longer an extra concern carried by the most committed person in the room. It becomes part of how the work is already funded, bought, specified, and improved.

The work is to widen what the current process can carry, without necessarily adding another process.

The chapters ahead

- **Chapter 12: The Fear of Finding Out** examines what happens to a system when fragmented evidence suddenly threatens to become an explicit corporate obligation.
- **Chapter 13: The Power to Say No** explores sponsorship and governance, and examines the gates that allow a team to stop or change work that cannot be delivered responsibly.
- **Chapter 14: Levers of Change** tracks how a commitment moves through specifications and change-order loops to become a repeatable default.

- **Chapter 15: Mapping Progress** introduces a six-rung progress scale to measure whether a practice is actually deepening, choice by choice, without waiting for perfect data.

Part 1: Acknowledge and Part 2: Assess helped us see the pattern. Part 3: Adopt asks how that evidence will change the work.

Undark advertisement, 1921

United States Radium Corporation

CHAPTER 12

THE FEAR OF FINDING OUT

How can uncomfortable evidence move into action instead of avoidance?

Over the last decade, I have spent a lot of time across the table from executives, trying to map how human dignity survives the baseline math of today's commerce. In those rooms, I have rarely encountered open hostility toward social value. No one sits at a mahogany desk and actively demands exploitation; to do so would be a breach of basic corporate etiquette. Instead, my conversations almost always begin with a highly polished politeness. Leaders nod, lean forward over their laptops, and tell me with complete sincerity: Yes, we must understand this better. Yes, we should find a way to track it.

But over the years, I have learned to watch for the exact moment the presentation screens are turned off.

The moment the conversation shifts from high-level principles to resources and capital, the pleasantries evaporate and a much colder calculation takes over the room. The air changes, and the same question always surfaces, the one that drives the underlying panic of the enterprise: "What happens if we find something?"

The question is a proxy for a domino chain of more practical questions. For example, a report showing widespread harm at a main supplier instantly becomes a legal risk no one has set money aside for. Or evidence that a project praised for helping a community is in fact pushing residents out forces an expensive change of course. Meanwhile, the team that found the data lands in the firing line, and the main contract, the client relationship, and the next budget all come under risk of being lost.

> ***Once evidence becomes specific, it turns into an active responsibility. Someone has to own it, fund the response, and decide whether it changes where the money goes.***

FOFO

> ***FOFO, or "fear of finding out," is an informal term for the anxiety that makes people skip medical tests or avoid looking at their bank accounts. Imported into the business world, it offers a useful way to describe a structural defense mechanism.***

We often treat FOFO as a localized boardroom anxiety, a type of hesitation that surfaces the moment the presentation screens turn off. It runs deeper than that. FOFO is often a fault built into how companies are set up, the predictable response of a system with no channel strong enough to carry an uncomfortable finding. When a leadership team stalls over firsthand proof of labor abuses far down its supply chain, or of residents being pushed out, it is reacting to large costs it never planned for.

When human data is left out, the strain migrates along the paths of least resistance until it reaches whoever has the least power to refuse it. A project team may log a minor efficiency gain by value-engineering a healthier material out of a contract, clearing an immediate cost checkpoint while passing chemical exposures onto trade installers and intensive maintenance routines onto night cleaning crews. But when that social debt accrues interest, it routes back to the originating balance sheet disguised as an attrition premium, an insurance renewal, or a frontline retention crisis.

Resolving FOFO is a matter of commercial survival. The companies that refuse to look away are writing human protections directly into their documents, master specifications, and project budgets before anyone signs a deal. By making these social realities a requirement for doing business, they change what a supplier has to prove before it can work with them, and they do it before a regulator or an investor requires it of them.

Companies that stay blind to save a quick dollar may find themselves responding later, when investor expectations, regulation, or market practice make human-impact evidence harder to ignore. Because they waited, they inherit procurement rules, documentation requirements, and constraints that were designed by the firms that moved earlier. Not looking only defers the moment the capital is priced, and it tends to mean the terms are eventually set by someone else.

The radium girls

One of the most extreme historical examples of this pattern appears in the case of the U.S. Radium Corporation in the 1920s. The dial painters were young women, and the harm done to them was devastating.

The company manufactured glow-in-the-dark watch dials, a product that seemed almost magical in its time. The watches were useful, desirable, and commercially successful. To paint the tiny numbers cleanly, young women in the factory were instructed to bring their brushes to a fine point with their lips before dipping them into radium paint. The method was called "lip, dip, paint."

The women were told the material was safe. Some treated the glow as a novelty, painting their teeth or nails before going out after work. But inside their bodies, the radium was accumulating in bone. Over time, workers began suffering from severe anemia, bone deterioration, jaw necrosis, and other devastating illnesses associated with radium poisoning.

Here the story becomes relevant to the question of evidence. U.S. Radium did not suffer from a simple absence of data. The company commissioned an independent investigation by the Harvard industrial hygiene expert Cecil Drinker to examine the factory conditions. When Drinker's research identified serious harm among the dial painters, the evidence created a problem the company could no longer treat as abstract.

If the findings were accepted, they would force action: changes to production, responsibility for sick workers, legal exposure, public scrutiny, and financial cost. The evidence described harm, and in describing it, created an obligation the company could no longer sidestep.

Instead of using the findings to protect the remaining workers or build a route toward remediation, company leadership altered the report before submitting it to the Department of Labor, presenting a version stating that every woman was in perfect health. The report was a forgery.

Whatever the motive, the company chose institutional self-protection over worker safety and falsified the evidence. It faced large, unplanned costs and responded by protecting itself rather than the women carrying the harm. The same survival reflex fires in boardrooms today. The stakes in most of those rooms today are different and should not be equated with the physical devastation suffered by the dial painters.

The 1920s can look like a relic of a more savage, unregulated era, though the thread running underneath is what keeps the case current. Workplace protections have changed dramatically since the 1920s. The organizational reflex underneath the case, however, remains recognizable: evidence can still be resisted when accepting it creates an immediate obligation to act. When a firm has built no pathway strong enough to receive an uncomfortable finding, its default setting is self-defense through deliberate ignorance. The crisis is rarely that a company cannot find out what is happening. The crisis is a structural effort to avoid what finding out would force it to do.

This is the first place we encounter the two tools of Part 3: the gates and the levers. **A gate is a threshold where a decision is approved or dropped, and a lever is one of the ordinary inputs, such as a brief, plan, or specification, that carries intent up to that threshold.**

FOFO is what happens at a gate when no lever has been built to carry the evidence through it. The truth arrives, finds no channel prepared to receive it, and is turned away by a system that has built nowhere to put what it has learned. No one in the room has to choose cruelty for this to happen; the absence of a channel does it for them.

The friction of truth

In a system built for speed and consistency, friction looks like a fault. Real evidence introduces friction because it forces the room to stop and look at variables that cannot be easily solved by a formula or a standard checklist.

Sometimes organizations challenge data responsibly to ensure its integrity; sometimes they challenge it simply to avoid taking action. When a finding threatens a timeline or a protected margin, the firm often spends significant energy trying to audit the methodology, minimize the sample size, or move the problem to a "softer room" where it can no longer interrupt the schedule.

Silence is a decision

This institutional self-defense has a recognizable form in daily meetings, and it wears a polite, understated, bureaucratic face, and never needs the raised voice of open hostility to do its work. A question of human consequence is raised without the paperwork that would give it standing, the room pauses, and the phrase that closes it is the one described earlier in this book: “let’s take that offline”.

The concern is moved out of the room where the active decision is being made, the meeting continues, and the choice passes unchanged. Named that way, the sequence is easy to see: uncomfortable evidence is raised, it is moved to a softer room, and the decision passes with its original shape intact. This is effective because it sounds collaborative, and sometimes it genuinely is. But when it serves instead to move the issue out of the room where the decision is made, the concern loses its force without anyone having to argue against it.

> ***In Malayalam, my mother tongue, we have a phrase: Mounam sammatham. It translates to silence as agreement.***

In the polite silence of a corporate meeting, this holds a double meaning. When a team stays quiet after an uncomfortable risk is raised, the silence itself becomes a decision, a collective agreement to proceed with the status quo.

Sociologists describe this as strategic ignorance: the deliberate arrangement of information flows so that an institution and its leadership remain insulated from uncomfortable realities. Not knowing can be useful. It keeps the schedule clean, keeps the contract moving, and keeps the decision-maker free of any immediate obligation.

When the messenger becomes the friction

If the organization has not built a route for uncomfortable evidence, the person who surfaces the issue can easily become the issue. With nowhere for the discomfort to travel, it lands on the messenger instead. This tension catches up with people in every part of the business:

- **The designer** who flags a spatial layout flaw that compromises safety but threatens the drawing-phase schedule.
- **The procurement officer** who notices a suspiciously low vendor bid that clears the basic compliance checklist but signals deep labor extraction down the value chain.
- **The sustainability lead** whose supply-chain audit uncovers an environmental or labor risk that complicates a major vendor relationship.
- **The community liaison** who reports genuine local resistance to a development project during the planning and approval phase.
- **The facilities worker** who notes a chronic maintenance hazard in a service corridor that requires an unbudgeted capital fix.

When an individual raises these issues within a system that has no slot to receive them, they are often treated as the person who complicated the plan, when in fact they are the one protecting the initiative. That is a gate with no lever behind it. The next chapter takes up what it would take to build one, so that the person who surfaces a problem is not left carrying it alone.

The route for improvement

A public promise is easy to make and easy to mistake for a process. A public pledge can pile pressure on a firm to look serious without building the plain, unglamorous routes that acting seriously takes. The result is decoupling, a split where the front of the house adopts the right language while the spreadsheets at the back stay fully out of step with it.

Courage on its own is never enough, because courage is not infrastructure.

For social value to survive a cost crunch, an uncomfortable finding needs a built path to travel. That path is made of levers and gates, and the chapters that follow build it one tool at a time.

The Syndics of the Drapers' Guild, 1662

Rembrandt van Rijn

CHAPTER 13

THE POWER TO SAY NO

What can stop a problem from being carried into the next phase?

In January 2016, nine tonnes of brickwork peeled away from the exterior facade of Oxgangs Primary School in Edinburgh and collapsed into the courtyard. It was pure coincidence that the space was empty; had the wall buckled a few hours later, the courtyard would have been filled with children.

The fault behind the collapse was small and specific. A brick facade is meant to be secured to the structural wall behind it by metal wall ties. At Oxgangs, those ties were missing in some places, and where they did exist, they were set too shallow, failing to reach the 50-millimeter depth required to bind the bricks to the building. The outer skin of the building was essentially standing on its own, and in a winter storm, it came away in a single sheet.

The immediate aftermath was swift. The City of Edinburgh Council ordered the urgent closure of 17 schools across the city, forcing the sudden relocation of more than 7,600 pupils.

On paper, these buildings had cleared every checkpoint. But a structural wall does not spontaneously collapse. The building failed at the masonry, and it had failed earlier at the gates, in a sequence of unchecked decisions that ran silently for years before the wall gave way. The collapse arrived at the end of that sequence, the last event in a chain that had been forming long before the bricks let go.

Decades earlier, and an ocean away, another building carried a hidden defect of its own. The Citicorp Center in Manhattan had been finished and occupied for about a year when a Princeton engineering student named Diane Hartley, working on her senior thesis, calculated the tower's response to diagonal winds and found structural stresses far higher than the figures the design engineer's own office had calculated. She took the question to the firm. The tower's structural engineer, William LeMessurier, re-examined his design and discovered that the construction team had substituted bolted joints for the welded ones the design called for, leaving the tower highly vulnerable to a strong wind.

For nearly two decades afterward, the story of the tower's midnight repair was told without her. In the popular telling, the student was always a man. Hartley only found out what her thesis had set in motion when she happened to watch a documentary about the building, many years later.

The flaws in Edinburgh and the flaw in Manhattan were close cousins, each buried behind a finished surface, each completely invisible to the people inside. What separated them was what happened after the flaw was found.

The load has to go somewhere

A building teaches us a simple rule of physics: the load has to go somewhere.

Pull a column out of a structural plan to save money, and the weight of the roof does not vanish; it re-routes onto the beams and columns that remain. If those elements have capacity to spare, the architecture stands. If they are already near their limit, stress gathers in places never designed to carry it, and the system begins to deform long before a crack shows in the drywall.

The same logic runs through organizations. The pressure of a cut budget or a compressed schedule travels until it reaches whoever has the least power to refuse it: a facilities team, a supplier, an installer, or a neighborhood. We rarely see it happen because the savings and the consequences land in different columns owned by different departments, far enough apart that no one in the room sees both halves of the trade at once. One department records a clean victory while the rest of the enterprise absorbs the burden, and nobody has to be lying for the truth to go missing.

The mechanism here is an ordinary one. The example of the 40-floor headquarters from Chapter 1 swapped in a synthetic vinyl floor to clear a cost checkpoint, logged the savings, and celebrated it as a purchasing win. The trade installers then spent weeks breathing solvent-based glues to hold the compressed delivery date, the occupants absorbed the long tail of chemical outgassing, the slow release of fumes from new materials, and the night cleaning crews inherited a stripping-and-buffing routine they would have to repeat for years.

The people in that room were doing their jobs well. What none of them held was the authority to carry the whole pattern, so the pattern carried itself downward onto the people least equipped to say no. The missing piece was an instrument capable of seeing the whole pattern at once.

We often expect the people who first notice a problem to fix it: the inspector who sees the defect, the supplier who sees the impossible lead time, the facilities worker who sees the hazard. Then we give them no structural way to act on what they have seen. Seeing a problem and being able to rebalance the work around it are two different powers, and we hand out the first while withholding the second.

> ***A gate is a condition or checkpoint where evidence meets the authority to act. It is the specific checkpoint where a project can actually be changed.***

The rest of this chapter is an attempt to find those places before the load does.

Four gates for impact

What we are looking for is the restoration of a feedback system the project was supposed to have. In construction, this takes the familiar form of a stage-gate sequence, dividing a project into clear, sequential phases separated by hard checkpoints. But the form matters less than the test. A real gate is an investment checkpoint with the authority to halt the work. The common failure is the toothless gate, where a project is waved through because the checkpoint has no clear criteria, no authority, and no discipline to stop it.

Before any phase advances, a project must navigate four distinct gates:

- **Sponsorship:** Asking who has the authority to step in and say no when an uncomfortable issue is being buried.
- **Budget:** Testing whether a stated human commitment has been funded, or if it exists only as a slogan.
- **Timeline:** Asking whether project speed can actually slow down when it starts to cause physical or operational harm.
- **Feedback:** Testing whether what the finished building teaches is allowed to reopen and correct a funded decision.

A project rarely arrives with all four gates strong at once, and it does not need to. The gates work like the structure itself, where a beam with capacity to spare can carry the load of a column that has been removed. A sponsor with real authority can protect a budget that comes in thin. A generous schedule can absorb a feedback loop that was slow to close.

What a project cannot survive is the condition where every gate is already pushed to its limit, because then there is nothing left in reserve, and the next constraint comes to rest directly on a person. We need to know which gate is still carrying the load and protect it before the weight arrives.

Gate 1: Sponsorship

The sponsorship gate is the route an inconvenient finding travels from the person who sees it to the person who can act on it.

The distinction we tend to miss is between a champion and a sponsor. A champion lends visibility and enthusiasm but can only carry a concern as far as the next person who has the power to refuse it. A sponsor is a named, senior leader who holds the authority and the budget to change the work, and who has agreed in advance to own the issue when it lands.

Where that figure is absent, a finding is seldom refused outright. Instead, an inspector logs the same installation variance week after week, the note is condensed for the coordination meeting, condensed again for the client, and by the time it reaches a desk with real authority, it has shrunk from a major risk into a minor line item. No one actively buried it; the structure simply had no one positioned to catch it while it was still loud enough to act on.

In practice, a sponsorship gate is working when you can point to a senior leader who has agreed in advance to own the issue, a clear path for the finding to travel upward without being condensed, and a clear answer to who is allowed to make the final decision once it gets there.

Gate 2: Budget

The budget gate tests whether a commitment has money behind it. A commitment that clears the design meeting but not the budget meeting exists only on paper.

This pattern is easy to see outside of construction as well. An organization announces a new safety standard, a fair-pay commitment, or a supplier-vetting requirement, and everyone in the launch meeting agrees it matters. Then, no budget line is created to pay for the extra staff time, the audits, or the higher-cost suppliers it requires. No one voted the commitment down; it simply never got funded.

The same holds inside a project. A lower-toxicity product, a commissioning budget, or a maintenance headcount rarely loses an argument at the cost meeting. It is simply left unfunded, and an unfunded specification stays a note and never becomes a decision in the building.

We see the clearest version of this in the split every design team knows: an organization commits capital to high-performance mechanical systems to clear a design-stage sustainability checklist, and then, when the budget tightens late, finds the savings on the operating side, reducing the commissioning, the calibration, the training, and the people who would have run it. The building is handed over with highly capable equipment but no funding for training, leaving the facilities team to fall back on manual overrides and sealed vents. The building might have scored well on the design checklist, but the people running it had to live with a different reality.

Gate 3: Timeline

The timeline gate tests whether project speed is allowed to slow once it begins causing harm. A fixed date with a compressed timeline keeps the same amount of work while stripping out the time the work needed.

That time has to come from somewhere, and in construction it can be absorbed by the people doing the assembly. A late design change reaches the field, and the plan updates within the hour, which looks like agility, until we notice that the opening date will not move with it. The time needed to absorb the change cannot expand, so it contracts the work instead. Installers re-sequence under intense pressure, tear out finished work to re-route conduit, and spend their safety buffers to meet a date none of them set.

A timeline gate is working when the schedule can actually be stopped, when there are pause points somebody has the authority to call, lead times that cannot be compressed below what the work needs, and a review that must happen before a late change order is absorbed.

Gate 4: Feedback

The feedback gate tests whether what the finished building teaches is allowed to change what was already decided. Feedback that is collected but cannot reopen a funded decision stays a record and corrects nothing.

Some healthcare layouts streamline travel paths or departmental adjacencies on paper while creating unexpected walking burdens in daily operations. A time and motion study across 36 hospitals found that medical-surgical nurses walked a median of about three miles in a shift, with some walking closer to five, every shift, year after year. Walking burden and fatigue may surface in staff surveys, but by then, the building belongs to a separate management budget, and the number is read as a staffing matter, and no one treats it as evidence about the design.

The industry has created tools to tackle this. Post-occupancy evaluations look at how a finished building performs in real life rather than on paper. Soft Landings goes a step further, keeping the design and delivery team attached to the project after handover so the people who developed the specifications are still around when the operational problems pop up.

The trouble is that neither framework is standard practice, and neither one gives a team the actual authority to go back and fix a decision once the capital budget is closed.

Listening is only useful when we have decided what the listening is allowed to change. The people who hold that knowledge are rarely the ones the reporting chain is built to hear. Nurses in a hospital can usually name a layout problem years before it reaches a facilities report, because they read the building every shift through their own fatigue. The feedback gate works only when that reading is treated as evidence, not complaint.

Reading the cases through the gates

With the four gates in hand, we can go back to the two buildings and see what we could not see before. Edinburgh is what it looks like when every gate is already at its limit. Citicorp is the same structure read forward, turning on a single gate that held under load.

Gate	Edinburgh	Citicorp
Sponsorship	No senior route with the standing to challenge; warnings thinned on the way up	The design engineer had the standing to reach top leadership directly
Budget	Quality assurance and client-side inspection capacity were severely underfunded	Emergency capital was immediately released to fund the fix
Timeline	Construction speed was pursued without the capacity to pause and inspect	The schedule was immediately reopened for overnight welding and repair
Feedback	Performance failures only surfaced after the schools were occupied	The occupied building was opened up to act on the student's findings

Table 15. Reading the Edinburgh and Citicorp cases through the four gates

The two buildings tell a story about capacity, not about one careful team and one careless one. One system had a gate with enough authority in reserve to pull the others open behind it; the other had four gates already spent before the work began. Seen this way, the difference stops being a matter of who cared, which is a question that leads nowhere, and becomes a matter of which gates were strong, which is a question we can actually act on.

Designing the pathway

The work begins with the humbler act of looking, of finding these four gates in a real project and asking honestly how much pressure each one can actually withstand. Most projects will find at least one gate near its limit. This is a beginning, and it settles nothing on its own, because a gate we can name is a gate we can fund, slow, or staff before the next constraint arrives.

For the values we care about to survive a cost crunch, the truth has to have somewhere to go. The first step asks no one to be braver; it builds the place the truth can travel to, and we now know where to look for it.

Garden Scene, Tomb of Ipuy, ca. 1290–1224 BCE

Norman de Garis Davies, facsimile of a wall painting at Deir el-Medina

CHAPTER 14

LEVERS OF CHANGE

How do better choices make it into budgets, specifications, and contracts?

Every project, product, and initiative takes shape through hundreds of small decisions. We often imagine that a project's ethical direction is settled in a boardroom or a high-level charter. In practice, that direction is carried through a submittal log, the running record of what a contractor proposes to install, plus a messy spreadsheet, a site review, and an open file on a desktop.

Some of these decision points are highly visible:

- The master request for proposals (RFP), the formal document through which an organization invites and evaluates bids
- The municipal climate action plan
- The building certification scorecard
- The technical specification
- The supplier code of conduct

Others slip by almost unnoticed: a response to a request for information (the routine query a contractor sends when a drawing or requirement is unclear); a tender scoring question; a material substitution form; a Division 01 clause (the general requirements section at the front of a construction specification); or the standard procurement phrase allowing an "approved equal."

> ***These small moments are exactly where human impact either enters the work or is left outside it. They carry a commitment toward the gates described in the previous chapter, where it can be funded, protected, revised, or left behind.***

Where intent meets execution

Change becomes practical when it reaches the people already using these documents every day.

- **Contractors** do not build from corporate aspirations. They build from drawings, schedules, prices, contracts, submittals, technical clarifications, and change orders.
- **Cities** do not implement equity in the abstract. They implement it through budgets, capital projects, housing programs, transit investments, procurement rules, and reporting cycles.
- **Architects** do not simply purchase better materials. They specify what procurement permits, what the submittal proves, what estimating can defend, and what facilities can maintain.

A decision made early can create a long chain of consequences. A shortened lead time reaches procurement, the prime contractor, the subcontractor, and finally the people doing the work. Each person may be making a defensible choice within their role. The combined effect can still be a double shift, rushed installation, or a safety margin that softly disappears.

Adoption means finding the points where that chain can be interrupted before the burden reaches the people with the least room to absorb it.

> ***The point is not to create a new administrative process. It is to help the documents already guiding the work carry a fuller account of the impact on people.***

This chapter looks at five familiar leverage points where we can make those adjustments.

Lever 1: Procurement

Procurement is one of the most direct ways to make social value operational because it controls access to contracts and capital. It is a sequence of highly practical filters:

- An early market inquiry or supplier questionnaire asks who may be capable of doing the work.
- The RFP asks what bidders propose to deliver.
- The scoring matrix decides which qualities carry weight.
- Early contractor engagement tests whether the requirement is workable.

- The contract determines whether the requirement is funded.
- Delivery review checks whether the promised benefit appeared in practice.

Procurement carries weight because scoring and contracts hold genuine commercial force.

When an organization claims social value matters but forces bidders to compete strictly on price, schedule, and experience, that commitment dissolves. Often, tenders include a single, vague question: "Describe your approach to social impact."

The answers are often broad because the question is broad. Bidders may describe volunteering, workforce diversity, or local hiring without explaining what will change in this particular contract. The buyer is then left with little basis for comparing one proposal with another.

Governments have used different mechanisms to give social commitments commercial or institutional weight. The United Kingdom has done so through procurement scoring, while India's Companies Act routes responsibility through corporate spending, board oversight, and disclosure rather than tender evaluation.

The gate before the score

Weighting is useful for comparing added value. It is less appropriate for deciding whether basic protections apply. A proposal should not be able to compensate for a serious wage, safety, or labor-practice concern by scoring well elsewhere.

Minimum requirements can therefore sit before the scoring stage. A bidder that cannot demonstrate wage compliance, credible dust controls, or transparent subcontracting practices does not proceed to the financial comparison.

Price is considered only after the proposal has met the minimum conditions required for responsible delivery.

Try this

Add one focused question to a future tender asking bidders to identify:

- The frontline groups the work will affect
- The material risks or benefits for those groups
- The evidence they will provide
- The person responsible for acting on the findings
- The stage at which the issue will be reviewed

Test the question with contractors before issuing the tender. Their response will tell you whether the requirement is clear, proportionate, and possible within the proposed schedule. If it is workable, give it enough weight to affect the award. If it is not, revise the requirement or the commercial conditions rather than asking bidders to promise what the contract will not support.

Lever 2: Climate and sustainability plans

Municipal climate action plans and corporate resilience roadmaps are proving grounds for whether environmental ambition translates into lived human benefits. The lever reads the same at both scales.

A serious plan may begin with carbon accounting, but it quickly reaches housing affordability, household energy costs, transit access, extreme heat, flooding, green jobs, and community trust.

Often, a city commits to decarbonization and environmental justice in its opening pages while its implementation tables track only physical outputs:

- Megawatts of renewable energy
- Vehicle miles traveled
- Tree canopy
- Waste diversion
- Metric tons of carbon reduced

These measures matter, but they do not show how the benefits and burdens are distributed. Without that second layer, equity remains an intention rather than a guide to implementation.

Our internal review of 30 municipal and metropolitan climate action plans across six global regions found that nearly every plan used equity language, but only a minority measured who benefited and who paid rather than tracking physical outputs alone. This was an internal analysis; the scoring rubric, city list, and selection method are on file with the author and available on request.

The next step is to place distribution alongside environmental performance.

- Who experiences the immediate relief created by cooler streets?
- Who receives the financial savings from energy retrofits?
- Who gains reliable, step-free access to clean transportation?
- Who is protected from displacement when green infrastructure increases nearby land values?

This is how a just transition becomes a working discipline. It connects the move toward a low-carbon economy with the workers, households, and neighborhoods most likely to carry the cost of change.

Try this

Choose one action in a current sustainability or resilience plan that is measured only through an environmental indicator. Add:

- The population most affected
- The likely human benefits and risks
- The accountable owner
- The source of evidence
- The route for affected people to contribute information
- The point at which the action will be reviewed and adjusted

This does not require rebuilding the plan. It adds human impact to a structure that already exists.

Lever 3: Technical specifications

The technical specification is where high-level strategy becomes a buildable requirement, making it the lever closest to the physical outcome.

An executive strategy can promise healthy air, a rating system can reward transparency, and a designer can prefer a responsible product, but procurement will ultimately buy exactly what the master specification permits. The specification is where a human outcome becomes something a project team can require, verify, and defend.

Consider a team that selects a healthier and more responsibly made product early in design. Late in the project, a substitution request arrives with a cheaper alternative.

The original product may have been selected for several reasons:

- Lower emissions
- Safer installation
- Better durability
- Easier maintenance
- Greater ingredient transparency
- A take-back pathway
- Stronger labor documentation

But if those qualities were never written into the specification, the substitution is assessed mainly on cost, appearance, and technical compatibility.

The team may approve the substitute as equal because the document never defined which human or environmental qualities had to remain equal.

A stronger specification places the required evidence in Division 01 and in the relevant technical sections. The documentation should match the material's actual risks.

Material category	Primary human and environmental risk	Required specification focus
Paints and wet adhesives	Volatile organic compounds (VOCs) affecting installers' respiratory health	Strict VOC limits and indoor emissions verification
Engineered stone and quartz	Silica dust exposure causing worker silicosis	Verified factory and site dust controls and manufacturing disclosures
Structural timber	Illegal logging and deforestation	Forest traceability and chain-of-custody documentation
Commercial flooring	Chemical maintenance burden and hazardous exposure	Lower toxicity maintenance, installer safety, and circular take-back pathways

Table 16. Material categories, human risk, and required specification

This approach is beginning to scale across the building industry. Gensler's Product Sustainability Standards establish performance criteria across high-impact product categories. The Common Materials Framework, developed by mindful MATERIALS, is a shared structure across human health, climate health, ecosystem health, social health and equity, and circularity. It was developed by a cross-disciplinary group beginning in 2021 and publicly endorsed in November 2023 by the American Institute of Architects, the International Living Future Institute, the International WELL Building Institute, and the U.S. Green Building Council.

A shared vocabulary makes material requirements easier for manufacturers to anticipate and for project teams to repeat.

Try this

Select one high-impact material category on an active project. Identify the human risks that matter across manufacture, installation, use, maintenance, and removal. Then write those protections into the specification.

For flooring, this might include:

- Material-health disclosure
- Low-emissions verification
- Installer-safety instructions
- Safer maintenance procedures
- Durability expectations
- Manufacturer take-back information

Substitutions can still go ahead; writing these protections into the specification simply makes the basis of equivalence clear.

Lever 4: Certifications and lifecycle evidence

Building certifications matter less for the plaque than for the decisions required to earn it.

Each prerequisite, feature, or credit can change something the project team was already going to decide:

- What gets specified
- What receives funding
- Which evidence must be submitted
- What gets measured after occupancy
- Who is accountable for performance

The right requirement can carry a human question into the brief, specification, submittal log, or operating plan. That is what makes a scorecard useful.

Under cost and schedule pressure, project teams naturally favor credits that are easier to document and less expensive to deliver. The result may be a strong overall score that says little about the project's most significant human risks. The response is to keep the rating system and choose the requirements most likely to improve the actual conditions of the project.

Lifecycle thinking has expanded through several complementary approaches:

- **Environmental Life Cycle Assessment (LCA):** Tracks environmental footprints across extraction, manufacturing, transport, use, and disposal.
- **Cradle to Cradle:** Examines how materials can support health, reuse, and technical or biological nutrient cycles.
- **Social Life Cycle Assessment (S-LCA):** Applies lifecycle thinking to people and communities.

In an internal review of building products, I found that material-health documentation was widely available, while information about labor conditions in manufacturing and supply chains was far harder to trace. Many manufacturers disclose corporate policies and supplier codes. Fewer disclose:

- Findings from third-party audits
- Wage-remediation cases
- Worker-voice channels
- Living-wage verification
- Product-specific labor information

To shape how a team uses certification, begin with the project's most material human risks, then select the credits, features, or documentation pathways that make those risks visible and actionable.

Try this

Review an active certification scorecard and identify three requirements most likely to improve human conditions. For each one, ask:

- Will this change the design?
- Will it change the specification?
- Will it influence procurement?
- Will it require meaningful evidence?
- Will it change how the building is operated?

A credit with no effect on any of these may still have value, but it is unlikely to be the strongest lever for human impact.

Lever 5: The pilot

Large institutional changes can be difficult to introduce across an entire organization at once. A pilot provides a contained starting point to test out a requirement, method or approach:

- One product category
- One vendor tender
- One floor plate
- One project site
- One engagement method

A well-designed pilot lowers the cost of learning. It allows a team to test a requirement, understand its practical effects, and improve it before wider adoption.

The weakness of many pilots is that they succeed and then remain isolated. The team completes the exercise, publishes the case study, and returns to the previous specification or procurement process. The learning never changes the next project.

A useful pilot therefore begins with an integration pathway. Before the work starts, the team should define:

- What risk or question is being tested?
- What evidence will be collected?
- Whose experience will count as feedback?
- What result would justify expansion?
- What result would require revision or stopping?
- Which standard document will change if the pilot succeeds?

The pilot brief should name the future default it is trying to influence. For example, a team may want to test product-level social disclosure without delaying procurement. It could begin with resilient flooring and ask manufacturers to submit:

- Verified material-health documentation
- Take-back information
- Installer-safety guidance
- Relevant supplier-labor outcomes

The project then becomes a place to learn which requirements are clear, which evidence is available, and which requests create unnecessary burden. The revised requirement can then move into the next procurement template.

Try this

Choose one contained opportunity and write the learning question before work begins. For example: Can we require product-level social disclosure in one material category without delaying procurement or reducing supplier participation?

Name the template, specification, policy, or review process that will be updated if the pilot works. Without that next step, the pilot may produce insight without producing adoption.

The levers across the five sites

Site	Procurement	Climate or sustainability plans	Specification	Certification or lifecycle evidence	Pilot
People	Ask bidders to identify affected workers, staffing assumptions, safety controls, grievance routes, and evidence behind an absolute quality gate	Add worker protections, extreme heat exposure limits, affordability baselines, mobility links, and health indicators to plan actions	Specify technical requirements for safe installation, maintainability, service personnel access, rest spaces, ergonomics, and indoor air quality	Choose credits or features that directly improve health, comfort, safety, accessibility, worker well-being, and post-occupancy feedback loops	Test a workload balance, contractor safety protocol, or direct worker-voice process on one contained project or site
Place	Ask contractors how site delivery affects physical access, community disruption, service clearways, neighbors, and the surrounding public-realm	Use climate plan findings to connect emissions reduction directly to heat mitigation, flooding relief, clean transit links, housing quality, and public health	Specify accessibility standards above code, acoustics, daylighting, external shade, intuitive wayfinding, cleaning access, and facilities maintenance capacity	Use rating frameworks only where optimization credits actively improve the physical working and living conditions of the place	Pilot a structured post-occupancy evaluation or inclusive design review on one building, floor plate, or public space

Product	Ask bidders what human risks the product creates across raw ingredient manufacturing, installation, daily use, facility maintenance, and end of life	Add material health disclosures, circularity metrics, repair access pathways, and social lifecycle priorities directly to product development roadmaps	Require EPDs, HPDs, Declare labels, Cradle to Cradle certificates, GREENGUARD, FSC, S-LCA evidence, installer safety guidance, repair sheets, and take-back logistics	Use LCA for environmental footprints, Cradle to Cradle for material health and circularity, and S-LCA to follow people across the product lifecycle	Pilot product-level social disclosure and transparency within one specific material category before making it a standard requirement
Partners	Use RFIs to learn what criteria suppliers can reliably meet, what liquidity support they require, and what buyer practices generate systemic delivery risk	Add supplier engagement strategies, responsible sourcing protocols, fair payment speed practices, and executive buyer accountability to the master plan	Specify responsible sourcing frameworks, vendor documentation, audit findings, ethical recruitment verification, and clear remediation pathways	Use third-party vendor audit mechanisms only when they rigorously match the documented labor and extraction risks of the value chain	Pilot accelerated payment velocities, bidirectional supplier feedback loops, or independent worker-voice platforms with one vendor group

Public Good	Ask bidders how project execution creates durable local benefit, minimizes disruption, expands civic access, and preserves community trust	Use climate and just transition findings to connect decarbonization capital directly to quality job creation, affordability, health access, and neighborhood resilience	Specify genuine public-space access, local wealth-benefit tracking, universal design, permanent maintenance funding, and binding anti-displacement covenants	Use community-oriented rating systems only when the verified credits actively shape equitable governance, ongoing access, and local benefit sharing	Pilot formal community co-governance, disaggregated local hiring tracking, or accessible public benefit reporting on a single project site

Table 17. The five levers across the five sites

The next line

Institutional change can sound larger than the decisions through which it actually happens. In practice, it may begin with one RFI question, one procurement threshold, one climate-plan metric, one specification clause, one certification requirement, one pilot brief, one substitution rule, or one reporting field.

The point is not to create a new administrative process. It is to help the documents already guiding the work carry a more complete account of its impact on people.

The practical test comes when the project becomes expensive, late, politically difficult, or commercially inconvenient. Does the human commitment still appear in the requirements, the budget, the evidence, and the approval process?

If it does, the commitment has become part of how the work is delivered. If it disappears, the next task is not to question whether people cared enough. It is to strengthen the document or decision point that was unable to carry it.

Study of Clouds, 5 September 1822

John Constable

CHAPTER 15

MAPPING PROGRESS

How do we measure progress without waiting for perfect data?

In the natural world, the accounting of survival is kept with a certain brutal honesty. A Douglas fir under prolonged water stress does not decide to shed a branch; it simply lets it go. Its outermost branches are the most vulnerable points in its plumbing. As the water columns inside them break under tension, those branches die back and eventually fall.

Losing them is less an amputation than a triage, and the tree does not always survive the crisis. But the feedback is immediate and entirely without sentiment. Living systems persist not because they possess an ideology of endurance, but because they are unable to ignore the truth of their own strain.

Organizations are much better at separating a decision from the conditions it creates. The choice may appear in one budget, while its consequences surface months later in another department, another contract, or another person's working day.

Measurement can therefore create a misleading sense of progress. Tracking a condition and improving it are not the same thing.

A sophisticated dashboard may show that an organization is collecting more data without showing whether people's conditions have changed. To know which way we are moving, we have to watch two things at once: how good the outcome actually is for people, and how deeply the practice is built into the way we work.

A project can produce an exceptional human outcome through individual heroism or a lucky combination of variables, yet remain entirely fragile because the system has no way to repeat it. Conversely, a corporate program can be meticulously audited, certified, and tracked, while continuing to pass an unmeasured tax down its supply chain. Progress requires seeing both.

The two instruments

Two tools help us read these dimensions separately. They look at the same decision from different angles:

- **The People Positive Spectrum:** This is the outcome tool. It asks what the decision is producing for people in practice.
- **The Progress Scale:** This is the adoption tool. It asks how deeply the practice has entered the documents, budgets, responsibilities, and review processes that guide everyday work.

The two tools are best read together as a two-axis map. One axis runs from risk (where the human outcome is still unknown) toward a positive outcome that has been achieved. The other runs from a fragile, one-off success toward a practice embedded deeply enough to have a strong chance of surviving a sudden budget cut or a change of leadership.

A positive outcome sitting on a fragile base is a success that may not be reliably repeated. An embedded practice with an unknown outcome is a well-established process whose effects are still unclear.

The goal is to move every major decision toward the corner where a good outcome and a durable practice hold at the same time.

Evaluating the outcome

Categorizing a human outcome as extractive, neutral, or positive begins with an unmapped baseline: risk.

Risk is where we begin when the evidence is incomplete. The data may be missing, fragmented, unverified, or disconnected from the experiences of the people affected. A cost saving may be recorded without any way to connect it to the compressed schedule, higher workload, or reduced safety margin that followed.

Once we establish a clear line of sight, the Spectrum evaluates what the evidence shows:

- **People Extractive:** The system generates commercial value or speed by drawing down human capacity, safety, health, or local staying power faster than people can recover.
- **People Neutral:** The system satisfies basic regulatory compliance and meets legal criteria, but its frame is too narrow to see or protect the wider network of lives it alters.
- **People Positive:** The system intentionally designs stable, equitable human conditions into how value is created, delivered, maintained, and shared from the very beginning.

Evaluating the depth of application

While the Spectrum diagnoses the human condition, the Progress Scale tracks how durable our response is. It measures whether a value can survive a sudden budget cut or a leadership transition, mapping organizational maturity across six distinct stages:

- **Stage 0: Absent.** No one owns the issue. Nobody tracks it, nobody is asked about it, and it appears in none of the documents that govern the day-to-day work.
- **Stage 1: Mentioned.** The value is spoken about in a high-level public statement, a marketing brochure, or a corporate social responsibility report, but nothing is funded behind it.
- **Stage 2: Defined.** The commitment is written into a formal policy or a supplier code of conduct, but it has not yet entered the project budget or delivery process.
- **Stage 3: Operationalized.** The intent enters the practical work itself, appearing as a specific supplier requirement, a design guideline, or an active step somebody performs.

- **Stage 4: Measured.** Someone is actively tracking the metric closely enough that the organization would immediately notice if the human conditions began to degrade.
- **Stage 5: Embedded.** The metric is built into the review gates that have the authority to halt a project, into contingency funds set aside to fix what goes wrong, and into the public reporting that makes it visible outside the company. This gives the practice its strongest chance of holding when budgets tighten or leadership changes.

The scale does not measure moral worth. A practice can sit at Stage 4 and still reveal a fundamentally extractive outcome.

The goal is to ask these questions of project choices:

- Are we creating better conditions for people?
- Is the organization becoming better able to protect, correct, and repeat those conditions when pressure arrives?

The progress map

The two tools can be used together across the five sites of human consequence introduced in Part 2.

The map below puts the framework on a single page. It can be filled in one row at a time, for one decision. Most teams will only need to populate two or three rows at once.

Site	Human outcome	Adoption depth	Risks and unknowns	Feedback source	Next correction
People	Risk / Extractive / Neutral / Positive	Stage 0–5	Where is physical fatigue or unmeasured turnover accumulating behind broad corporate averages?	Trade workers, subcontractors, facilities crews, shift managers, disaggregated HR logs	Adjust staffing assumptions, re-sequence shifts, and fund safety buffers
Place	Risk / Extractive / Neutral / Positive	Stage 0–5	Which wings, service corridors, or maintenance routes force users to spend energy compensating for poor design?	Occupants, overnight cleaners, technicians, transient visitors, local route testing	Reopen design specifications, reallocate maintenance capital, and modify layouts
Product	Risk / Extractive / Neutral / Positive	Stage 0–5	What hazardous chemical exposures, supply chain liabilities, or end-of-life disposal costs does our product carry?	Trade installers, fabricators, component suppliers, municipal waste handlers	Substitute toxic chemistry, reformulate specifications, and structure take-back paths

Partners	Risk / Extractive / Neutral / Positive	Stage 0–5	Where are our aggressive payment terms or compressed lead times forcing vendors to squeeze their own workforces?	Direct suppliers, secondary subcontractors, confidential worker-voice channels	Accelerate payment velocities, lock in stable lead times, and adjust contract pricing
Public Good	Risk / Extractive / Neutral / Positive	Stage 0–5	Who is being economically thinned out, displaced, or excluded as a direct result of our investment?	Neighborhood residents, independent local businesses, historical civic data	Fund local covenants, allocate below-market space, and shift governance power

Table 18. The progress map across the five sites

The feedback loop

A progress map remains useful only if the information moving through it can change what happens next. That requires a feedback loop with a clear path from evidence to decision and from decision to correction.

An effective loop moves through five steps:

1. **Listen:** Gathering direct evidence from the people closest to the condition, including those with the least authority to change or refuse it.

2. **Interpret:** Placing that evidence alongside financial, scheduling, safety, and operating data to understand what may be producing the strain.

3. **Decide:** Taking the evidence to a decision point where someone has the authority to change the budget, schedule, scope, specification, or contract.

4. **Act:** Making the correction, such as revising a contract clause, changing a specification, adjusting staffing, or funding a safeguard.

5. **Verify:** Returning to the people who raised or experienced the issue to check whether the change improved the condition.

When a feedback loop breaks, the failure often happens at the third step, the transition from interpretation to decision. An organization may listen carefully and document what it hears but send the findings to a team with no authority or funding to respond.

Listening can build trust, clarify what happened, and help people feel heard. The loop is not complete, however, until the evidence is allowed to influence a decision. Before gathering feedback, the organization should be clear about what can be changed, who can authorize it, and how the response will be communicated.

From feedback to remedy

When an active feedback loop reveals that harm or widespread extraction has already occurred, the response must go beyond recording the issue. There needs to be a defined path for remedy and material repair.

This is where a general community benefit must be separated from a specific remedy owed to the people who carried the cost. A corporate grant, a local mural, or a public park may be highly valuable additions to a neighborhood, but they are acts of goodwill that do not directly amount to reparations.

> ***Benefit and remedy are related, but they are not interchangeable. When a company causes or contributes to harm, international standards recognize a responsibility to cooperate in providing a remedy for the adverse impact.***
>
> ***In human rights law, the term reparations is generally associated with grave, systematic, or historical violations and can include restitution, compensation, rehabilitation, and guarantees that the harm will not recur. Most project or***

corporate remedies do not operate at that scale, so the terms should not be used interchangeably.

A general benefit is offered broadly. A remedy is directed toward the people who experienced the specific harm.

A development that prices out a block of low-rent tenants and then opens a beautiful public plaza on the site has created something real. The plaza does not, by itself, remedy the displacement. It does not restore housing, financial footing, or decision-making power to the people who had to leave.

Remedy begins by naming exactly what was taken, depleted, or made invisible. This might include land surrendered without a fair return, labor underpaid or made unsafe, a neighborhood destabilized by rising costs, a subcontractor forced to finance a buyer's cash flow, or a community left holding the maintenance bill after the value has moved on.

It then asks who benefited, who carried the cost, and what would materially repair the harm. That response may involve moving capital, land, governance authority, protection, or a share of future financial value toward the people and places that carried the burden.

In the built environment, that can look like a community land trust, long-term affordable commercial space, a binding anti-displacement covenant, a funded environmental cleanup, supplier repayment, wage restitution, or a voting governance seat for the people most affected.

Each changes the distribution of value or authority. That is what distinguishes a material correction from a response that is primarily symbolic.

Honest proof

Requests for greater precision can be legitimate, especially when evidence will support a public claim, legal conclusion, or consequential investment decision. Weak evidence can create its own harm.

But uncertainty should not become a reason to ignore conditions that are already visible. The absence of a complete global dataset does not prevent an organization from responding to a clear local pattern of delayed payments, unsafe work, or repeated strain.

Honest proof requires us to be clear about what we know, how we know it, what remains uncertain, and which boundaries our evidence covers.

We do not need a perfect, multi-tier global supply-chain record to notice that current payment terms are pushing a local supplier toward insolvency. We do not need a multi-year academic study to respond when a compressed construction schedule is producing repeated safety shortcuts on site.

At the same time, the response should remain proportionate. A warning signal may justify investigation, an interim safeguard, or a pause. It may not yet justify a sweeping public conclusion about an entire organization or supply chain.

Moving outward

As these measures enter ordinary reviews, budgets, and project documents, better conditions become less dependent on a particular champion or an unusually generous budget. They become easier to protect and repeat.

But keeping that progress locked inside a single organization or a single project team is not enough. A practice can be perfectly mapped and governed internally and still fail to shift the broader industry if the insight remains stranded in a local shared drive.

The next question is how that learning travels, first across the rooms and teams of the organization itself, and then outward into the wider field. It has to travel without being reduced to vague claims, overstated beyond the evidence, or buried in technical language that the next person cannot use.

Recap of Part 3

A system does not change when we write a better mission statement. It changes when we alter the defaults that govern its daily execution.

Part 3 focused on the practical, unglamorous work of building human consequence into the checkpoints and administrative tools that guide our projects and organizations.

We traced how uncomfortable data can trigger organizational self-defense, and how to build structural pathways that let truth travel safely from the field to the executive desk. We looked at the gates that must hold when a project faces budget and timeline compression, and we mapped the specific administrative levers we can pull on any given Tuesday to rewrite the instructions of the built world.

Four points to carry forward

- **Evidence Needs a Route.** If the organization does not have an administrative path strong enough to carry uncomfortable evidence, the person who uncovers a risk will always be treated as the problem. We must protect the messenger by structuring the escalation path in advance.
- **A Gate Needs Authority.** A real project gate must hold the contractual authority to halt progress, reject a bid, or delay a schedule when basic human baseline conditions are breached. Checkboxes that cannot stop a project are just administrative theater.

- **Procurement Is a Powerful Lever.** What we say we care about in the design presentation is irrelevant if our contract terms force our suppliers to squeeze their people to survive. Social value begins in the pricing model and the payment terms.
- **Maturity Becomes Visible Under Pressure.** A progressive practice is only truly embedded when it remains protected during a cost crunch. If a human protection is the first thing to be value-engineered out when margins tighten, it was never operationalized; it was merely tolerated.

With the diagnostic tools, gates, and levers established, the organization has a stronger way to turn human evidence into action. The next challenge is transmission: how learning moves across teams, survives handoffs, and becomes useful outside the project or organization that produced it.

Instrument	Type	Function	Sample Checkpoint
Sponsorship	Gate	Authority to act on and resolve critical, uncomfortable findings	A named executive committed to owning the issue before it arises
Budget	Gate	Verification that a social commitment has direct financial backing	A dedicated, non-discretionary funding line in the master cost sheet
Timeline	Gate	The structural ability to slow schedules when speed causes harm	Non-penalized schedule relief clauses for subcontractor safety
Feedback	Gate	The authority of operational data to alter funded design defaults	Post-occupancy evaluations that trigger updates to master specifications

Procurement	Lever	The translation of values into commercial bidding requirements	Mandatory gateway filters that disqualify extractive bidders before scoring
Specifications	Lever	The codification of human baselines into legally binding contracts	Division 01 documentation requirements that prevent cheap substitutions

Table 19. Selected gates and levers of system adoption

PART 4

AMPLIFY

A project goes well, and then nothing comes of it. The budget battles are fought and won, the material specifications hold, the suppliers are treated fairly, and the job is delivered. Everyone shakes hands and moves on to the next thing.

The project folder is archived on a shared drive. A few months later, another team encounters a similar decision without the benefit of what was already learned. The earlier evidence remains accurate and useful, but it doesn't always reach the people who need it. A better way was demonstrated once without becoming easier to repeat.

In forest ecology, a fallen tree becomes what ecologists call a nurse log, a physical seedbed that stores moisture and nutrients, giving the next generation of seedlings a place to take root and grow. The tree keeps feeding the forest long after it is gone, but only because the forest floor is designed to receive it.

When we work on a responsible project, we are trying to create that kind of "nurse log." The templates we write, the budgets we defend, and the contracts we sign are proof that a better way works.

But proof doesn't travel on its own.

Without a clear path for that information to move, our wins remain isolated. They stay trapped in project folders, vulnerable to the next cost-cutting review or a change in leadership.

Part 4 is about building the channels that let our progress travel so it can lead to more progress. We do this by starting inside our own teams before we try to change the wider field:

- **Translation:** How to make our data legible to the next room down the corridor, especially the finance and procurement teams who hold the next decision.
- **Reporting:** How to package what we learned so it is portable and easy for another team to pick up and use, without flattening it into corporate PR spin.
- **Precedent:** How to turn an internal project win into an industry-wide standard, so the next company has the permission they need to do the same thing.

The Turkish Letter Writer, 1840

Sir David Wilkie

Left unfinished at the artist's death

CHAPTER 16

SPEAK THE LANGUAGE OF THE ROOM

How do we translate human-impact evidence to make it easy for decision-makers to use?

Seven years into my career, shortly after moving from one continent to another for a new position, I sent this email to a colleague:

> *Dear Mary,*
>
> *Please send over the spec document from yesterday's project meeting.*
>
> *Best,*
> *Gayathri*

Where I had spent my entire professional life up to that point, an email like this was standard. It was clear, direct, and respectful of a colleague's time. I valued her schedule enough not to waste it with a longer preamble, so I told her exactly what I needed. The expected response from her was just three letters and an attachment:

PFA, short for "please find attached."

There wouldn't be an introduction or a sign-off in the response either.

Instead, my supervisor called me into her office that afternoon. In the careful tone people use when delivering awkward feedback, she told me my new colleagues had found my email rude.

I remember sitting there, running the words back through my mind like a document search, looking for the error. The facts were right. The request was clear. I hadn't been unkind.

What I had missed, I gradually realized, was the unwritten social choreography the new room required before a request could even be processed: the warm opener, the hope that they were doing well, the framing of a direct ask as a polite invitation. None of this was written down anywhere. There was no way to know I had gotten it wrong until after the message had already been received negatively. The information itself was sound; what tripped me up were the unwritten rules of how it had to be packaged to be received.

There is a name for this in Amharic, the language of highland Ethiopia. Säm-ənna wärq, or "wax and gold," describes a form of poetry where the surface words carry one obvious meaning, while a second, deeper meaning waits underneath for those who know how to look for it.

The phrase comes from the goldsmith's bench. A wax model is packed in clay, the wax is heated until it melts and runs out, and molten gold is poured into the hollow space left behind. The wax is not a trick or a disguise; it is the mold that decides what shape the gold will take.

> ***Translation inside a company works the same way. The core issue, the reality on the ground, is the gold, and it stays constant. What changes is the wax, the surface form the argument has to take before a particular room can receive it. If you get the mold wrong, the substance has nowhere to settle.***

My brief email carried the gold but none of the wax, so it did not have a shape that could easily be understood.

The route into the right room

A team can run a strong study, prove their case, and still watch it fizzle out three doors down because they delivered it in a language the next department cannot use. Before your proof can shift a wider market, it first has to survive the trip down your own hallway, moving from the room that uncovered the problem to the rooms that hold the budget and the schedule. This is where real change starts: the unglamorous, daily work of making evidence legible to the next person who has to act on it.

This pattern repeats whenever someone tries to bring human evidence into a business decision. Sometimes the evidence stalls even when the facts are sound and the issue matters, because it does not yet connect to the responsibilities of the people receiving it.

When I worked on the WELL Building Standard, a large part of my job was translating medical and public health research into the practical language of design, construction, and building operations. The science itself was rarely new. Data on indoor air quality, lighting, sleep disruption, and cognitive performance had existed for decades in medical journals. The gap was that the people designing and building commercial properties were looking at entirely different dashboards, with different incentives, margin pressures, and definitions of success.

My first few presentations went badly. I stood in rooms full of experienced architects, engineers, and contractors and essentially told them that their standard, compliant way of doing things was making people sick. I showed academic papers. I brought in scientists.

Project leads told me the standards I was suggesting were unrealistic, expensive, and clearly written by academics who had never had to meet a construction schedule in the wild. The annoying part was that they were right.

Their resistance had nothing to do with the quality of the science. Many of them had the same technical background as I did. The problem was the shape the argument had taken. From their side of the table, it looked less like a solution and more like a verdict that had already been reached without them.

I had to learn how to talk about these issues differently. The conversation changed only when I stopped trying to prove the science and started translating it into the metrics they were already responsible for. The data hadn't changed, but the route into the right room had.

Over time, as the translation improved, the friction eased. We learned how to talk about human outcomes in a way that actually helped project teams do their jobs and defend their budgets, without making them feel like their entire careers were being put on trial. WELL has since scaled across more than 130 countries and billions of square feet of real estate. That kind of scale requires aligned capital and early adopters, but beneath it all, it requires thousands of tedious, precise translations.

Evidence does not move across an industry simply because it is true. It moves because it becomes useful to the people who are responsible for the next decision.

Lost in translation

Working inside a large company can feel like a game where everyone is using the same words but meaning entirely different things. The person trying to protect the people on the ground is almost never the person making the final financial call. That distance is where the message gets lost.

If you present the same evidence about supply chain labor conditions or indoor air quality to five different departments, you will hear five different sets of questions, shaped by what each department is responsible for:

- **The sales lead** is trying to hit a demanding revenue target while fending off a new competitor. She is calculating whether your claim gives her an edge to close a deal or just adds friction to a time-sensitive pitch.
- **The finance director** is balancing cash flow during a period of volatile interest rates. He runs your numbers through immediate risk exposure, making sure unexpected costs don't mess up an upcoming credit review.
- **The operations manager** is navigating a tight labor shortage with a lean site team. His eye slides straight to capacity, calculating whether his crew can absorb new compliance routines without quitting.
- **The legal counsel** is focused on regulatory precedent. She scans your data for liability exposure, trying to insulate the firm from long-term litigation risks.
- **The regional director** is evaluating whether your ethical sourcing pathway is buildable under current shipping bottlenecks, or if it risks leaving his job site stranded without materials.

None of these people are hostile to the human argument. Their reactions are practical reflections of the outcomes they are accountable for under pressure.

The risk is presenting the case as though every part of the organization evaluates evidence through the same logic. A strong moral case and a strong operational case can support each other, but they do not automatically take the same form.

There is a persistent gap between what a company says it values and what its daily operating systems protect. Sincerity alone does not bridge this gap. The evidence also needs to be usable in the room that holds the decision, not the room where you gathered the data.

What translation requires

> ***Translation is not a way of softening the truth; it makes the truth legible to the people who have to sign off on it, which means understanding what they are already on the hook to defend.***

Consider the difference between two ways of presenting the same finding:

- **Version A:** "Workers in poorly lit service areas experience higher rates of fatigue and injury, which is a basic dignity concern."
- **Version B:** "Poor lighting in service corridors may increase safety risk and contribute to accidents, fatigue, and avoidable maintenance disruption. We should examine incident reports, turnover data, and rework costs to determine the operational exposure in this building."

The second version keeps the human reality intact and connects the human cost directly to the financial and operational gears of the company. It gives the decision-maker a practical, defensible reason to act.

The strongest case may use both versions: the human reason the condition matters and the operational reason the organization can act on it.

One useful test is whether the evidence helps the person responsible do one or more of these five things:

- **Defend a Budget:** Show how protecting conditions prevents a cost spike elsewhere.
- **Reduce a Risk:** Ground the human impact in terms of legal, operational, or insurance liabilities.
- **Protect a Specification:** Give the team the exact metrics they need to defend ethical materials from being value-engineered out.
- **Improve a Delivery Outcome:** Tie the human data directly to project quality, schedule preservation, or team capacity.
- **Explain Value to a Skeptical Client:** Package the impact as a clear commercial or reputational asset they can easily defend.

Evidence is more likely to influence a decision when it helps the person responsible understand both why the issue matters and what action is available to them. Without that connection, even important findings may be acknowledged without changing the decision.

An argument that works in a room already aligned around the issue may not work in a room carrying different responsibilities. The first can begin with shared values. The second may need to begin with shared constraints, such as cost, safety, quality, legal duty, or delivery.

For progress to hold across the organization, the evidence has to work in both kinds of rooms. The goal is to keep the human reality intact while connecting it directly to the decision already being made.

Moving forward

When we treat translation as a professional discipline rather than a workaround, we rely less on individual courage or corporate goodwill. It helps us map the rooms, identify the constraints, and do the translation work before the meeting even starts.

When the evidence does not change the decision, the next step is to understand why. The barrier may be translation, but it may also be authority, funding, timing, conflicting incentives, or an unwillingness to act. Better translation can address the first. It cannot substitute for the others.

Where the issue is one of translation, we revise the approach. Where the barrier lies elsewhere, we need to strengthen the gate, change the commercial conditions, or bring the evidence to someone with the authority to act.

The Geographer, 1669

Johannes Vermeer

CHAPTER 17

MAKE PROOF PORTABLE

How does one project's proof become the next project's starting point?

Chapter 16 was about translating human-impact evidence so the person holding the next decision can actually understand it. This chapter is about what happens after that meeting ends.

An argument that convinces one team in one room still has to survive being handed off to another team, on another project, months down the line, without you there to defend it. Translation makes proof readable; portability keeps it usable once it changes hands.

> *The problem underneath both is the same: proof stays where it was made unless someone builds it a route.*

Somewhere inside your company's network, a finished pilot report sits untouched in a nested folder. Meanwhile, in a meeting room three doors down, a group of project managers is arguing about the exact budget problem that the report already solved.

Re-solving problems that another team has already addressed consumes time, money, and institutional attention.

We see this happen across organizations. A design team runs a successful healthy-materials pilot. They answer the main technical and practical questions raised by the project. The new flooring performs beautifully under heavy foot traffic, the maintenance crew confirms it's easy to clean, and the staff feedback is positive.

But three months later, the next project hits a budget crunch. Because the data from that successful pilot was never turned into a permanent procurement rule for the estimating team, the new project managers revert to the lower-cost conventional material during a late-night cost-cutting session.

One team gained a useful case study, while the next team made its decision without access to the evidence behind it.

> ***A useful report has to do three jobs: it gathers scattered evidence, connects it directly to decisions, and leaves behind proof that the next team can actually use. Reporting usually focuses on the first.***

Stranded proof

When leaders talk about proving the business case for treating people better, they may assume they need to commission expensive new research. They brace themselves for a long, slow climb to prove something from scratch.

Often, however, the proof your teams have already generated is stranded before it can reach the next decision-maker.

This happens constantly when certifications are treated as the conclusion of one team's work rather than as evidence other teams can use. A study of office buildings by the MIT Real Estate Innovation Lab found that properties carrying a health-focused certification commanded rents between 4.4% and 7.7% higher per square foot than uncertified buildings, a premium that remained even after accounting for the building's age, location, or other green ratings.

The study suggests that the market can recognize this value. But inside many developer organizations, the evidence may not reach the commercial teams positioned to use it.

The design and construction teams get the plaque on the wall and complete their part of the work. Meanwhile, the leasing team pitches the building using existing sales materials because the certification data was not translated into a toolkit they can use. Some of the commercial value may therefore remain unrealized because the proof stayed with the team that produced it.

The data is siloed, not missing

The standard complaint about "social" data in business is that it is too soft, too qualitative, and too hard to pin down. In reality, that data already exists in concrete form. It simply sits in silos, scattered across systems that may not connect.

If you look across any company, the human data is already there. It is sitting in safety logs, supplier reviews, HR exit interviews, community feedback forms, accessibility audits, and procurement spreadsheets. The problem is that these fragments live in entirely different systems, formatted for different audiences, with no line of sight between them.

The disconnect between facilities and human resources offers a useful illustration.

A building engineer, trying to hit a tight energy-efficiency target, reduces the fresh air ventilation rates during the hottest summer weeks. On the engineer's spreadsheet, he just saved the company thousands of dollars in utility costs.

On the floor above, the HR team is trying to figure out why mid-afternoon productivity is tanking, employee headaches are spiking, and people are leaving early. They have employee survey scores and desk usage data, but they have no access to the ventilation logs.

Both teams are looking at the same problem from opposite sides of a wall, and neither has a system built to connect the dots. A substantial body of building-science research links ventilation and indoor air quality with cognitive performance, yet those data may never reach the department trying to understand the symptoms.

Proof doesn't look like proof when it is locked in a room that doesn't know how to read it.

What a report is actually for

This requires us to ask a different question from the one that often guides corporate reporting. The standard question is: What are we required to disclose?

The people-positive question is: After this report is written, what can the next project team, procurement lead, estimator, or community partner do differently because this proof now exists?

A report that answers the second question serves an additional purpose. It maps exactly where human impact lives inside the company's existing data. It draws a traceable, evidence-based connection between the maintenance log and the occupant's health, between a supplier's payment terms and a labor violation three tiers down, and between a genuine community engagement process and the speed of your next municipal approval.

It presents those connections in a form that can defend a budget, protect a specification, clarify a risk, or support the human case for action. That is the difference between a report that records what happened and one that also helps shape what the next team does when pressure rises.

The portable handoff

A practical approach to reporting treats the document as a handoff to the next team. This means that the primary audience is the next project team, ahead of any auditor, investor, or public relations firm: the people who will inherit the budget templates and specifications left behind, and who need to understand exactly what those choices will produce on the ground.

Including that audience changes what the report needs to contain. Instead of sorting the findings by compliance categories, we can organize them by how they affect decisions:

- What do we know now that we didn't know before?
- What specific project choice does this knowledge protect or improve?
- Who needs to receive this data before the next design or budget cycle begins?

This turns scattered fragments into connective tissue. The maintenance log links to employee health. The payment terms link to supplier stability. The community review links to the construction timeline.

When we make proof portable, we turn temporary wins into institutional memory. A lesson that survives one handoff can survive a second, and eventually, the practice stops depending on any single champion to keep it alive.

Farhad Carves a Milk Channel for Shirin, 1524 to 1525

Attributed to Shaikh Zada

CHAPTER 18

PROOF BECOMES PERMISSION

What turns a successful pilot into a precedent others can use?

There is a reason the same proof that inspires one room can fail in another. Early believers buy possibility, while the practical majority waits for proof that an idea survives ordinary constraints, and the same evidence rarely serves both.

> *This distinction matters. Being first proves that something can happen under exceptional conditions. The work of amplification is proving that it can happen again under ordinary ones.*

What leadership makes possible

It is tempting to equate leadership in this field with being first, with the courage to do something before others do. That is one dimension, and not the most durable one. Proof becomes generative when it makes the next better decision easier for someone else to take.

A certification that ends at a plaque proves something happened once, but may leave the next team, client, or supplier without enough information to repeat the result under similar pressure. A certification that becomes usable proof, that gives the next procurement officer something to cite in a budget review and the next developer something to show a skeptical investor, has done something meaningfully different. It has changed what the room is able to do.

This is where proof becomes permission. Permission here means a precedent that shifts the weight of the default, so the next team inherits an argument someone else has already made, with the evidence left where it can be found.

The blue diode

Early in my career, long before I was looking at building scorecards or carbon ledgers, my job was to walk the baking pavement of Dubai carrying a heavy, black hard-shell sample case filled with light-emitting diodes.

Long before I worked in social sustainability and healthy buildings, I was the person in the room with the strange blue light. It was the late 2000s. In the Middle East, lighting meant the rich, golden, heat-generating flood of halogen and incandescent bulbs. What I was pulling out of my foam-lined case looked like an alien artifact. When I clicked the battery pack, the diode cast a sharp, cold, spectral, slightly sickly 6000-Kelvin blue, a very cool blue-white color temperature, across the mahogany conference tables of the city's top architecture and design practices.

I would sit between lighting designers, electrical engineers, and project directors, and watch their enthusiasm evaporate. They did not care about my rehearsed pitch on solid-state physics or theoretical 50,000-hour lifespans. They looked at the blue tint reflected on their skin and asked two devastatingly practical questions: how bright does it actually get, and why does it make everyone look like a corpse?

At that time, you could not sell LED fixtures to an ordinary building. The clients most willing to consider them were innovators prepared to accept the uncertainty that came with being early. My commercial breakthrough was not a standard office block; it was the region's very first LEED-certified mosque.

The client who was building that mosque did not buy the LED because its light quality was superior to halogen. It objectively was not. They bought it because the sheer, radical possibility of a light source that drew a fraction of the standard wattage captivated them, and because they wanted the symbolic vanguard of the LEED plaque on the wall. They were willing to accept a slightly strange color temperature to test what the future might offer.

When researchers first mapped how new ideas travel through a culture, they drew a bell curve of adopter categories: innovators, early adopters, the early majority, the late majority, and laggards. In the textbook diagram, it looks tidy, as though an innovation rolls downhill under its own momentum, handed cleanly from one group to the next.

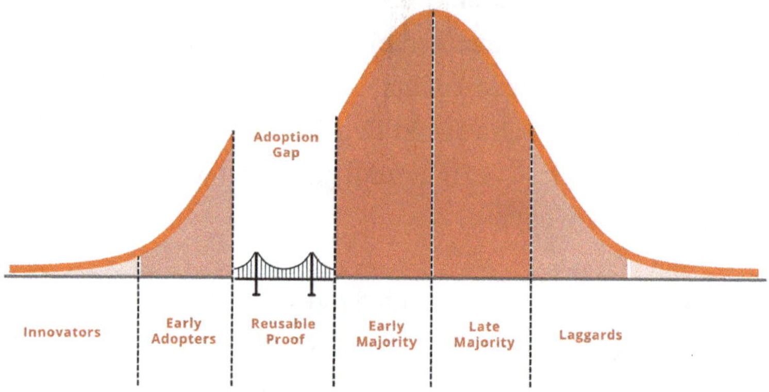

In the real world, there is no clean handoff. Instead, there is a difficult transition between the visionary buyer who wants the future and the pragmatist who has to make it work on Monday. In my industry, that chasm sits directly between the client who commissions a landmark mosque and the project manager who has to fit out a standard 400-unit residential tower.

When I finally got my low-energy tech onto the desk of that residential project manager, they looked at it with total, unblinking sobriety.

They were not hostile to the concept of saving energy. They were responsible for a different set of risks. The mosque client had accepted the uncertainty of an early application. The project manager at the tower could not afford an unbudgeted electrical glitch, a delay, or a subcontractor who did not know how to install it.

So, they looked at my specification sheet and asked the grounded questions that keep the physical world running:

- What happens to this light fixture when the ceiling cavity hits 50°C (122°F) in August?
- If one diode fails, do I have to rip out the entire custom plasterboard cove to fix it?
- Will your manufacturing plant still exist in 36 months to honor this warranty, or are you going to leave me with 4,000 dead blue lights I cannot find replacement parts for?

A cautious adopter is often labeled a laggard or an obstacle to progress. That label misses the responsibility the project manager is carrying. That project manager was the immune system of the building. Their skepticism was the entirely rational behavior of a professional who had watched a dozen beautiful, world-saving architectural innovations turn into operational problems the moment they met the reality of a site.

The innovator may buy the vision. The early adopter may buy the story. The early majority is more likely to require operating proof.

Fast forward 20 years. Today, if you walk into an electrical distributor in Dubai, London, or Tokyo to buy a standard lightbulb, you do not ask the clerk if it is a solid-state light-emitting diode. You just ask for a warm white screw-cap. The strange blue light became a warm glow. The fixture's design addressed many of those early objections, and unit costs fell dramatically.

The market moved as the technology improved, costs fell, and regulation accelerated adoption. It no longer required the buyer to accept exceptional uncertainty. This is a useful parallel for the movement of verified social value today.

Right now, our field has made progress among innovators and the early adopters. We have our equivalent of the regional flagship mosques: the bespoke pilot projects, the celebrated community benefit agreements, the high-profile living-wage developments that win the civic awards. These projects have demonstrated what is possible. The unfinished work is translating that story into the ordinary mechanics of the early majority.

We see the blueprint for this transition operating in the material health movement. When an architecture practice large enough to move the market writes a material standard into its own project specifications, the decisive move is administrative as well as declarative. They translated the fragmented demands of material sustainability into performance criteria across a defined set of commonly specified building product categories. They took the strange blue light of material chemistry and formatted it into a standard specification submittal. When an architectural practice of that scale embeds a standard into its own documents, the product manufacturer no longer has to wonder whether the market genuinely wants a Health Product Declaration. For covered product categories, the disclosure may become a condition of consideration.

This is the same approach we explored in the previous two chapters, now operating at market scale rather than inside one company. Translation made the human argument legible, portable reporting kept it usable past the first handoff, and here that same proof hardens into a specification other firms have to meet.

The practical majority

Once an idea begins to cross from early adoption into broader use, the proof has to leave something behind for the next person trying to make the same decision under less favorable conditions.

The useful artifact is the reusable proof: the specification language, the supplier pathway, the budget defense, the decision memo, the tenant explanation, the manufacturer signal, the procurement rule, the data field, or the reporting pathway that lets the next team move faster than the first one did.

The better question after any milestone is what conditions it improved for the next project. A strong process leaves behind a stronger supplier pathway, a more confident client, a team that knows how to do the work again, a precedent others can cite, and evidence that better choices can survive real-world constraints. The proof is what the work changed, what it made easier to defend, and what it allows the next person to do without starting from zero.

Every hard moment in a project, a process that had to shift, a product that had to be replaced, a budget that had to hold through a cost review, contains a question worth asking: did that moment cause any change that endured once the project ended? If yes, capture it. If not, ask why the next project had to start from scratch.

From proof to precedent

Standards rarely arrive fully formed from a central authority. They codify what practitioners have already learned to do because the work demanded it. Diffusion is shaped not only by direct interpretation but by the work that surrounds adoption: what a practice is believed to mean, who is seen using it, and which channels carry it across organizations. The methodologies that early systems accept, the data fields they require, and the forms of verification they normalize become the baseline that later organizations work within. Organizations entering later often work within requirements and methods shaped by the earlier adopters.

A practice becomes durable when it no longer depends on one unusually committed person carrying it alone. When a single analyst modifies an intake spreadsheet to defend a budget, or a purchasing manager alters a contract specification to protect a supply line under live conditions, a practice has crossed a threshold. It begins moving from an individual request into a requirement that colleagues across the organization can apply. The goal is a system that depends less on heroics.

Complete evidence may be necessary for some legal, public, or enterprise-wide claims. But requiring comprehensive coverage before making any bounded operational change can delay action even where the available evidence already supports a proportionate response. During that delay, existing conditions remain in place.

The alternative is disciplined transparency. The real hazard is proof that is presented to be more complete than it is. When evidence is incomplete, uncertainty should narrow the scope of the claim, not halt the execution. An occupant feedback survey showing recurring complaints about acoustic distraction supports a case for acoustic improvement without needing to be a comprehensive study of every occupant group. A localized supplier pilot demonstrating better labor outcomes within a specific material category supports a case for extending that standard to similar categories without needing to cover the entire supply chain first. The useful test is whether the evidence is strong enough to support the decision at hand, and honest enough to say so.

Case study

In late 2024, IKEA's German business pledged 6 million euros to a hardship fund being established by the German government to compensate victims of forced labor under the East German regime in the 1970s and 1980s. Furniture made under those conditions had entered IKEA's supply chain, and the company had commissioned an independent historical review that confirmed it. The pledge was widely reported as the first payment of its kind into the fund, and victims' advocates framed it as a precedent they hoped would move other companies that had benefited from the same forced labor.

The contribution was not a legal settlement. It was a voluntary acknowledgment of a historical harm that had occurred decades earlier.

The historical review and contribution show what acknowledgment can look like decades after the harm occurred. Separately, IKEA has built systems including the IWAY supplier code, reporting paths, and worker-protection requirements intended to identify and address current supply-chain risks. Those systems do not erase the historical harm, but they demonstrate the kind of ongoing infrastructure organizations need if they are to surface problems earlier and respond before the consequences compound. Without such systems, an organization has fewer opportunities to identify and address harm before its human and financial consequences grow.

Acts of acknowledgment and remedy change what the market treats as possible. They demonstrate what acknowledgment, remedy, and learning systems can look like in practice, and they shift what the next organization believes it is permitted to do. They function as market signals about the permission structure of the field.

That is the process this chapter has been describing, seen from the outside. One company's acknowledgment becomes a reference point that changes what the next firm can be asked to do, and gives others an example they can assess, challenge, or build upon.

The question worth asking at the end of any significant project is what it changed for the next person or the next organization. What did this make easier? For the next project team, the next procurement lead, the next supplier, the next standard-setter, the next organization trying to make the same case in a different room?

A people-positive approach

A people-positive approach to proof is designed from the beginning for the skeptics. This means that when a pilot is completed, the documentation captures not only what was achieved but what made the achievement repeatable under ordinary conditions: which supplier was used, what the cost differential was, how the specification survived value engineering, what objections arose, and how they were answered.*

This is the kind of proof broader adoption requires. Organizations often document the outcome more fully than the route. A people-positive approach records both.

It also means being honest about what the proof cannot yet support. Claims that extend beyond the evidence can weaken trust in both the current finding and the next one. When an initiative states clearly what the evidence shows, where its limits sit, and which decisions it can reasonably support, it leaves the next team with something they can use.

* *In construction, value engineering is a cost-review process that often looks for savings through material or system substitutions.*

Recap of Part 4

Part 4: Amplify followed proof as it moved across rooms, teams, organizations, and industries. The question was whether human-impact evidence could be produced and, beyond that, whether it could travel far enough to shape the next decision.

In the early environmental movement, progress often appeared as a series of isolated acts of corporate stewardship: one energy retrofit, one recycled-packaging pilot, or one volunteer cleanup day. Wider adoption became possible when those efforts were translated into shared methods such as lifecycle assessments, verified disclosures, and carbon-accounting protocols. These tools made performance easier to compare, communicate, and carry from one organization to another.

Part 3: Adopt built the internal infrastructure, the gates and levers that help social value survive when a budget tightens or a timeline slips. Part 4 turned outward. It asked how evidence could leave the project where it was produced and become useful to the next team, organization, or industry. When local learning is translated into shared language, usable data, standard documents, and repeatable protections, people-positive practices become easier to adopt, defend, specify, and repeat.

Points to carry forward

- **Proof Makes Action Easier To Defend.** We do not need perfect certainty before we act. But we do need to be precise about what the evidence shows, what it does not, and how far the claim can travel. The perfection trap keeps a weak default in place by making every change wait for impossible

completeness. Responsible proof narrows the claim, names the limits, and responds to clear signs of human strain.
- **Trust Is A Working Condition.** Trust is often treated as free until it runs out. An operating model that depends on frontline workers absorbing exhaustion in silence, or sourcing teams not looking too closely, is drawing down a reserve it may not know how to rebuild. The cost becomes visible only when people stop stretching, suppliers stop cooperating, or concerns stop being raised.
- **Shared Protections Make It Safer To Speak.** A subcontractor, designer, or small supplier may recognize an unsafe shortcut or impossible timeline long before the risk reaches leadership. Raising it alone can cost them the contract, the relationship, or future work. Amplification requires shared safeguards, including realistic capacity limits, protected escalation routes, and contract terms that distribute responsibility, so identifying a problem does not leave one person carrying the commercial consequences.

An honest accounting of social value does not depend on louder statements of care. It asks organizations to examine what their current decisions treat as unpriced or outside the frame.

Across the four parts of this book, that work has moved through a sequence:

- **Acknowledge** what current instruments leave out.
- **Assess** where the consequences appear.
- **Adopt** the gates and levers that allow evidence to change the work.
- **Amplify** what has been learned so the next team and organization can move further.

Together, these practices give human dignity a more durable place in design, procurement, operations, reporting, and governance.

Wiosna (Spring), 1933

Leon Wyczółkowski, interior of the artist's studio at Gościeradz

CONCLUSION: START HERE

In forest ecology, the survival of a tree depends less on the quality of its seed than on whether the conditions exist to receive it. The seed carries everything the tree needs. What it cannot carry is the route.

When we share methodology, name data limits, describe what failed, and document what changed, we build something the next team can actually use rather than a report they file and start over. Every isolated team that begins without that transparency starts from zero, not because the previous work did not exist but because it was never formatted to travel.

Evidence needs to disperse.

In the early 1990s, the waste pickers of Pune were treated as a nuisance the city would rather not see. They collected and sorted what the municipal system failed to recover, and for that they were called thieves, turned away from neighborhoods, and harassed. The city's contracts, sanitation budgets, and records had no line for them at all.

Who they were is not incidental to how they were treated. Waste picking in India has long been structured by caste. In Pune it was done overwhelmingly by Dalit women, members of communities historically oppressed under the caste system, most of them from the Mahar and Matang communities, for whom caste discrimination had already closed the doors to almost everything else. The city's instruments had no line for them, and that was not an accidental omission. The work had been assigned to people whose invisibility was a large part of why it was assigned to them.

They did not wait for the categories to change. In 1993, they organized as the Kagad Kach Patra Kashtakari Panchayat (KKPKP), a union of waste pickers, and created the record of work the city had never formally counted.

Through their union, the waste pickers helped build the evidence the city had never collected. A 2001 study commissioned by the International Labour Organization mapped Pune's recycling chain, documented the material they diverted from landfill, and quantified the millions of rupees their work saved the city in transport costs.

In 2008, SWaCH, a worker-owned cooperative that grew from the union, entered a formal agreement with the city to collect segregated waste from Pune residents. Rani Shivsharan, a waste picker who now sits on the SWaCH board, describes what shifted. Once, she says, they would not have dared to speak in front of two people. Now they argue their case in front of 500.

They built a record that could enter the city's budgets and contracts and used it to claim greater authority over the work they were already doing. Their experience demonstrates this book's argument more directly than any corporate example could.

Goodwill alone rarely protects a value inside an unaligned

system. It becomes more durable when it has a route into the records, budgets, and decisions that govern the work. The waste pickers of Pune wrote a new record, claimed their seat at the table, and changed the rules of the room. That is this book's argument at the scale where it matters most.

What comes next

This book began with an octopus arranging shells outside its den, an animal operating through a form of intelligence our instruments were slow to read. We did not fail to see the octopus because the behavior was hidden. We failed because our categories of recognition were too narrow.

The work ahead is to update the tools. When we build the human impact axis that records the physical, contractual, and spatial conditions required to keep human capacity intact, we begin reading the whole document.

This work is already visible in rewritten procurement questions, revised certification rules, community commitments carried into delivery meetings, supplier contracts that fund the standards they require, and reports that finally name what the old system was built to ignore.

The starting point

> ***A people-positive starting point begins with one decision. A single decision where human consequence is already visible but missing from the operating system. The discipline is***

to name what is known, name what is still unknown, and format both in a way that protects something specific: a budget line, a specification, a supplier standard, a community commitment, or a procurement criterion. That is enough to begin.

The decisions already in front of any organization this week contain these moments. Someone is setting a timeline whose pressure may be absorbed by a subcontractor with little room to refuse it. Someone is selecting a material whose installation burden has never been measured. Someone is writing a community engagement report whose findings will never reach the design brief for the next project. Someone is accepting a price from a supplier whose margin makes the human standard being demanded impossible to meet.

We begin not by redesigning the whole system, but by finding the last movable moment before a decision hardens into a contract, a budget, a specification, a schedule, or a burden someone else has to carry.

Sustaining our core

Starting with one decision sounds manageable. It stays manageable only if we do not have to reopen and defend that same decision on every project that follows. This is where exhaustion connects to the wider argument of this book. When better outcomes depend on repeated personal effort rather than a changed default, the organization is paying for progress with human endurance. The standard holds only as long as someone is in the room to insist on it. Everything around that person stays the same.

One of the most serious constraints on this work is exhaustion.

We are trying to solve generational problems inside quarterly systems. That friction has a human cost. An initiative that depends on a single advocate working long hours and fighting the same familiar battles on every project is not yet embedded. It is being carried. When that person burns out, changes roles, or steps back, much of the practice leaves with them. This is not a personal failure. It shows that the change was stored in an individual rather than built into the process.

A process that requires constant personal force to succeed repeats the extractive pattern it is trying to correct. It may deliver a better outcome while draining the health, attention, and endurance of the person responsible for producing it. If progress depends on perpetual heroics, it is not durable.

Making proof portable offers a practical way to conserve human energy. It moves knowledge out of one person's memory and into documents and frameworks other people can use. When we have to rebuild the case for a responsible supplier every Tuesday morning, the cost of adoption is being paid through repeated human effort. Without changing the default, we carry the same argument from room to room. When the requirement is written into the standard RFP, the next project begins with it already in place. We can then focus on improving the outcome rather than defending its right to exist.

Small wins become durable when they change the default. Good conversations can open doors, but they cannot hold those doors open once everyone returns to the pressure of an ordinary day. Progress becomes easier to repeat through small, practical adjustments: a question added to an RFP, a new field in a report, an expectation funded upfront in the contract, or a post-occupancy lesson carried into the next brief.

> ***We need to design processes for ordinary working days, when people are tired, busy, or behind schedule. These ordinary processes can turn a temporary victory into a usable default, so the next person does not need an unusual level of strength to create the same outcome.***

A path forward

We build what we can see, but we inhabit what our tools are allowed to ignore.

Throughout this book, we have traced a single pattern across modern commerce: when our primary systems of measurement screen out the human element to keep the spreadsheet clean, the cost migrates along the paths of least resistance until it lands on people with the least room to pass it on.

The pressures are real. Every manager and executive operates inside competitive markets, tight margins, and volatile supply chains. When a capital budget tightens, keeping people safe can appear as an added expense, especially when the cost of the alternative is recorded somewhere else.

The goal is to widen what the spreadsheet and the decision process are able to hold. It means walking the actual site, opening the contracts, and looking at the parts of the building that rarely appear in the main report: the loading docks, the service corridors, the backstairs where invisible labor keeps the place upright.

Walking toward a people-positive future

None of this requires a grand vision. It is a question added to a tender document, a payment term shortened to 30 days, or a clause specifying what a substitute has to prove before anyone can call it equal. It is done in ordinary documents, on ordinary afternoons, by people who are already tired and behind schedule.

This may sound modest. That is part of its strength. Transformation rarely arrives all at once. It trickles in through the next email, the next review, and the question of what we decide our tools should carry.

So, what if it carried a more people-positive approach? What if our specs asked about the air quality during installation? What if a rushed schedule was recorded as a cost rather than a saving, in the same decision record and with enough weight to influence the choice? What if the person who cleans the building after hours appeared once, anywhere, in the documents that decided how the building would be designed?

The goal is that none of us has to be a hero on a rainy Thursday. Better processes are not the whole solution, but they reduce the amount of personal courage and energy required to make a responsible choice.

The tools we were handed do not set the limits of our responsibility. They only show us the limits of what the current process has been designed to count.

Acknowledgments

This book was written over nearly three years and through more seasons than I expected. It followed me to sunny windows in Redwood City, monsoons in Kerala, the bright sun of Dubai and Kona, chilly flights, and tables crowded with chargers, cups, and a fairly ambitious range of snacks.

Had someone told me at the beginning how long it would take, I probably would never have started. I am notoriously impatient, which is an inconvenient quality for someone who works on systems change. This book exists because the people below brought patience, judgment, encouragement, and love to the years when I needed all four.

To the book team: Eli Keren, my editor, read this manuscript with patience, candor, and extraordinary care. He told me when an argument needed more evidence, when a chapter had lost its way, and when I was using several pages to avoid writing one direct sentence. He treated the book seriously from the beginning, including during the long period when it was still a very large Word document. Eli, thank you for seeing what the book could become and for helping me get it there. Your care for the ideas, the writing, and the reader made me a better writer.

Nvard Yerkanian gave the book its visual life. She worked through my endless opinions about the cover, the illustrations, the diagrams, the size of the building, every possible shade of blue, and what exactly counted as "terracotta." She understood what I was reaching for, even when my feedback arrived as screenshots, arrows, and cryptic sentences such as "warmer, but with more contrast." Thank you for bringing so much imagination, patience, and beauty to this book. I will always be grateful that you cared as much as I did about how it entered the world.

Hanna Domingo kept everything else at Liveable running while I disappeared into the manuscript.

To the people who shaped the ideas: I have had the privilege of working with remarkable people across lighting, manufacturing, product development, architecture, public health, sustainability, real estate, and social impact. They welcomed me into factories, hospitals, offices, classrooms, construction sites, and community rooms. They showed me how decisions were made and trusted me with the stories that the official version often left out.

Many of the central questions in this book grew from my years at the International WELL Building Institute. I am grateful to the colleagues, researchers, advisers, practitioners, and project teams who helped build WELL and the WELL Equity Rating. Together, we wrestled with how to turn health, dignity, and equity into requirements that could survive budgets, schedules, and real projects. That work changed the direction of my life.
To the clients, collaborators, advisers, and practitioners whose experiences informed the People Positive framework, thank you for sharing the realities of your work. Your questions, skepticism, honesty, and practical judgment kept the ideas grounded as they developed.

I am also grateful to everyone who read chapters, questioned the language, sent research, opened doors, made introductions, and told me when I was still being too abstract. Some of you had to tell me more than once.

To my friends and family: Ansil, Michelle, Sarah, and Kimberly, thank you for accepting long silences followed by messages containing several months of information at once. I cannot tell you how much your calls and messages meant during this time.

And to the many friends, family members, colleagues, and quiet encouragers who sent a note, shared a meal, read a page, made an introduction, or simply made these three years easier, thank you.

To the places where I wrote: Jersey City is where the book first took shape, before I had written a single word. Redwood City gave me the sunny window where much of it was eventually written. Kerala gave me family meals, food that tasted like home, and regular reminders that life continued beyond my laptop. Dubai gave me bright sunlight, shawarmas, and the familiar feeling of returning to a place that made me. Kona gave me shave ice, and an appreciation for how land, ocean, people, and life continually shape one another, and how little in this world exists on its own.

I acknowledge that Redwood City is located on the unceded ancestral homeland of the Ramaytush Ohlone peoples, Jersey City sits within Lenapehoking, the homeland of the Lenape peoples, and Hawaiʻi is an Indigenous place whose people are Kānaka Maoli.

I am grateful for the time I spent in each of these places and aware that my time within them is one small part of a much longer history.

To my family: My parents gave me a life across countries, languages, cultures, and ways of seeing. Growing up between places taught me to notice who belongs easily, who must translate, and who is repeatedly expected to adapt. Those questions entered this book because they entered my life first.

Amma and Acha, thank you for giving me both roots and range. You taught me to work hard, remain curious, and keep finding my way in unfamiliar places. I carry more of you into my work than I probably say often enough.

My brother, Gautam, maintained a steady supply of memes. Their quality varied considerably. His confidence in them did not. Thank you for making sure nothing stayed serious for too long, and for always being one message away.

My husband, Sandeep, lived through every version of this manuscript, from the earliest scattered notes to printed chapters, cover proofs, launch spreadsheets, and sentences I continued changing after announcing that I was finished. During that time, he managed more than his share of our life, patiently gave up more weekends than either of us had planned, and brought me boba tea with impressive regularity.

Thank you for believing in this book when I was exhausted by it, for protecting the time I needed, and for making our life feel steady while mine was organized around a manuscript.

My dogs, Luna and Sky, were my constant companions. They are the goodest girls and the main reason I stepped outside on many days. Luna believes most problems require a snack. Sky prefers that I throw a ball. Either way, they do not find the laptop half as interesting as I do, and sometimes I needed that reality check.

Finally, to you, dear reader: To every person trying to make a building, product, organization, or community more people-centered while working inside systems that are slow to change, thank you.

This book was written for you.

BONUS TOOLS

Big shifts tend to arrive as small administrative adjustments: a budget line trimmed during a cost review, or a note proposing that a specification be "simplified."

The following pages are helpful for keeping human outcomes visible in a fast moving project. The reference guide below helps you choose the right lens for the decision in front of you. The People Positive Decision Check helps you catch trade-offs while options are still fluid. The meeting prompts belong in your next project review, where the questions that matter most tend to go unasked. Adapt these tools to your situation. Use the prompts in meeting agendas, mark up these pages, anchor them in your briefs, contracts, and operating plans.

When a project decision begins to shift, walk through these five steps to identify whether it is shifting in a people-positive direction:

1. Locate the impact: use the five sites.
2. Evaluate the outcome: map it across the People Positive Spectrum.
3. Clarify responsibility: apply the Circles of Responsibility.
4. Anchor it in delivery: identify the Gates and Levers.
5. Design for durability: use the Progress Scale.

Bring in the Just Transition Matrix whenever carbon or climate goals and human realities intersect.

A Reference Guide

A map for choosing the right lens for the right moment.

Framework	What It Clarifies	When To Use It
The five sites	Where impacts are landing across People, Place, Product, Partners, and Public Good.	You need to look beyond obvious occupants and assess wider human outcomes.
The People Positive Spectrum	Whether a decision operates as extractive, neutral, or people-positive in practice.	A commitment sounds strong on paper, but you need to test what survives under financial or time pressure.
The Just Transition Matrix	Environmental performance and human outcomes evaluated together.	A climate or sustainability solution risks passing hidden burdens to workers, suppliers, or communities.
The Circles of Responsibility	What you control directly, shape through relationships, or influence downstream.	An issue feels too large, systemic, or boundary-spanning to assign immediate ownership.
Gates and Levers of Adoption	Which gate must review the choice and which lever (document or process) carries it forward.	An intentional decision needs to survive the friction of procurement, budgeting, and execution.
The Progress Scale	Depth of integration, from absent to fully embedded.	You need to distinguish a high-level pledge from a repeatable operational habit.

The People Positive Decision Check

Use this check when a proposed change to budget, schedule, scope, specification, or delivery model could impact people beyond the project team, extending to the people who deliver the work or live with the consequences.

1. Name the change

What is changing?

☐ Budget ☐ Timeline ☐ Scope ☐ Specification

☐ Delivery Approach ☐ Proposed Alternative

☐ Other: ______________________________

Why is this change being proposed?

---

2. Locate the impact

Focus on the areas most likely to experience the consequences of this change. You do not need to fill in every dimension.

People: Could this affect workload, safety, health, time, dignity, or well-being?

People or groups affected: ______________________________

Place: Could this affect physical comfort, use of the space, operational conditions, maintenance, or accessibility?

Conditions affected: ______________________________

____

Product: Could this affect or change manufacturing processes, installation, daily use, repairability, or end-of-life removal?

Lifecycle stage affected: ___________________________

____

Partners: Could this affect commercial pricing, lead times, margins, safety buffers, or supplier capacity?

Partners affected: _______________________________

____

Public Good: Could this affect local access, community benefit, affordability, displacement, or shared resources?

Wider effects: __________________________________

3. Check the gate

A gate is the formal checkpoint where a decision can be approved, revised, paused, or redirected. Which gate must review this change?

Sponsorship: Is the person approving the change aware of the broader consequences?

☐ Yes ☐ No ☐ Unclear

Budget: Have the change and its impacts been adequately funded so the costs are not pushed downstream?

☐ Yes ☐ No ☐ Unclear

Timeline: Does the revised schedule allow for proper execution, safety checks, and consultation?

☐ Yes ☐ No ☐ Unclear

Feedback: Have people delivering, maintaining, or experiencing the project been considered?

☐ Yes ☐ No ☐ Unclear

Gate requiring review: ______________________________

Person with authority: ______________________________

4. Update the lever

A decision agreed in a room but absent from project governance will rarely survive implementation. Which formal document or process must carry this decision into delivery?

☐ Brief ☐ Budget ☐ Schedule

☐ Procurement Criteria ☐ Specification

☐ Contract ☐ Change Order ☐ Operating Procedure

☐ Other: ______________________________

5. Next steps and governance log

Change under consideration:

____

Five sites impacted:

____

Gate requiring review:

____

Document or process requiring update:

____

Information still needed:

____

Person responsible:

____

Target review date:

____

Key question: "Which gate must review this change, and which project document must be updated before it moves forward?"

Meeting Prompts

Especially during times of evolving project plans, these questions serve well for everyday team meetings. Use them to surface any human impacts that might be unexamined.

When the timeline shifts

- Which handoffs, safety checks, or review steps are being compressed by this schedule?
- Has the delivery team directly evaluated these revised dates?
- Are our core staffing and lead-time assumptions still realistic?
- Where will the updated schedule, and its trade-offs, be formally recorded?

When the budget shrinks

- What specific scope, material, or quality element is being removed or deferred?
- Who absorbs the practical impact of that reduction?
- Do any safety, performance, accessibility, or maintenance assumptions change as a result?
- Which briefs, specifications, or commercial contracts need immediate updates?

When “value engineering” is proposed

- What non-negotiable performance requirements must this alternative still satisfy?

- Has this substitution been evaluated across installation, daily use, repairability, and end-of-life?
- What hard data or evidence do we still need before calling this option equivalent?
- Who has formal sign-off authority for this switch?

When evaluating a people-positive alternative

- Who specifically experiences the benefit of this approach?
- What direct evidence supports the proposed positive outcome?
- What are the cost, operational, schedule, and maintenance implications?
- Can we integrate this option now, run a pilot, or embed it into a future phase?

When responsibility feels fuzzy

- Which parts of this issue sit within our direct control?
- What can we shape through commercial agreements and contracts?
- What sits beyond our immediate boundary, and how can we use our leverage effectively?
- Who has the authority to act on each component?

Before you wrap the meeting

- What was explicitly decided today?
- What remains open or unresolved?
- Who owns the next step, and when is it due?
- Where will this decision be formally documented?

A single well-timed question in a review can keep a critical requirement from dissolving somewhere between the meeting and the final contract.

Bringing People Positive into Practice

Continue the work online

People Positive continues online through free tools, research, conversations, and practical examples for people putting these ideas to work.

Take the People Positive Check, download the worksheets and meeting prompts, read The Impact Edit, and listen to Changing Tomorrow. New research, case studies, and resources will be added as the work develops.

makeitliveable.com/peoplepositive

Help carry People Positive forward

Books do not change systems on their own. People do, usually by bringing one useful question into a room where it has not been asked before.

If this book helped you see a decision differently, I would be grateful if you carried that thinking into your work.

- Use one of the meeting prompts on a live project.
- Share the book with someone who controls a budget, specification, contract, or procurement decision.
- Leave a review so other people working on these questions can find it.
- Tell me what you tried, what changed, and where the framework fell short.

Sometimes one question or one change to an existing document is enough to begin. Sometimes the evidence is scattered, no one quite owns the issue, and the better outcome is still vulnerable to cost, timing, or competing priorities.

That is where Liveable is usually brought in. We help teams bring the evidence together, turn what they learn into decisions and systems they can stand behind, and communicate the work in a way that holds up under scrutiny.

The aim is the same throughout: make the better outcome easier to protect, repeat, and explain.

Find the tools, share your experience, or work with us at: makeitliveable.com/peoplepositive

About the Author

Gayathri Unnikrishnan is the founder of Liveable, a social sustainability practice that helps organizations understand, improve, and communicate how their buildings, products, and operations affect people.

Before founding Liveable, Gayathri led standard-development work at the International WELL Building Institute, where she helped develop WELL v2 and co-led the WELL Equity Rating. WELL is now applied across more than 6 billion square feet in over 137 countries.

Her career has spanned electrical engineering, manufacturing, product development, architectural lighting design, standards, and sustainability strategy across India, the Middle East, Europe, and the United States. That experience shaped her interest in the gap between what organizations say they value and what their budgets, specifications, contracts, and procurement systems actually protect.

Gayathri has been named a Living Future Hero and serves as an advisor to Executive Council of the ITU/WMO/UNESCO-IOC Joint Task Force on SMART Subsea Cables. She holds a degree from NIT Calicut and a master's degree in architectural lighting design from KTH Royal Institute of Technology, where she was a Swedish Institute Scholar. She also completed the Stanford LEAD program at Stanford Graduate School of Business.

She lives in Redwood City, California, with her husband and their two dogs, Luna and Sky.

APPENDICES

Appendix A: Glossary

The glossary is organized in four sections. The first section introduces the central concepts that are explored and utilized across the entire book. The second section clarifies which distinctions are crucial for the framework, especially when similar wording might suggest varied duties, decision-making power, or types of execution. The third section clarifies key terminology from the realms of design, construction, procurement, and reporting. The final section defines terms specific to how design, procurement, and construction professionals use them day to day.

The working vocabulary

- **People Positive:** An operating state in which human benefit is designed into how performance is achieved, rather than applied as a correction after harm occurs. A people-positive system is not flawless; it is structurally equipped to perceive, respond to, and remediate human burdens as they arise.
- **People Positive Spectrum:** The diagnostic framework used to evaluate system performance under pressure, prioritizing actual outcomes over stated values. Measured across three coordinates, extractive, neutral, and positive, it represents a direction of travel rather than a static score.
- **Risk:** The systemic baseline of operating without knowledge, where data is missing, fragmented, unverified,

or insulated from those affected by a decision. Because an invisible cost cannot be priced, risk is an active liability rather than a neutral starting point.

- **People Extractive:** An operating state that generates value for one group by depleting the health, safety, dignity, time, or resilience of another, consuming human capacity faster than it can regenerate. Extraction is independent of intent; a system can be extractive even when every actor within it behaves reasonably.
- **People Neutral:** An operating state that avoids overt harm and complies with regulations governing recognized stakeholders but fails to examine the wider human consequences of how value is produced. This is the baseline of compliance: bounded, risk-averse, and uncurious about what lies outside the frame.
- **The Five Sites:** The five operational environments where social value is generated and evaluated: People, Place, Product, Partners, and Public Good. They are diagnostic focal points rather than moral categories.
    - **People:** The complete network of workers, occupants, and transients a system relies upon to function, as distinct from the narrower subset it formally accounts for.
    - **Place:** The physical environment and the specific conditions of access, exposure, safety, and physical agency it enforces.
    - **Product:** The physical or functional output a system yields, whether a material object, a building, or a service.
    - **Partners:** The supply chain of contractors, vendors, and labor brokers executing the work, and the

commercial terms that dictate whether they can perform responsibly.

  - **Public Good:** The regional legacy of a project, measured by whether neighboring communities can continue to live, work, govern, and belong after the development is complete.

- **Workforce, Occupants, Transients:** The three human networks supporting any system. The workforce operates it; the occupants are its intended users; the transients service, traverse, or are affected by it without formal recognition. A single individual may transition between these roles depending on where the data boundary is drawn.
- **Assumed User:** The baseline demographic around whom a space, product, or service is implicitly designed. Exposing the assumed user is the most direct method for identifying systemic exclusions.
- **Circles of Responsibility:** A diagnostic framework categorizing social outcomes by proximity to organizational decision-making. Direct responsibility governs conditions set internally; shared responsibility governs conditions shaped through commercial agreements; extended responsibility governs conditions set in motion beyond operational boundaries.
- **Thrive Pyramid:** An evaluative model measuring whether a workforce is supported by material conditions rather than narrative promises. Composed of five sequential tiers: safety, compensation, environment, development, and purpose. Because upper tiers cannot compensate for a compromised foundation, providing a well-being initiative (tier five) to workers unable to safely report hazards (tier one) represents a structural failure.

- **Gates:** Operational checkpoints where a project is authorized, financed, deferred, or terminated. A functional gate possesses the contractual authority to halt progress; a cosmetic gate lacks criteria or teeth, waving projects through. This book explores four gates:
    - **Sponsorship Gate:** The formal escalations pathway routing critical findings to a designated executive who has agreed, in advance, to own and act on the issue.
    - **Budget Gate:** The financial verification of a social commitment. A target that passes design review but is stripped at cost review was never funded, only described.
    - **Timeline Gate:** The operational mechanism allowing schedules to adjust when speed generates human harm. When deadlines are absolute, the pressure is inevitably absorbed by the workforce.
    - **Feedback Gate:** The structural allowance for post-occupancy or post-use data to reopen funded design decisions. Surveying without the power to adjust defaults is a registry of complaints, not a correction.
- **Levers:** The administrative mechanisms, briefs, specifications, budgets, and contracts, that translate intent into system architecture before decisions solidify. Levers supply the criteria for gates; because they are mundane, they are often overlooked, making them the primary site of intervention.
- **The pilot:** The smallest operational iteration of the feedback gate. A pilot is structurally useful only if its brief dictates, prior to mobilization, how master specifications or contract templates will be modified upon success. A

pilot that yields only a case study while leaving standard procurement defaults untouched is marketing.

- **Progress Scale:** A maturity model assessing operational integration rather than performance. Tier 0 (Absent), Tier 1 (Mentioned), Tier 2 (Defined), Tier 3 (Operationalized), Tier 4 (Measured), and Tier 5 (Embedded). Only Tier 5 integration survives value engineering or budget constraints.
- **Progress Map:** The analytical interface crossing the People Positive Spectrum with the Progress Scale. It evaluates both current human outcomes and the system's capacity to replicate them.
- **People Positive Decision Check:** A pre-commitment diagnostic run over design, procurement, or policy decisions before they are codified into budgets or contracts.
- **Social Debt:** The unrecorded human liabilities accrued when an organization underpays for the physical or social capacity it draws upon. Like financial or technical debt, social debt compounds, returning to the balance sheet as attrition, quality failure, litigation, or community opposition.
- **The Hidden Ledger:** The unmonetized balance sheet of human consequences generated by an enterprise. While the corporate ledger records the savings, the hidden ledger documents who absorbed the cost.
- **The Sleep Subsidy:** The unpriced reserve of human rest extracted by organizational cultures that mandate constant availability. The cost of this extraction is carried by individuals and ultimately externalized to public health systems.
- **The Health Externalization:** The transfer of health costs from the employer generating them to external actors,

including public healthcare infrastructure, private households, or subsequent corporate fiscal years.

- **The Care Gap:** The domestic labor that sustains the recognized workforce. Unpriced and unrecorded, this labor operates as the foundational subsidy for formal economic activity.
- **The Three Scales of Application:** The three focal sizes through which social diagnostic tools are deployed: the building (localizing conditions in space), the product (scaling conditions across a value chain), and the organization (codifying conditions in governance and briefs).
- **The Feedback Metabolism:** The complete cycle required to close an informational feedback loop: listen, interpret, decide, act, and verify. Operational failures typically occur at the decision phase, when field data is received by actors lacking the authority to reallocate funds.
- **Symmetrical System:** A supply chain or operational architecture designed so that commercial or scheduling pressure cannot be externalized downward without immediate cost to the contracting party. Characterized by a shared speed limit matching physical human capacity, visible margins preventing predatory pricing, and protected friction allowing risk escalations without contractual penalty.
- **The Perfection Trap:** The demand for absolute empirical certainty prior to intervention. It operates as a strategic delay mechanism, masquerading as scientific rigor while preserving extractive default settings.
- **Responsible Proof:** An evidentiary standard that qualifies its own limits, acting on clear indicators rather than

holding out for absolute certainty, while strictly bounding claims to what the data actively supports.

Key distinctions

- **Human impact** and **social value:** The distinction is one of scale, resolution, and distribution. Human impact is the direct benefit or burden experienced in an individual life (health, safety, time, dignity, agency). Social value is the cumulative pattern those individual impacts form when scaled across a project, product, policy, or organization. Human impact is the material; social value is the distribution of that material.
- **Benefit** and **remedy:** A benefit is a positive externality offered generally to a population. A remedy is a targeted correction owed to those who have carried a direct, uncompensated cost for a project to succeed. Creating a public plaza after pricing out a neighborhood's tenants is a benefit, but it provides zero remedy to the displaced.
- **Remedy** and **reparations:** Under international human rights frameworks, remedy is the corrective action required when a business causes or contributes to harm. Reparations is a distinct, formal legal designation reserved for grave, state-level, or systematic violations. Capital projects should avoid borrowing the term "reparations" to prevent diluting its specific historical and legal meaning.
- **Compliance** and **extraction:** These states are not mutually exclusive. An enterprise can be fully compliant with local labor laws, industry standards, and building codes while remaining highly extractive, because compliance merely establishes a regulatory floor.

- **Participation** and **power:** The difference between consultation and agency. Participation is the invitation to offer comment; power is the structural capacity to alter design, budget, procurement, and tenure. High consultation metrics do not demonstrate social value; altered decisions do.
- **Champion** and **sponsor:** A champion generates visibility and enthusiasm but lacks executive authority, carrying concerns only as far as the next gatekeeper. A sponsor holds budget authority and contract ownership, having committed in advance to resolve systemic issues. Confusing a champion with a sponsor is how human risks are neutralized.
- **Engagement** and **feedback loop:** Data collection is not a loop. A feedback loop exists only when performance data has the structural authority to reopen funded design or procurement decisions, and when an executive is contractually obligated to act on the output.
- **Harm prevention** and **social value:** The distinction between risk mitigation and net-positive impact. Harm prevention (due diligence) establishes the human rights floor by mitigating negative impacts. Social value addresses the subsequent question: who benefits from the intervention and who carries the operational burden. A system cannot be classified as people-positive if active, unresolved harms persist within its boundary.

Concepts and terms from the field

- **Decoupling:** The formal adoption of policies to satisfy external expectations while daily operations remain unchanged. This mechanism allows an organization to produce a sustainability report while leaving its procurement spreadsheets untouched.

- **Revealed Preference:** The economic principle that an actor's actual priorities are demonstrated by choices made under constraint rather than statements made in comfort. The budget reconciliation meeting, not the mission statement, is where organizational value is revealed.
- **Strategic Ignorance:** The systematic management of information flows to insulate an institution from liability or uncomfortable knowledge.
- **Organizational Silence:** A systemic pattern in which employees withhold operational or ethical insights because reporting them is perceived as personally risky or structurally futile.
- **Ghost Acreage:** The external agricultural land base required to sustain a domestic population's consumption. Used here as the conceptual predecessor to modern corporate carbon and social accounting boundaries that obscure their supply-chain dependencies.
- **Externality:** A cost or benefit generated by an economic activity that is borne by third parties and not reflected in the market price of the transaction.
- **Technical Debt:** The long-term compound penalty an organization incurs by choosing a rapid, low-quality fix over a robust structural solution. Social debt functions via the same compounding mechanism, applied directly to human infrastructure.
- **The Fissured Workplace:** The operational strategy whereby lead firms shed direct employment, shifting workforce liabilities and regulatory compliance down through tiers of subcontractors.

- **Human Rights Due Diligence (Hrdd):** The continuous management process through which an enterprise identifies, prevents, mitigates, and accounts for actual and potential adverse human rights impacts within its operations and supply chains, in accordance with the UN Guiding Principles.
- **Just Transition:** A framework ensuring that the societal shift to a low-carbon economy is managed equitably, protecting affected workers, households, and communities from bearing disproportionate structural costs.
- **Double Materiality:** The reporting principle requiring organizations to disclose both how sustainability risks impact their financial performance (outside-in), and how their operations impact society and the environment (inside-out).
- **Anchor Institution:** A highly capitalized, place-based organization, such as a hospital, university, or municipal headquarters, whose scale and permanent physical presence link its economic survival to the local community.

Trade practice

- **Value Engineering (VE):** A late-stage design review intended to optimize cost by substituting equivalent materials or systems. In practice, the point in procurement where unpriced social, labor, and environmental value is stripped from a project.
- **Approved Equal:** Contractual language permitting a general contractor to substitute an alternative product for the specified brand. Substitution matches performance only to the extent that the original specification defined

it; if a specification is silent on installer safety or chemical exposure, the substitute is legally equal.

- **Specification:** The legally binding contract document dictating material, performance, and execution standards for construction. It is the primary lever of physical delivery, overriding loose design narratives.
- **Submittal:** The product data, shop drawings, or samples sent by a contractor for architectural approval prior to installation. The submittal log is the administrative record of whether specified social standards were verified or bypassed.
- **Request for Information (RFI):** A formal query sent by a contractor to resolve ambiguities in construction documents. The RFI volume serves as an administrative audit trail of what the initial design failed to anticipate.
- **Request for Proposals (RFP):** The procurement document inviting vendor bids. When combined with a weighted evaluation matrix, it is the primary administrative lever holding commercial force.
- **Change Order:** A contract modification adjusting a project's scope, cost, or schedule. Executing a change order without adjusting the timeline is a unilateral decision to extract uncompensated time from the workforce.
- **Division 01:** The front-end general requirements section of a construction specification. It is the primary lever for embedding mandatory social, labor, or reporting obligations across all trades.
- **Critical Path:** The sequential scheduling of key project activities that directly dictates the minimum completion timeline. Delays on the critical path compress subsequent schedules, converting temporal delays into extreme working pressure on final trades.

- **Back-of-House:** The service, maintenance, and logistics zones of a building (loading docks, corridors, mechanical rooms). These represent the primary workspace of the service workforce, where environmental, light, and acoustic performance are least monitored.
- **Supplier Tiers:** The organizational layers of a supply chain. Tier 1 represents the direct contracting entity; Tier 2 represents the contractor's suppliers, moving sequentially back to raw extraction. Due diligence and accountability often drop precipitously at each step.
- **Post-Occupancy Evaluation (POE):** The empirical assessment of a building's performance, occupancy experience, and systems operation after handover. POE data is structurally useless unless integrated into a feedback gate that can adjust future specifications.
- **Capital Stack:** The structured layering of debt and equity financing supporting a real estate development. Its configuration dictates which design commitments are secured and which are classified as discretionary as margins narrow.
- **Embodied Carbon:** The lifecycle greenhouse gas emissions generated by the extraction, manufacture, transportation, assembly, and eventual demolition of building materials.
- **Scope 1, 2, and 3:** The emissions reporting boundaries established by the Greenhouse Gas Protocol (2001). Direct emissions (Scope 1), purchased utility emissions (Scope 2), and value chain emissions (Scope 3).
- **Life Cycle Assessment (LCA):** A standardized methodology for evaluating the environmental impacts of a product or material across its entire lifespan.

- **Social Life Cycle Assessment (S-LCA):** A corresponding methodology assessing the human, labor, and community impacts of a product across its entire global supply chain.
- **Environmental Product Declaration (EPD):** A standardized, third-party-verified document declaring a material's lifecycle environmental impacts, based on an LCA.
- **Health Product Declaration (HPD):** A standardized disclosure detailing a product's chemical composition and associated toxicological risks.

Appendix B: Standards Referenced

Workforce and human capital

ISO 30414:2025, Human Resource Management: Requirements and Recommendations for Human Capital Reporting and Disclosure. Geneva: International Organization for Standardization, 2025. Supersedes ISO 30414:2018, which is withdrawn, and restructures its reporting areas. Covers 11 areas: workforce composition; diversity; costs; productivity; health, safety and well-being; leadership, culture and engagement; compliance, ethics and workforce relations; recruitment; mobility and succession planning; workforce turnover; and skills, capabilities and development.

GRI Topic Standards, 400 series (Social). Amsterdam: Global Reporting Initiative. Cite by individual standard and its own revision year, not as a block. The most relevant here are GRI 401: Employment (2016); GRI 402: Labor/Management Relations (2016); GRI 403: Occupational Health and Safety (2018), substantially revised; GRI 404: Training and Education (2016); GRI 405: Diversity and Equal Opportunity (2016); GRI 407: Freedom of Association and Collective Bargaining (2016); GRI 408: Child Labor (2016); GRI 409: Forced or Compulsory Labor (2016); GRI 413: Local Communities (2016); GRI 414: Supplier Social Assessment (2016). See also GRI 3: Material Topics (2021), which governs how any of these are selected. The GSSB's revision of the labor-related Topic Standards is in progress and is expected to supersede several of these; readers should confirm which edition governs.

ILO fundamental conventions. The ten are C029 Forced Labour (1930), C087 Freedom of Association and Protection of the Right to Organise (1948), C098 Right to Organise and Collective Bargaining (1949), C100 Equal Remuneration (1951), C105 Abolition of Forced Labour (1957), C111 Discrimination, Employment and Occupation (1958), C138 Minimum Age (1973), C182 Worst Forms of Child Labour

(1999), and C155 Occupational Safety and Health (1981) with C187 Promotional Framework for Occupational Safety and Health (2006), the last two designated fundamental in 2022. See also C189 Domestic Workers (2011), which is not a fundamental convention but bears directly on the care gap described in Chapter 7. Geneva: International Labour Organization. See also the ILO Declaration on Fundamental Principles and Rights at Work (1998, amended 2022 to include a safe and healthy working environment).

Living wage benchmarks. There is no single global standard. The most widely used methodologies are the Anker Methodology, published as Richard Anker and Martha Anker, Living Wages Around the World: Manual for Measurement (Cheltenham: Edward Elgar, 2017), operationalized by the Global Living Wage Coalition; and, in the United Kingdom, the Real Living Wage rates published annually by the Living Wage Foundation. Readers should note these produce different numbers and are not interchangeable.

Engagement survey instruments. Gallup Q12 and the State of the Global Workplace series (Washington, DC: Gallup, published annually) and Workday Peakon Employee Voice are proprietary commercial products, not open standards. Their methodologies are not fully published, and their benchmarks are not externally auditable. They are used here as widely adopted market instruments, not as neutral measurement.

Health, safety, and the physical environment

ANSI/ASHRAE Standard 62.1-2025, Ventilation and Acceptable Indoor Air Quality. Atlanta: ASHRAE, 2025. Supersedes the 2022 edition. Establishes the Ventilation Rate Procedure, under which required outdoor air is a function of both occupancy and floor area.

ANSI/ASHRAE Standard 55-2023, Thermal Environmental Conditions for Human Occupancy. Atlanta: ASHRAE, 2023.

ISO 7730:2025, Ergonomics of the Thermal Environment: Analytical Determination and Interpretation of Thermal Comfort. Geneva: ISO, 2025. Replaces the 2005 edition and remains built on Fanger's predicted mean vote model.

ISO 45001:2018, Occupational Health and Safety Management Systems: Requirements with Guidance for Use. Geneva: ISO, 2018, incorporating Amendment 1:2024 on climate change considerations.

Occupational Safety and Health Administration, U.S. Department of Labor. Recordkeeping and reporting requirements at 29 CFR Part 1904; construction standards at 29 CFR Part 1926; respirable crystalline silica standard at 29 CFR 1926.1153.

WELL Building Standard, v2. New York: International WELL Building Institute, https://standard.wellcertified.com. A proprietary, fee-based certification. IWBI has announced a unification of its programs, One WELL, for 2026; readers should confirm the operative version.

Fitwel. New York: Active Design Advisors, Inc. (Adai), a subsidiary of the Center for Active Design, https://www.fitwel.org. Proprietary, fee-based.

RESET Standard, https://www.reset.build. Proprietary, sensor-based, focused on continuously monitored indoor air quality.

UL Verified Healthy Building program. Northbrook, IL: UL Solutions. Proprietary.

LEED v5. Washington, DC: U.S. Green Building Council, https://www.usgbc.org/leed. Proprietary, fee-based. Ratified March 2025; projects may still register under LEED v4.1 until June 30, 2027.

Living Building Challenge 4.1 (2024) and Living Product Challenge. Seattle: International Living Future Institute, https://living-future.org.

Accessibility

2010 ADA Standards for Accessible Design. Washington, DC: U.S. Department of Justice. Comprising 28 CFR Part 36, subpart D, together with the 2004 ADA Accessibility Guidelines at 36 CFR Part 1191, Appendices B and D. Appendix D to 28 CFR Part 36 contains the superseded 1991 Standards and should not be cited for current requirements.

Approved Document M, Access to and Use of Buildings, Volumes 1 and 2. London: Ministry of Housing, Communities and Local Government (2015, as amended; Volume 2 incorporates 2024 amendments). Part M of the Building Regulations 2010.

ISO 21542:2021, Building Construction: Accessibility and Usability of the Built Environment. Geneva: ISO, 2021.

United Nations, Convention on the Rights of Persons with Disabilities (2006), Article 9 (Accessibility).

Post-occupancy evaluation

Leesman Index. London: Leesman Limited, a subsidiary of HqO, Inc. since June 2022, https://www.leesmanindex.com. A proprietary commercial workplace-experience survey; the Leesman Index Score (Lmi) is a 0–100 composite whose algorithm is not publicly disclosed.

CBE Occupant Survey. Berkeley: Center for the Built Environment, University of California, Berkeley, https://cbe.berkeley.edu/research/

occupant-survey/. Research-based and more transparent in methodology than the commercial alternatives.

Product, material, and lifecycle

ISO 14040:2006 and ISO 14044:2006, Environmental Management: Life Cycle Assessment. Geneva: ISO, 2006, as amended (ISO 14040/Amd 1:2020; ISO 14044/ Amd 1:2017 and Amd 2:2020).

ISO 14025:2026, Environmental Statements and Programmes for Products: Environmental Product Declarations (EPDs). Geneva: ISO, 2026. Replaces ISO 14025:2006, which is withdrawn. The basis for Environmental Product Declarations.

EN 15804:2012+A2:2019, Sustainability of Construction Works: Environmental Product Declarations, Core Rules for the Product Category of Construction Products. Brussels: CEN, 2019, with corrigendum AC:2021.
Health Product Declaration Open Standard, v2.3. Wakefield, MA: HPD Collaborative,
https://www.hpd-collaborative.org.

Declare label and the Red List. Seattle: International Living Future Institute, https://living-future.org/declare/. Requires disclosure of intentionally added ingredients to 100 parts per million.

JUST label, version 3.0 (launched May 2024). Seattle: International Living Future Institute. A voluntary social equity disclosure program for organizations, not products, organized around 21 indicators across six categories: Diversity, Inclusion, Compensation, Health, Benefits, and Stewardship. Procurement sits inside Stewardship as Indicator 21. ILFI states that JUST involves no third-party verification and is not a certification.

GREENGUARD and GREENGUARD Gold certification. Northbrook, IL: UL Solutions. Chemical emissions criteria for indoor products.

Forest Stewardship Council Principles and Criteria for Forest Stewardship, FSC-STD-01-001 V5-3. Bonn: FSC International. A further revision is in progress.

Cradle to Cradle Certified Product Standard, v4.1 (2025). San Francisco and Amsterdam: Cradle to Cradle Products Innovation Institute.

UNEP, Guidelines for Social Life Cycle Assessment of Products and Organizations, 2020 edition. Paris: UNEP Life Cycle Initiative, 2020. The reference methodology for Social LCA, now complemented by ISO 14075:2024, Environmental Management: Principles and Framework for Social Life Cycle Assessment (Geneva: ISO, 2024).

mindful MATERIALS Common Materials Framework (CMF). https://www.mindfulmaterials.com/cmf-reference-guide. Organizes material-sustainability data from more than 150 certifications and ecolabels around five impact areas aligned with the AIA Architecture & Design Materials Pledge: human health, climate health, ecosystem health, social health and equity, and circular economy. Developed by a cross-disciplinary group convened from 2021; the AIA, ILFI, IWBI, and USGBC formally aligned around it in a joint announcement of November 2023. It is a mapping framework, not a certification.

California Air Resources Board, Airborne Toxic Control Measure to Reduce Formaldehyde Emissions from Composite Wood Products (Phase II); and US EPA, Formaldehyde Standards for Composite Wood Products, TSCA Title VI, 40 CFR Part 770.

Procurement, supply chain, and due diligence

ISO 20400:2017, Sustainable Procurement: Guidance. Geneva: ISO, 2017. Guidance, not a certifiable requirements standard.

OECD, Due Diligence Guidance for Responsible Business Conduct (Paris: OECD, 2018); and the sector guidance, notably OECD Due Diligence Guidance for Responsible Supply Chains in the Garment and Footwear Sector (2017).

United Nations Human Rights Council, Guiding Principles on Business and Human Rights (New York and Geneva: United Nations, 2011). The foundation of human rights due diligence, and of the distinction between remedy and benefit drawn in Chapter 15.

Better Buying Purchasing Practices Index (BBPPI). Developed by the Better Buying Institute; Cascale acquired the Institute's key assets in February 2025 and now runs the program. See Cascale, Better Buying Purchasing Practices Index (BBPPI) Report, 2025 (Amsterdam: Cascale, November 2025). Notable because it is one of the very few instruments that scores the buyer rather than the supplier: Tier 1 suppliers anonymously rate their brands and retailers across seven categories. Individual buyer scorecards are confidential to subscribers; only aggregated results are published, and the sector covered is apparel, footwear and household textiles.

SA8000 Standard (2026). New York: Social Accountability International, https://sa-intl.org. Supersedes SA8000:2014; mandatory for new certifications from January 2027, with certificates against the 2014 edition phased out by 2029.

Sedex Members Ethical Trade Audit (SMETA), 7.0 methodology (2024). London: Sedex, https://www.sedex.com. SMETA 6.1 is legacy and being phased out. A social audit methodology, not a certification. The limits of audit-based assurance are discussed in Chapter 10.

EcoVadis sustainability ratings. Paris: EcoVadis, https://ecovadis.com. Proprietary; scores a company's submitted policies and documentation, which is not the same as scoring its conduct.

KnowTheChain benchmarks. https://knowthechain.org. Published by Business & Human Rights Resource Centre.

UK Modern Slavery Act 2015, s.54 (transparency in supply chains); California Transparency in Supply Chains Act 2010; and EU Directive 2024/1760 on Corporate Sustainability Due Diligence (CSDDD), Official Journal of the European Union, OJ L, 2024/1760, 5 July 2024, as amended by Directive (EU) 2025/794 and by the Omnibus amending Directive (EU) 2026/470, which raised the thresholds to 5,000 employees and EUR 1.5 billion turnover, removed the harmonized civil liability regime, and moved transposition to July 2028 with application from 2029.

Disclosure and reporting

GRI Universal Standards (2021): GRI 1: Foundation; GRI 2: General Disclosures; GRI 3: Material Topics. Amsterdam: Global Reporting Initiative, 2021.

IFRS S1, General Requirements for Disclosure of Sustainability-related Financial Information, and IFRS S2, Climate-related Disclosures. London: IFRS Foundation, International Sustainability Standards Board, 2023. The ISSB has absorbed the SASB Standards, which remain in use for industry-specific metrics.

European Sustainability Reporting Standards (ESRS), in particular ESRS S1 (Own Workforce), ESRS S2 (Workers in the Value Chain), ESRS S3 (Affected Communities), and ESRS S4 (Consumers and End-Users). Brussels: EFRAG / European Commission, Delegated Regulation (EU) 2023/2772, as amended. A revised and substantially simplified set of ESRS was adopted by the European Commission in July 2026, optional for FY2026 reporting and mandatory from FY2027; readers should confirm the operative version. These are the most directly relevant existing instruments to the five sites this book describes, and the double materiality principle they carry is the closest regulatory analogue to the Spectrum.

B Corp Certification. Philadelphia, PA: B Lab, https://www.bcorporation.net. Proprietary and fee-based. New certification standards published in April 2025 replace the cumulative 80-point B Impact Assessment with mandatory performance requirements, phasing in from 2026.

Public good and community

International Finance Corporation, Performance Standards on Environmental and Social Sustainability (Washington, DC: IFC, 2012), in particular PS1 (assessment and management), PS4 (community health and safety), PS5 (land acquisition and involuntary resettlement), and PS7 (Indigenous Peoples). The operative international benchmark for environmental and social impact assessment on financed projects; the Performance Standards are under formal review as of 2026.

UK Cabinet Office, Procurement Policy Note 06/20: Taking Account of Social Value in the Award of Central Government Contracts (2020), superseded by PPN 002 (February 2025), mandatory for in-scope procurements from 1 October 2025. Retains the minimum 10% social value weighting.

Social Value Model (UK), the scoring framework attached to PPN 06/20, replaced under PPN 002 by an updated model organized around the government's five missions.

Government of India, Companies Act 2013, Section 135 (Corporate Social Responsibility) and the Companies (CSR Policy) Rules, 2014, as amended.

Community benefit agreements and community land trusts are contractual and legal instruments rather than standards, and there is no single authority governing them. For the standard reference on CBAs, see Julian Gross, Greg LeRoy, and Madeline Janis-Aparicio, Community Benefits Agreements: Making Development Projects Accountable (Good Jobs First and the California Partnership for Working Families, 2005). On CLTs, see John Emmeus Davis, ed., The Community Land Trust Reader (Cambridge, MA: Lincoln Institute of Land Policy, 2010).

Participatory budgeting likewise has no governing standard. For the reference account of the Porto Alegre model and its diffusion, see Gianpaolo Baiocchi, Militants and Citizens: The Politics of Participatory Democracy in Porto Alegre (Stanford: Stanford University Press, 2005).

Appendix C: Notes and Sources

Sources and References

This book draws on published research, official reports, and primary documents, cited below. Where a scene is reconstructed, the note identifies the evidence the reconstruction is based on. Where a project or a person could be identified, details have been altered. Contested figures and published ranges are described as such in the text, and research of my own that is not yet published has been disclosed as "internal analysis."

Introduction

Scheel, David, et al. "Octopus Engineering, Intentional and Inadvertent." Communicative & Integrative Biology 11, no. 1 (2017): e1395994. https://doi.org/10.1080/19420889.2017.1395994.

Scheel, David, et al. "A Second Site Occupied by Octopus tetricus at High Densities, with Notes on Their Ecology and Behavior." Marine and Freshwater Behaviour and Physiology 50, no. 4 (2017): 285–291. https://doi.org/10.1080/10236244.2017.1369851.

King, Stephanie L., and Vincent M. Janik. "Bottlenose Dolphins Can Use Learned Vocal Labels to Address Each Other." Proceedings of the National Academy of Sciences 110, no. 32 (2013): 13216–13221. https://doi.org/10.1073/pnas.1304459110.

Janik, Vincent M., Laela S. Sayigh, and Randall S. Wells. "Signature Whistle Shape Conveys Identity Information to Bottlenose Dolphins." PNAS 103, no. 21 (2006): 8293–8297. https://doi.org/10.1073/pnas.0509918103.

Garvey, Kathy Keatley. "Nighty-Night, Mr. Bumble Bee!" Bug Squad. University of California Agriculture and Natural Resources. https://ucanr.edu/blog/bug-squad/article/nighty-night-mr-bumble-bee.

van Doorn, Wouter G., and Uulke van Meeteren. "Flower Opening and Closure: A Review." Journal of Experimental Botany 54, no. 389 (2003): 1801–12. https://doi.org/10.1093/jxb/erg213.

Poole, Joyce H., et al. "The Social Contexts of Some Very Low Frequency Calls of African Elephants." Behavioral Ecology and Sociobiology 22, no. 6 (1988): 385–392. https://doi.org/10.1007/BF00294975.

Eleuteri, Vesta, et al. "Multimodal Communication and Audience Directedness in the Greeting Behaviour of Semi-Captive African Savannah Elephants." Communications Biology 7 (2024): 472. https://doi.org/10.1038/s42003-024-06133-5.

Pardo, Michael A., et al. "African Elephants Address One Another with Individually Specific Name-Like Calls." Nature Ecology & Evolution 8 (2024): 1353–1364. https://doi.org/10.1038/s41559-024-02420-w.

Emlen, Stephen T. "Migratory Orientation in the Indigo Bunting, Passerina cyanea: Part I: Evidence for Use of Celestial Cues." The Auk 84, no. 3 (1967): 309–342. https://doi.org/10.2307/4083084.

Emlen, Stephen T. "The Stellar-Orientation System of a Migratory Bird." Scientific American 233, no. 2 (August 1975): 102–111. https://doi.org/10.1038/scientificamerican0875-102.

Directive (EU) 2026/470 of the European Parliament and of the Council of 24 February 2026 (the "Omnibus I" Directive). Published in the Official Journal of the European Union, 26 February 2026, and in force from 18 March 2026, amending

Directive (EU) 2024/1760 on Corporate Sustainability Due Diligence and the Corporate Sustainability Reporting Directive.

Nightingale, Florence. Notes on Hospitals, 3rd ed. London: Longman, 1863.

Nightingale, Florence. "Diagram of the Causes of Mortality in the Army in the East" (1858). Published in Notes on Matters Affecting the Health, Efficiency and Hospital Administration of the British Army. London: Harrison and Sons, 1858.

The Collected Works of Florence Nightingale. University of Guelph.

International Energy Agency. World Energy Investment 2025. Paris: IEA, June 2025. https://www.iea.org/reports/world-energy-investment-2025.

International Energy Agency. Net Zero Roadmap: A Global Pathway to Keep the 1.5 °C Goal in Reach — 2023 Update. Paris: IEA, September 2023. https://www.iea.org/reports/net-zero-roadmap-a-global-pathway-to-keep-the-15-0c-goal-in-reach.

World Resources Institute and World Business Council for Sustainable Development. The Greenhouse Gas Protocol: A Corporate Accounting and Reporting Standard. Washington, DC: WRI/WBCSD, 2001; revised edition 2004.

Chapter 1: What Is Social Value?

Abraham, Meera. Two Medieval Merchant Guilds of South India. New Delhi: Manohar, 1988.

Dale, Stephen F. "The Geography, Economy and Society of Indian Diasporas." In Regional Routes, Regional Roots? Cross-Border Patterns of Human Mobility in Eurasia, 1–12. Comparative Studies on Regional Powers 14. Sapporo: Slavic Research Center, Hokkaido University, 2013.

McKinnon, E. Edwards. "Continuity and Change in South Indian Involvement in Northern Sumatra: The Inferences of Archaeological Evidence from Kota Cina and Lamreh." In Early Interactions between South and Southeast Asia: Reflections on Cross-Cultural Exchange, edited by Pierre-Yves Manguin, A. Mani, and Geoff Wade, 137–60. Singapore: Institute of Southeast Asian Studies, 2011.

Sherry, Bennett. "Indian Ocean Routes." OER Project. https://www.oerproject.com/OER-Materials/OER-Media/HTML-Articles/Origins/Unit5/Indian-Ocean-Routes

Stein, Burton. "The Economic Function of a Medieval South Indian Temple." Journal of Asian Studies 19, no. 2 (1960): 163–176, https://doi.org/10.2307/2943547.

Subbarayalu, Y. "The Tamil Merchant-Guild Inscription at Barus: A Rediscovery." In Histoire de Barus, Sumatra: Le site de Lobu Tua, I. Études et documents, edited by Claude Guillot, 25–33. Cahier d'Archipel 30. Paris: Association Archipel, 1998.

Vosmer, Tom. "Fibre and Wood: Sewn Boats in Oman and the Indian Ocean." In Connected Hinterlands: Proceedings of Red Sea Project IV. International Journal of Nautical Archaeology, 2019. https://doi.org/10.1111/1095-9270.12371

Vosmer, Tom. "The Jewel of Muscat: Reconstructing a Ninth-Century Sewn-Plank Boat." In Shipwrecked: Tang Treasures and Monsoon Winds, edited by Regina Krahl et al. Washington, DC: Arthur M. Sackler Gallery, Smithsonian Institution; Singapore: National Heritage Board, Singapore Tourism Board, 2010.

A working definition

Austin, James, Howard Stevenson, and Jane Wei-Skillern. "Social and Commercial Entrepreneurship: Same, Different, or Both?" Entrepreneurship Theory and Practice 30, no. 1 (2006): 1–22., https://www.researchgate.net/publication/307773106_Social_and_Commercial_Entrepreneurship_Same_Different_or_Both

Phills, James A., Kriss Deiglmeier, and Dale T. Miller. "Rediscovering Social Innovation." Stanford Social Innovation Review 6, no. 4 (2008): 34–43.

Samuel, Flora, and Kelly Watson. "Social Value of the Built Environment." Buildings and Cities 4, no. 1 (2023): 938–947, https://doi.org/10.5334/bc.399.

Wade-Benzoni, Kimberly A., Harris Sondak, and Adam D. Galinsky. "Leaving a Legacy: Intergenerational Allocations of Benefits and Burdens." Business Ethics Quarterly 20, no. 1 (2010): 7–34.

The hidden costs of a choice

National Institute for Occupational Safety and Health. Current Intelligence Bulletin 48: Organic Solvent Neurotoxicity. DHHS (NIOSH) Publication No. 87-104. Cincinnati: NIOSH, 1987. https://www.cdc.gov/niosh/docs/87-104/default.html.

National Institute for Occupational Safety and Health. Health Hazard Evaluation Report HETA 95-0209-2515. Cincinnati: NIOSH, 1996. https://www.cdc.gov/niosh/hhe/reports/pdfs/1995-0209-2515.pdf.

National Institute for Occupational Safety and Health. Protecting Workers Who Use Cleaning Chemicals. DHHS (NIOSH) Publication No. 2012-126. Cincinnati: NIOSH, 2012. https://www.cdc.gov/niosh/docs/2012-126/default.html.

Occupational Safety and Health Administration. "Solvents: Hazard Recognition." https://www.osha.gov/solvents/hazards.

Zock, Jan-Paul, Dolores Vizcaya, and Nicole Le Moual. "Update on Asthma and Cleaners." Current Opinion in Allergy and Clinical Immunology 10, no. 2 (2010): 114–120, https://doi.org/10.1097/ACI.0b013e32833733fe.

Chapter 2: The Missing Thread

Junta Constructora del Temple Expiatori de la Sagrada Família. "Cross Lands in Sky above Barcelona." Press release, February 20, 2026. https://sagradafamilia.org/en/-/una-creu-que-arriba-al-cel-de-barcelona.

Samuel, Flora, and Kelly Watson. "Social Value of the Built Environment." Buildings and Cities 4, no. 1 (2023): 938–947, https://doi.org/10.5334/bc.399.

The waves of corporate responsibility

Bowen, Howard R. Social Responsibilities of the Businessman. New York: Harper & Brothers, 1953.

Carroll, Archie B. "The Pyramid of Corporate Social Responsibility: Toward the Moral Management of Organizational Stakeholders." Business Horizons 34, no. 4 (1991): 39–48, https://doi.org/10.1016/0007-6813(91)90005-G.

Five ways of seeing human impact

Allen, Joseph G., et al. "Associations of Cognitive Function Scores with Carbon Dioxide, Ventilation, and Volatile Organic Compound Exposures in Office Workers." Environmental Health Perspectives 124, no. 6 (2016): 805–812.

ASHRAE. Position Document on Indoor Carbon Dioxide. 2022.

Boivin, Diane B., and Charles A. Czeisler. "Resetting of Circadian Melatonin and Cortisol Rhythms in Humans by Ordinary Room Light." NeuroReport 9, no. 5 (1998): 779–782.

Brown, Timothy M., et al. "Recommendations for Daytime, Evening, and Nighttime Indoor Light Exposure to Best Support Physiology, Sleep, and Wakefulness in Healthy Adults." PLOS Biology 20, no. 3 (2022): e3001571.

Du, Bowen, et al. "Indoor CO2 Concentrations and Cognitive Function: A Critical Review." Indoor Air 30, no. 6 (2020): 1067–1082.

Gładyszewska-Fiedoruk, Katarzyna. "The Concentration of Carbon Dioxide in Conference Rooms." International Journal of Environmental Science and Technology 16, no. 12 (2019): 8031–8040.

Radune, Jenni, et al. "Speech Is Special: The Stress Effects of Speech, Noise, and Silence During Tasks Requiring Concentration." Indoor Air 31, no. 6 (2020): 1350–1360.

Monk, Timothy H. "The Post-Lunch Dip in Performance." Clinics in Sports Medicine 24, no. 2 (2005), https://doi.org/10.1111/ina.12733.

Persily, Andrew, and Lilian de Jonge. "Carbon Dioxide Generation Rates for Building Occupants." Indoor Air 27, no. 5 (2017): 868–879.

Satish, Usha, et al. "Is CO2 an Indoor Pollutant?" Environmental Health Perspectives 120, no. 12 (2012): 1671–1677.

O. Seppänen, et al. "Ventilation and Performance in Office Work." Indoor Air 16, no. 1 (2006): 28–36.

Yin, Jie, et al. "Effects of Biophilic Indoor Environment on Stress and Anxiety Recovery: A Between-Subjects Experiment in Virtual Reality." Environment International 136 (2020): 105427.

Costanza-Chock, Sasha. Design Justice: Community-Led Practices to Build the Worlds We Need. Cambridge, MA: MIT Press, 2020, https://doi.org/10.7551/mitpress/12255.001.0001.

Fainstein, Susan S. The Just City. Cornell University Press, 2010.

Talen, Emily. Design for Diversity: Exploring Socially Mixed Neighborhoods. Oxford: Architectural Press, 2008.

American Bar Association Center for Human Rights. Tainted Stones: Bonded Labor and Child Labor in the India-U.S. Sandstone Supply Chain. Washington, DC: ABA, 2020. https://www.americanbar.org/groups/human_rights/reports/tainted-stones--bonded-labor-and-child-labor-in-the-india-u-s--s/.

Ruggie, John G. Guiding Principles on Business and Human Rights: Implementing the United Nations "Protect, Respect and Remedy" Framework. New York: United Nations, 2011.

Hodges, Rita Axelroth, and Steve Dubb. The Road Half Traveled: University Engagement at a Crossroads. East Lansing: Michigan State University Press, 2012.

Serafeim, George. "Social-Impact Efforts That Create Real Value." Harvard Business Review, September–October 2020.

The connective tissue

George, Gerard, et al. "Understanding and Tackling Societal Grand Challenges Through Management Research." Academy of Management Journal 59, no. 6 (2016): 1880–1895.

Bridging to action

Elkington, John. "25 Years Ago I Coined the Phrase 'Triple Bottom Line.' Here's Why It's Time to Rethink It." Harvard Business Review, June 25, 2018.

Phills, James A., Kriss Deiglmeier, and Dale T. Miller. "Rediscovering Social Innovation." Stanford Social Innovation Review 6, no. 4 (2008): 34–43.

Social Value International. The Social Value Principles. London: Social Value International, 2021.

Case study: 20 Fenchurch Street

"Land Secs Comes Up with Fix for Walkie Scorchie." Construction Enquirer, February 12, 2014. https://www.constructionenquirer.com/2014/02/12/land-secs-comes-up-with-fix-for-walkie-scorchie/.

"'Walkie-Talkie' Skyscraper Melts Jaguar Car Parts." BBC News, September 2, 2013. https://www.bbc.co.uk/news/uk-england-london-23930675.

"Walkie-Talkie Skyscraper to Have Screen Put Up to Stop Rays." BBC News, September 3, 2013. https://www.bbc.co.uk/news/uk-england-london-23948811.

Danks, Ryan, Joel Good, and Ray Sinclair. "Assessing Reflected Sunlight from Building Facades : A Literature Review and Proposed Criteria." Building and Environment 103 (2016): 193–202."

Speroni, Alberto, et al. "Experimental Assessment of the Reflection of Solar Radiation from Facades of Tall Buildings to the Pedestrian Level." Sustainability 14, no. 10 (2022).

Chapter 3: How We Learned to Count

Beckert, Sven. Empire of Cotton: A Global History. New York: Vintage Books, 2014.

Martinez-Alier, Joan. The Environmentalism of the Poor: A Study of Ecological Conflicts and Valuation. Cheltenham: Edward Elgar, 2002.

Pomeranz, Kenneth. The Great Divergence: China, Europe, and the Making of the Modern World Economy. Princeton: Princeton University Press, 2000, Appendix F.

Wrigley, E. A. Continuity, Chance and Change: The Character of the Industrial Revolution in England. Cambridge: Cambridge University Press, 1988.

What measurement leaves out

Kennedy, Robert F. "Remarks at the University of Kansas." March 18, 1968. John F. Kennedy Presidential Library and Museum, https://www.jfklibrary.org/learn/about-jfk/the-kennedy-family/robert-f-kennedy/robert-f-kennedy-speeches/remarks-at-the-university-of-kansas-march-18-1968.

Waring, Marilyn. If Women Counted: A New Feminist Economics. San Francisco: Harper & Row, 1988.

Carbon becomes visible

World Resources Institute and World Business Council for Sustainable Development. The Greenhouse Gas Protocol: A Corporate Accounting and Reporting Standard. Washington, DC: WRI/WBCSD, 2001; revised 2004.

Chapter 4: The Omission

Sternberg, Esther M. Healing Spaces: The Science of Place and Well-Being. Cambridge, MA: Belknap Press, 2009.

Ulrich, Roger S. "View Through a Window May Influence Recovery from Surgery." Science 224, no. 4647 (1984): 420–421, https://doi.org/10.1126/science.6143402.

Ulrich, Roger S., et al. "A Review of the Research Literature on Evidence-Based Healthcare Design." HERD: Health Environments Research & Design Journal 1, no. 3 (2008): 61–125.

A promise is not a process

Meyer, John W., and Brian Rowan. "Institutionalized Organizations: Formal Structure as Myth and Ceremony." American Journal of Sociology 83, no. 2 (1977): 340–363, https://doi.org/10.1086/226550.

The budget is the test

Samuelson, Paul A. "Consumption Theory in Terms of Revealed Preference." Economica 15, no. 60 (1948): 243–253.

The system is working as planned

Deming, W. Edwards. Out of the Crisis. Cambridge, MA: MIT Center for Advanced Engineering Study, 1982.

The question taken offline

Morrison, Elizabeth W., and Frances J. Milliken. "Organizational Silence: A Barrier to Change and Development in a Pluralistic World." Academy of Management Review 25, no. 4 (2000): 706–725.

Chapter 5: The Cost Comes Back

House of Commons Business, Energy and Industrial Strategy and Work and Pensions Committees. Carillion: Second Joint Report of Session 2017–19, HC 769. London: House of Commons, 2018. https://publications.parliament.uk/pa/cm201719/cmselect/cmworpen/769/769.pdf.

Mor, Federico, Lorraine Conway, Djuna Thurley, and Lorna Booth. The Collapse of Carillion. Briefing Paper CBP-8206. London: House of Commons Library, 14 March 2018, updated 8 July 2026. https://commonslibrary.parliament.uk/research-briefings/cbp-8206/.

The cost returns

Boushey, Heather, and Sarah Jane Glynn. There Are Significant Business Costs to Replacing Employees. Washington, DC: Center for American Progress, 2012. https://www.americanprogress.org/article/there-are-significant-business-costs-to-replacing-employees/.

Coffey, Clare, et al. Time to Care: Unpaid and Underpaid Care Work and the Global Inequality Crisis. Oxford: Oxfam International, 2020. https://doi.org/10.21201/2020.5419.

Fish, Jennifer N. Domestic Workers of the World Unite! A Global Movement for Dignity and Human Rights. New York: NYU Press, 2017.

Gallup. State of the Global Workplace: 2026 Report. Washington, DC: Gallup, 2026. https://www.gallup.com/workplace/349484/state-of-the-global-workplace.aspx

Goh, Joel, Jeffrey Pfeffer, and Stefanos A. Zenios. "The Relationship Between Workplace Stressors and Mortality and Health Costs in the United States." Management Science 62, no. 2 (2016): 608–628, https://doi.org/10.1287/mnsc.2014.2115.

GOV.UK. "Maternity Pay and Leave." https://www.gov.uk/maternity-pay-leave.

Hafner, Marco, et al. Why Sleep Matters: The Economic Costs of Insufficient Sleep. A Cross-Country Comparative Analysis, RR-1791-VH. Santa Monica: RAND Corporation, 2016. https://www.rand.org/pubs/research_reports/RR1791.html.

International Labour Organization. C189: Domestic Workers Convention, 2011 (No. 189), adopted 16 June 2011.

Pfeffer, Jeffrey. Dying for a Paycheck: How Modern Management Harms Employee Health and Company Performance, and What We Can Do About It. New York: HarperBusiness, 2018.

WIEGO. "A WIEGO Tribute to Myrtle Witbooi." 2023.

Work Institute. 2024 Retention Report. Franklin, TN: Work Institute, 2024.

Borrowing from human capacity

Cunningham, Ward. "The WyCash Portfolio Management System." In Addendum to the Proceedings on Object-Oriented Programming Systems, Languages, and Applications (OOPSLA '92), 29–30. New York: ACM, 1992. https://doi.org/10.1145/157709.157715.

Sculley, D., et al. "Hidden Technical Debt in Machine Learning Systems." Advances in Neural Information Processing Systems 28 (2015): 2503–2511.

Who can refuse?

Försäkringskassan. "Parental Benefit (Föräldrapenning)." https://www.forsakringskassan.se/english/parents/when-the-child-is-born/parental-benefit.

Weil, David. The Fissured Workplace: Why Work Became So Bad for So Many and What Can Be Done to Improve It. Cambridge, MA: Harvard University Press, 2014.

"Boeing to Sell Commercial Airplanes Operations in Kansas and Oklahoma to Onex." Boeing news release, February 22, 2005.

When responsibility crosses a boundary

National Transportation Safety Board. In-Flight Left Mid Exit Door Plug Separation, Alaska Airlines Flight 1282, Boeing 737-9 MAX, NTSB/AIR-25/04 (DCA24MA063), adopted June 24, 2025. https://www.ntsb.gov/investigations/AccidentReports/Reports/AIR2504.pdf.

Chapter 6: The People Positive Spectrum

The missing axis

International Labour Organization. Guidelines for a Just Transition Towards Environmentally Sustainable Economies and Societies for All. Geneva: ILO, 2015.

World Benchmarking Alliance. 2023 Corporate Human Rights Benchmark Insights Report. Amsterdam: WBA, November 2023. https://www.worldbenchmarkingalliance.org/latest/2023-corporate-human-rights-benchmark-insights-report.

Green is not automatically People Positive

"Comparative assessment of mass timber, structural steel, and reinforced concrete buildings under the 2021 IBC provisions." Building and Environment (2024). USDA Forest Service Treesearch record 67350, https://research.fs.usda.gov/treesearch/67350.

Cubbage, Frederick, Susan Moore, Thresa Henderson, and Michelle Araujo, "Costs and Benefits of Forest Certification in the Americas." In Natural Resources: Management, Economic Development and Protection, edited by Jeanette B. Pauling, 155–83. New York: Nova Science Publishers, 2009.

Forest Stewardship Council. FSC Standard for Group Entities in Forest Management Groups, FSC-STD-30-005 V2-0. Bonn: FSC International, 2020.

International Code Council. 2021 International Building Code, Section 602.4 and construction Types IV-A, IV-B, and IV-C. https://codes.iccsafe.org/content/IBC2021P1.

Puettmann, Maureen, et al. "Comparative LCAs of Conventional and Mass Timber Buildings in Regions with Potential for Mass Timber Penetration." Sustainability 13, no. 24 (2021): 13987, https://doi.org/10.3390/su132413987.

The floor of harm prevention

United Nations Human Rights Council. Guiding Principles on Business and Human Rights: Implementing the United Nations "Protect, Respect and Remedy" Framework. New York and Geneva: United Nations, 2011.

The pattern beneath the promise

People ex rel. Moloney v. Pullman's Palace Car Co., 175 Ill. 125 (1898).

United States Strike Commission. Report on the Chicago Strike of June–July, 1894. Washington, DC: Government Printing Office, 1895. https://www.loc.gov/item/2024771952.

Gutelius, Beth, and Sanjay Pinto. Pain Points: Data on Work Intensity, Monitoring, and Health at Amazon Warehouses. Chicago: Center for Urban Economic Development, University of Illinois Chicago, October 2023. https://cued.uic.edu/pain-points/.

People Neutral

KnowTheChain. 2023 Apparel and Footwear Benchmark.

Verité and the UN Global Compact. Eliminating Recruitment Fees Charged to Migrant Workers. 2015. https://unglobalcompact.org/library/3671.

The incentive objection

Bebchuk, Lucian A., and Roberto Tallarita. "The Illusory Promise of Stakeholder Governance." Cornell Law Review 106 (2020).

Business Roundtable. Statement on the Purpose of a Corporation, 2019.

Friedman, Milton. "The Social Responsibility of Business Is to Increase Its Profits." 1970.

Chapter 7: People

Origins

Bosma, Hans, et al. "Low Job Control and Risk of Coronary Heart Disease in Whitehall II (Prospective Cohort) Study." BMJ 314 (1997): 558–565.

Chadwick, Edwin. Report on the Sanitary Condition of the Labouring Population of Great Britain. London: HMSO, 1842.

Factory Act 1833 (UK), 3 & 4 Will. IV c. 103.

Karasek, Robert A. "Job Demands, Job Decision Latitude, and Mental Strain: Implications for Job Redesign." Administrative Science Quarterly 24, no. 2 (1979): 285–308.

Levitt, Steven D., and John A. List. "Was There Really a Hawthorne Effect at the Hawthorne Plant? An Analysis of the Original Illumination Experiments." American Economic Journal: Applied Economics 3, no. 1 (2011): 224–238, https://doi.org/10.1257/app.3.1.224.

Marmot, M. G., et al. "Employment Grade and Coronary Heart Disease in British Civil Servants." Journal of Epidemiology and Community Health 32, no. 4 (1978): 244–249.

Marmot, Michael G., et al. "Health Inequalities Among British Civil Servants: The Whitehall II Study." The Lancet 337, no. 8754 (1991): 1387–1393.

Marmot, Michael. The Status Syndrome: How Social Standing Affects Our Health and Longevity. New York: Times Books, 2004.

New York State Tenement House Act of 1901.

Ramazzini, Bernardino. De Morbis Artificum Diatriba. Modena, 1700; enlarged ed. Padua, 1713. English translation: Diseases of Workers, translated by Wilmer Cave Wright. Chicago: University of Chicago Press, 1940.

Riis, Jacob A. How the Other Half Lives: Studies Among the Tenements of New York. New York: Charles Scribner's Sons, 1890.

Roethlisberger, Fritz J., and William J. Dickson. Management and the Worker. Cambridge, MA: Harvard University Press, 1939.

In practice

Dublin, Thomas. Women at Work: The Transformation of Work and Community in Lowell, Massachusetts, 1826–1860. New York: Columbia University Press, 1979.

Eisler, Benita, ed. The Lowell Offering: Writings by New England Mill Women (1840–1845). New York: Harper & Row, 1977.

Villafañez Pérez, Itziar. "A Brief Chronicle of and Some Notes on the Bankruptcy Proceeding of Fagor Electrodomésticos S.Coop." International Journal of Cooperative Law 1 (2018). https://iuscooperativum.org/article/a-brief-chronicle-of-and-some-notes-on-the-bankruptcy-proceeding-of-fagor-electrodomesticos-s-coop/

Mondragon Corporation. Annual Report 2023. Arrasate-Mondragón: Mondragon Corporation, 2024.

Reuten, Geert. "The Mondragon Worker Cooperatives' Employment Record 1983–2019." Journal of Labor and Society 26, no. 3 (2023): 336–375.

The reality gap

Deloitte and Workplace Intelligence. As Workforce Well-Being Dips, Leaders Ask: What Now? Deloitte Insights, June 2023. https://www.deloitte.com/us/en/insights/topics/talent/workplace-well-being-research.html.

Trucker Bathroom Access Act, H.R. 2514, 119th Cong. (2025). https://www.congress.gov/bill/119th-congress/house-bill/2514.

Work Institute. 2024 Retention Report. Franklin, TN: Work Institute, 2024.

Chapter 8: Place

Rawson, Elizabeth. "Discrimina Ordinum: The Lex Julia Theatralis." Papers of the British School at Rome 55 (1987): 83–114.

Origins

Fanger, P. Ole. Thermal Comfort: Analysis and Applications in Environmental Engineering. Copenhagen: Danish Technical Press, 1970.

Goldsmith, Selwyn. Designing for the Disabled. London: RIBA, 1963.

Morawska, Lidia, et al. "How Can Airborne Transmission of COVID-19 Indoors Be Minimised?" Environment International 142 (2020): 105832, https://doi.org/10.1016/j.envint.2020.105832.

United Nations. Convention on the Rights of Persons with Disabilities, adopted 13 December 2006, entered into force 3 May 2008.

World Health Organization Regional Office for Europe. Indoor Air Pollutants: Exposure and Health Effects. EURO Reports and Studies 78. Copenhagen: WHO, 1983.

Yu, Ignatius T. S., et al. "Evidence of Airborne Transmission of the Severe Acute Respiratory Syndrome Virus." New England Journal of Medicine 350, no. 17 (2004): 1731–1739.

Li, Yuguo, et al. "Role of Air Distribution in SARS Transmission During the Largest Nosocomial Outbreak in Hong Kong." Indoor Air 15, no. 2 (2005): 83–95.

Access, exposure, agency

Allen, Joseph G., et al. Healthy Buildings: How Indoor Spaces Drive Performance and Productivity. Cambridge, MA: Harvard University Press, 2020.

Fanger, P. Ole. Thermal Comfort: Analysis and Applications in Environmental Engineering. Copenhagen: Danish Technical Press, 1970.

Lee, Gyu-Bin, et al. "A Comparative Field Study of Indoor Environment Quality and Work Productivity Between Job Types." International Journal of Environmental Research and Public Health 19, no. 21 (2022): 14332, https://doi.org/10.3390/ijerph192114332.

Morawska, Lidia, et al. "How Can Airborne Transmission of COVID-19 Indoors Be Minimised?" Environment International 142 (2020): 105832, https://doi.org/10.1016/j.envint.2020.105832.

Wargocki, Pawel, and David P. Wyon. "Providing Better Thermal and Air Quality Conditions in School Classrooms Would Be Cost-Effective." Building and Environment 59 (2013): 581–589.

Woods, V., and Peter Buckle. "Musculoskeletal Ill Health Amongst Cleaners and Recommendations for Work Organisational Change." International Journal of Industrial Ergonomics 36, no. 1 (2006): 61–72.

World Health Organization Regional Office for Europe. Indoor Air Pollutants: Exposure and Health Effects. EURO Reports and Studies 78. Copenhagen: WHO, 1983.

Wyon, DP. "The Effects of Indoor Air Quality on Performance and Productivity." Indoor Air 14, Suppl. 7 (2004): 92–101.

Zock, JP. "World at Work: Cleaners." Occupational and Environmental Medicine 62, no. 8 (2005): 581–584, https://doi.org/10.1136/oem.2004.015032.

Ventilation material

ANSI/ASHRAE Standard 62.1-2022. Ventilation and Acceptable Indoor Air Quality.

Seppänen, Olli, William J. Fisk, and Q. H. Lei. "Ventilation and Performance in Office Work."

Wargocki, Pawel, et al. "The Effects of Outdoor Air Supply Rate in an Office on Perceived Air Quality, Sick Building Syndrome (SBS) Symptoms and Productivity."

The temperature of the room

Criado Perez, Caroline. Invisible Women: Data Bias in a World Designed for Men.

ASHRAE. ASHRAE Position Document on Indoor Carbon Dioxide. Peachtree Corners, GA: ASHRAE, 2022. https://www.ashrae.org/file%20library/about/position%20documents/pd-on-indoor-carbon-dioxide-english.pdf.

Fanger, P. Ole. Thermal Comfort: Analysis and Applications in Environmental Engineering. Copenhagen: Danish Technical Press, 1970.

Kingma, Boris, and Wouter van Marken Lichtenbelt. "Energy Consumption in Buildings and Female Thermal Demand." Nature Climate Change 5, no. 12 (2015): 1054–1056, https://doi.org/10.1038/nclimate2741.

Parkinson, Thomas, Stefano Schiavon, Richard de Dear, and Gail Brager. "Overcooling of Offices Reveals Gender Inequity in Thermal Comfort." Scientific Reports 11 (2021): 23684, https://doi.org/10.1038/s41598-021-03121-1.

In practice

Fair Trade USA. "Factory Certification Standard." Oakland, CA: Fair Trade USA.

Fanger, P. Ole. Thermal Comfort: Analysis and Applications in Environmental Engineering. Copenhagen: Danish Technical Press, 1970.

"Saitex Scores High Marks for Environmental Efforts from Higg, B Lab." Sourcing Journal, 2023. https://wwd.com/sourcing-journal/sj-denim/saitex-vietnam-denim-manufacturer-higg-b-corp-impact-report-textile-waste-1238820807/

Morawska, Lidia, et al. "How Can Airborne Transmission of COVID-19 Indoors Be Minimised?" Environment International 142 (2020): 105832, https://doi.org/10.1016/j.envint.2020.105832.

Newsham, Guy, et al. "Do 'Green' Buildings Have Better Indoor Environments? New Evidence." Building Research & Information 41, no. 4 (2013): 415–434.

Quinan, Jack. Frank Lloyd Wright's Larkin Building: Myth and Fact, 2nd ed. Chicago: University of Chicago Press, 2006.

Joe, Tanuvi. "Sustainable Vietnam-Based Denim Factory Runs On Renewables, Builds An Inclusive Workplace." Green Queen Media, June 23, 2021. https://www.greenqueen.com.hk/sustainable-ethical-denim-factory-vietnam/.

"Saitex's New Project Offers Sustainable Work for People of All Abilities." Sourcing Journal, 2021.

"Behind Rekut." REKUT, https://rekut.org/pages/behind-rekut.

U.S. Green Building Council. LEED v4 for Building Design and Construction. Washington, DC: USGBC, 2013 (as updated).

World Health Organization Regional Office for Europe. Indoor Air Pollutants: Exposure and Health Effects: Report on a WHO Meeting, Nördlingen, 8–11 June 1982. EURO Reports and Studies 78. Copenhagen: WHO, 1983, 23–26. https://www.aivc.org/sites/default/files/airbase_1609.pdf.

Tracing the costs

Allen, Joseph G., et al. "Associations of Cognitive Function Scores with Carbon Dioxide, Ventilation, and Volatile Organic Compound Exposures in Office Workers: A Controlled Exposure Study of Green and Conventional Office Environments." Environmental Health Perspectives 124, no. 6 (2016): 805–812.

MacNaughton, Piers, et al. "Economic, Environmental and Health Implications of Enhanced Ventilation in Office Buildings." International Journal of Environmental Research and Public Health 12, no. 11 (2015): 14709–14722.

Return on Disability Group. The Global Economics of Disability: 2024 Annual Report. Toronto: Return on Disability, 2024.

Schroeder, Steven, and Edward Steinfeld. The Estimated Cost of Accessible Buildings. Washington, DC: US Department of Housing and Urban Development, 1979. Summarized in Independent Living Institute, "A Brief Survey of Studies on Costs and Benefits of Non-Handicapping Environments," https://www.independentliving.org/cib/cibrio94access.html.

United Nations Department of Economic and Social Affairs. Accessibility and Development: Environmental Accessibility and Its Implications for Inclusive, Sustainable and Equitable Development for All. New York: United Nations, 2013. https://www.un.org/disabilities/documents/accessibility_and_development_june2013.pdf.

U.S. Department of Transportation, Office of Inspector General. Estimates Show Commercial Driver Detention Increases Crash Risks and Costs, but Current Data Limit Further Analysis. Report No. ST2018019. Washington, DC: USDOT, January 31, 2018.

Yin, Michelle, Dahlia Shaewitz, Cynthia Overton, and Deeza-Mae Smith. A Hidden Market: The Purchasing Power of Working-Age Adults with Disabilities. Washington, DC: American Institutes for Research, 2018.

Chapter 9: Product

David, Alison Matthews. Fashion Victims: The Dangers of Dress Past and Present. London: Bloomsbury, 2015.

Jones, David E. H. "Arsenic and the Victorian Wallpaper." Chemistry in Britain (1982).

Whorton, James C. The Arsenic Century: How Victorian Britain Was Poisoned at Home, Work, and Play. Oxford: Oxford University Press, 2010.

Origins

Hamilton, Alice. Exploring the Dangerous Trades: The Autobiography of Alice Hamilton, M.D. Boston: Little, Brown, 1943.

International Organization for Standardization. ISO 14040:2006, Environmental Management — Life Cycle Assessment — Principles and Framework, and ISO 14044:2006, Environmental Management — Life Cycle Assessment — Requirements and Guidelines. Geneva: ISO, 2006.

McDonough, William, and Braungart, Michael. Cradle to Cradle: Remaking the Way We Make Things. New York: North Point Press, 2002.

United Nations Environment Programme. Guidelines for Social Life Cycle Assessment of Products and Organizations, 2020 ed. Paris: UNEP Life Cycle Initiative, 2020.

Following the product lifecycle

Cook, Ed, and Costas Velis. Global Review on Safer End of Engineered Life. London: Royal Academy of Engineering / Engineering X, 2021.

Corte Constitucional de Colombia. Auto 275 de 2011 (19 December 2011).

Goldman Environmental Prize. "Nohra Padilla." 2013. https://www.goldmanprize.org/recipient/nohra-padilla/.

Lau, Winnie W. Y., et al. "Evaluating Scenarios Toward Zero Plastic Pollution." Science 369, no. 6510 (2020): 1455–1461, https://doi.org/10.1126/science.aba9475.

Abizaid, Olga. ARB: Fighting for an Inclusive Model for Recycling in Bogotá. Manchester, UK: WIEGO / Inclusive Cities, 2015.

In practice

Fazio, Jane C., et al. "A Review of Silicosis and Other Silica-Related Diseases in the Engineered Stone Countertop Processing Industry." Journal of Occupational Medicine and Toxicology 20 (2025).

Fazio, Jane C., et al. "Silicosis Among Immigrant Engineered Stone (Quartz) Countertop Fabrication Workers in California." JAMA Internal Medicine 183, no. 9 (2023): 991–998.

Occupational Safety and Health Administration. "Respirable Crystalline Silica Focused Inspection Initiative in the Engineered Stone Fabrication and Installation Industries." 2023.

Public Health Watch. "Jury Awards $52.4M in Case Against Artificial Stone Countertop Makers." August 8, 2024. https://publichealthwatch.org/2024/08/08/jury-awards-52-4m-in-case-against-artificial-stone-countertop-makers/.

Testimony of Jose Francisco Andrade Peña before the California Occupational Safety and Health Standards Board, reported in Public Health Watch, May 2026. https://publichealthwatch.org/2026/05/21/california-ban-stone-countertops-workplace-epidemic-silicosis/.

Testimony of Leobardo Segura Meza before the California Occupational Safety and Health Standards Board, July 2023, reported by KQED. https://www.kqed.org/news/11956246/california-fast-tracks-rules-to-protect-stonecutters-from-horrible-deaths.

California Air Resources Board. Airborne Toxic Control Measure to Reduce Formaldehyde Emissions from Composite Wood Products, Phase II.

US Environmental Protection Agency. Formaldehyde Standards for Composite Wood Products, TSCA Title VI.

International Living Future Institute. Declare and the Living Building Challenge Red List.

International Living Future Institute. The JUST label, an organizational social equity transparency program launched in 2014 (JUST 3.0, 2024).

Cradle to Cradle Products Innovation Institute. Cradle to Cradle Certified Product Standard, Version 4.1. Oakland, CA: Cradle to Cradle Products Innovation Institute, 2024. https://c2ccertified.org.

Social Accountability International. SA8000 Standard: 2026. New York: Social Accountability International, 2026. https://sa-intl.org/resources/sa8000-standard/.

Chapter 10: Partners

Kuhn, Dieter. Science and Civilisation in China, Volume 5, Part 9: Textile Technology: Spinning and Reeling. Cambridge: Cambridge University Press, 1988.

Sims-Williams, Nicholas. "The Sogdian Ancient Letters." In The Silk Road: Trade, Travel, War and Faith, edited by Susan Whitfield with Ursula Sims-Williams. London: British Library, 2004.

Vainker, Shelagh. Chinese Silk: A Cultural History. London: British Museum Press, 2004.

Vaissière, Étienne de la. Sogdian Traders: A History, translated by James Ward. Leiden: Brill, 2005.

Origins

Distelhorst, Greg, Richard Locke, Timea Pal, and Hiram Samel. "Production Goes Global, Compliance Stays Local." Regulation & Governance 9 (2015): 224–242.

Fairtrade International. Published history of the Max Havelaar label, launched in the Netherlands in November 1988 by Solidaridad, working with the Mexican cooperative UCIRI.

Vandenbroucke, An-Sofie, et al. "The Portrayal of Effectiveness of Supplier Codes of Conduct." Regulation & Governance (2024).

Weil, David. The Fissured Workplace: Why Work Became So Bad for So Many and What Can Be Done to Improve It. Cambridge, MA: Harvard University Press, 2014.

The people behind a purchase

International Labour Organization. Founding conventions on hours of work, forced labor, and freedom of association, from 1919; and the ILO Declaration on Fundamental Principles and Rights at Work (1998).

Locke, Richard M. The Promise and Limits of Private Power: Promoting Labor Standards in a Global Economy. Cambridge: Cambridge University Press, 2013.

In Practice

American Bar Association Center for Human Rights. Tainted Stones: Bonded Labor and Child Labor in the India-U.S. Sandstone Supply Chain. Washington, DC: ABA, 2020.

Diaspora Co. "About." https://www.diasporaco.com/pages/about, and the company's published impact reporting.

Human Rights Watch. Human Rights in Supply Chains: A Call for a Binding Global Standard on Due Diligence. New York: HRW, 2016, and related reporting on sourcing practices and labor abuses.

International Labour Office. Purchasing Practices and Working Conditions in Global Supply Chains: Global Survey Results, INWORK Issue Brief No. 10. Geneva: ILO, 2017.

Apple Inc. People and Environment in Our Supply Chain: 2025 Annual Progress Report. Cupertino, CA: Apple Inc., 2025. https://s203.q4cdn.com/367071867/files/doc_downloads/2025/04/Apple-Supply-Chain-2025-Progress-Report.pdf.

Apple Inc. Supplier Responsibility 2013 Progress Report.

China Labor Watch. Study Casts Doubts on Apple's Ethical Standards. New York: CLW, 2016.

Fair Labor Association. Independent Investigation of Foxconn. Washington, DC: FLA, 2012.

Students and Scholars Against Corporate Misbehaviour (SACOM). Sweatshops Are Good for Apple and Foxconn, but Not for Workers. Hong Kong: SACOM, 2012.

Chapter 11: Public Good

Origins

Jacobs, Jane. The Death and Life of Great American Cities. New York: Random House, 1961.

Nihil novi (1505), Polish statute.

United Nations. Convention on the Rights of Persons with Disabilities, adopted 13 December 2006.

Nothing about us without us

Charlton, James I. Nothing About Us Without Us: Disability Oppression and Empowerment. Berkeley: University of California Press, 1998.

In Practice

Gravel, Ryan Austin. "Belt Line—Atlanta: Design of Infrastructure as a Reflection of Public Policy." Master's thesis (Master of Architecture and Master of City Planning), Georgia Institute of Technology, 1999. http://hdl.handle.net/1853/7400.

Gravel, Ryan, and Nathaniel Smith. Resignation letter to the board of the Atlanta BeltLine Partnership, September 26, 2016. Reproduced in Maria Saporta, "Ryan Gravel and Nathaniel Smith Resign from BeltLine Partnership Board over Equity Concerns," SaportaReport, September 26, 2016. https://saportareport.com/ryan-gravel-nathaniel-smith-resign-beltline-partnership-board-equity-concerns/.

Immergluck, Dan, and Tharunya Balan. "Sustainable for Whom? Green Urban Development, Environmental Gentrification, and the Atlanta Beltline." Urban Geography 39, no. 4 (2018): 546–62. https://doi.org/10.1080/02723638.2017.1360041.

Stafford, Leon. "Beltline Creator Gravel Resigns from Partnership." Atlanta Journal-Constitution, September 27, 2016.

Canterbury Earthquake Recovery Authority. Christchurch Central Recovery Plan. Christchurch: CERA, 2012.

Carlton, Sally. "Share an Idea, Spare a Thought: Community Consultation in Christchurch's Time-Bound Post-Earthquake Rebuild." Journal of Human Rights in the Commonwealth 1, no. 1 (2013).

Christchurch City Council. Share an Idea process reporting.

Gjerde, Morten. "Building Back Better: Learning from the Christchurch Rebuild." Procedia Engineering 198 (2017): 530–540.

Echeverri Restrepo, Alejandro, and Francesco M. Orsini. "Informalidad y urbanismo social en Medellín." In Medellín: Medio Ambiente, Urbanismo y Sociedad, edited by Michel Hermelin et al. Medellín: Universidad EAFIT, 2010.

Harboe, Lisbet, and Kristian Hoelscher. "Architecture, Politics and Peacebuilding in Medellín." Peacebuilding 11, no. 4 (2023): 403–424.

Harindranath, Arjun. "Medellín's Doomed Library: The Indefinite Closure of Biblioteca España." The Bogotá Post, October 8, 2018.

Sotomayor, Luisa. Medellín's Integrated Urban Projects: A Planning Tool to Reduce Socio-Spatial Inequality. Lincoln Institute of Land Policy Working Paper WP21LS1, 2021.

Public good at city scale

World Resources Institute. "In Ahmedabad, India, Women Are Climate Leaders" and Women's Action Towards Climate Resilience, Prize for Cities documentation.

Part 3: Adopt

Meadows, Donella. "Leverage Points: Places to Intervene in a System." Hartland, VT: The Sustainability Institute, 1999.

Ostrom, Elinor. Governing the Commons. Cambridge: Cambridge University Press, 1990.

Sen, Amartya. Development as Freedom. New York: Knopf, 1999.

Nussbaum, Martha C. Creating Capabilities: The Human Development Approach. Cambridge, MA: Belknap Press, 2011.

Chapter 12: The Fear of Finding Out

FOFO

Colino, Stacey. "You've Heard of FOMO. But Do You Have FOFO?" TIME, November 12, 2025. https://time.com/7332559/fofo-fear-of-finding-out/.

Clark, Claudia. Radium Girls: Women and Industrial Health Reform, 1910–1935. Chapel Hill: University of North Carolina Press, 1997.

Harvard T. H. Chan School of Public Health. "Deadly Occupation, Forged Report." Fall 2013 Centennial issue. https://hsph.harvard.edu/news/centennial-radium-forged-report/.

Moore, Kate. The Radium Girls: The Dark Story of America's Shining Women. Naperville: Sourcebooks, 2017.

Silence is a decision

McGoey, Linsey. "The Logic of Strategic Ignorance." British Journal of Sociology 63, no. 3 (2012): 533–555, https://doi.org/10.1111/j.1468-4446.2012.01424.x.

The Route for Improvement

Meyer, John W., and Brian Rowan. "Institutionalized Organizations: Formal Structure as Myth and Ceremony." American Journal of Sociology 83, no. 2 (1977): 340–363.

Morrison, Elizabeth W., and Frances J. Milliken. "Organizational Silence: A Barrier to Change and Development in a Pluralistic World." Academy of Management Review 25, no. 4 (2000): 706–725.

Chapter 13: The Power to Say No

99% Invisible. "Structural Integrity," episode 110 (2014).

Cole, John. Report of the Independent Inquiry into the Construction of Edinburgh Schools. Edinburgh: City of Edinburgh Council, February 2017. https://www.ciob.org/industry/policy-research/resources/report-independent-inquiry-into-construction-edinburgh-schools.

Morgenstern, Joe. "The Fifty-Nine-Story Crisis." The New Yorker, May 29, 1995, 45–53.

Four gates for impact

Bordass, Bill, Adrian Leaman, and Paul Ruyssevelt. "Assessing Building Performance in Use 5: Conclusions and Implications." Building Research & Information 29, no. 2 (2001): 144–157. https://doi.org/10.1080/09613210010008054

Way, Mark, and Bill Bordass. "Making Feedback and Post-Occupancy Evaluation Routine 2: Soft Landings." Building Research & Information 33, no. 4 (2005): 353–360.

Thomas, H. Randolph, and Ralph D. Ellis. Avoiding Delays During the Construction Phase of Highway Projects. NCHRP 20-24(12). Washington, DC: Transportation Research Board, 2001.

Weil, David. The Fissured Workplace: Why Work Became So Bad for So Many and What Can Be Done to Improve It. Cambridge, MA: Harvard University Press, 2014.

Hendrich, Ann, et al. "A 36-Hospital Time and Motion Study: How Do Medical-Surgical Nurses Spend Their Time?" The Permanente Journal 12, no. 3 (2008): 25–34.

Chapter 14: Levers of Change

Construction Specifications Institute. MasterFormat: Numbers and Titles, 2026 ed. Alexandria, VA: Construction Specifications Institute, 2026.

Dell'Isola, Alphonse J. Value Engineering: Practical Applications for Design, Construction, Maintenance & Operations. Kingston, MA: R.S. Means, 1997.

Samuel, Flora, and Kelly Watson. "Social Value of the Built Environment." Buildings and Cities 4, no. 1 (2023): 938–947.

Lever 1: Procurement

Cabinet Office. PPN 002: Taking Account of Social Value in the Award of Contracts. February 2025. https://www.gov.uk/government/publications/ppn-002-taking-account-of-social-value-in-the-award-of-contracts.

Cabinet Office. Procurement Policy Note 06/20: Taking Account of Social Value in the Award of Central Government Contracts. London: Cabinet Office, September 2020, applied from 1 January 2021.

Government of India. The Companies Act, 2013, Section 135 (Corporate Social Responsibility). Gazette of India, 2013.

Lever 2: Climate and sustainability plans

International Labour Organization. Guidelines for a Just Transition Towards Environmentally Sustainable Economies and Societies for All. Geneva: ILO, 2015.

Liveable. Internal analysis of 30 municipal and metropolitan climate action plans across six global regions, 2026, scoring each plan on the maturity of its social-outcome disclosure and measurement. Unpublished; rubric and city list on file with the author.

Lever 3: Technical specifications

Gensler. Gensler Product Sustainability (GPS) Standards, version 2.1. San Francisco: Gensler, 2025. https://www.gensler.com/gensler-product-sustainability-standards.

Gensler. "Gensler Product Sustainability Standards Reduce Environmental Impact of Architectural Interiors." Press release, September 24, 2024.

mindful MATERIALS. The Common Materials Framework. https://www.mindfulmaterials.com/a-common-language.

Lever 4: Certifications and lifecycle evidence

International Organization for Standardization. ISO 14040:2006, Environmental Management — Life Cycle Assessment — Principles and Framework, and ISO 14044:2006, Environmental Management — Life Cycle Assessment — Requirements and Guidelines. Geneva: ISO, 2006.

Liveable. Internal analysis of 30 building products across three complexity tiers, 2026, scoring the maturity of publicly available social-value disclosure from absent to embedded. Unpublished; scoring framework and product list on file with the author.

McDonough, William, and Braungart, Michael. Cradle to Cradle: Remaking the Way We Make Things. New York: North Point Press, 2002.

United Nations Environment Programme. Guidelines for Social Life Cycle Assessment of Products and Organizations, 2020 ed. Paris: UNEP Life Cycle Initiative, 2020.

Chapter 15: Mapping Progress

Leuschner, Christoph, and Meinzer, Frederick C. "Drought Resistance and Drought Adaptation of Douglas-Fir (Pseudotsuga menziesii): A Review." Perspectives in Plant Ecology, Evolution and Systematics 65 (2024): 125829, https://doi.org/10.1016/j.ppees.2024.125829.

Rood, Stewart B., et al. "Branch Sacrifice: Cavitation-Associated Drought Adaptation of Riparian Cottonwoods." Trees 14, no. 5 (2000): 248–257, https://doi.org/10.1007/s004680050010.

From feedback to remedy

United Nations General Assembly. Basic Principles and Guidelines on the Right to a Remedy and Reparation for Victims of Gross Violations of International Human Rights Law and Serious Violations of International Humanitarian Law, A/RES/60/147 (2005).

United Nations Human Rights Council. Guiding Principles on Business and Human Rights, Principles 22 and 29–31. New York and Geneva: United Nations, 2011.

Part 4: Amplify

Franklin, Jerry F., et al. "Tree Death as an Ecological Process." BioScience 37, no. 8 (1987): 550–556.

Harmon, Mark E., and Franklin, Jerry F. "Tree Seedlings on Logs in Picea-Tsuga Forests of Oregon and Washington." Ecology 70, no. 1 (1989): 48–59.

Chapter 16: Speak the Language of the Room

Levine, Donald N. Wax and Gold: Tradition and Innovation in Ethiopian Culture. Chicago: University of Chicago Press, 1965.

Mennasemay, Maimire. Qiné Hermeneutics and Ethiopian Critical Theory. Los Angeles: Tsehai Publishers, 2021.

The route into the right room

International WELL Building Institute. "Global WELL Adoption Experiences Unprecedented Growth, with 6 Billion Square Feet of Space Now Engaged." IWBI, July 2025. https://resources.wellcertified.com.

Lost in translation

Argyris, Chris, and Schön, Donald A. Theory in Practice: Increasing Professional Effectiveness. San Francisco: Jossey-Bass, 1974.

Chapter 17: Make Proof Portable

Stranded proof

Sadikin, Natasha, et al. The Financial Impact of Healthy Buildings. Cambridge, MA: MIT Real Estate Innovation Lab, 2020; SSRN working paper 2021.

The data is siloed, not missing

Seppänen, Olli, et al. "Ventilation and Performance in Office Work." Indoor Air 16, no. 1 (2006): 28–36.

Wargocki, Pawel, et al. "The Effects of Outdoor Air Supply Rate in an Office on Perceived Air Quality, Sick Building Syndrome (SBS) Symptoms and Productivity." Indoor Air 10, no. 4 (2000): 222–236.

Chapter 18: Proof Becomes Permission

The blue diode

Moore, Geoffrey A. Crossing the Chasm: Marketing and Selling High-Tech Products to Mainstream Customers. New York: HarperBusiness, 1991; 3rd ed. 2014.

Rogers, Everett M. Diffusion of Innovations, 5th ed. New York: Free Press, 2003.

From proof to precedent

Strang, David, and Soule, Sarah A. "Diffusion in Organizations and Social Movements: From Hybrid Corn to Poison Pills." Annual Review of Sociology 24 (1998): 265–290.

"East German Political Prisoners Made Some of Its Products, IKEA Admits." NPR, November 16, 2012. https://www.npr.org/sections/thetwo-way/2012/11/16/165263102/east-german-political-prisoners-made-some-of-its-products-ikea-admits.

Fortune. "IKEA Pledges €6 Million to Victims of Forced Labor in East Germany." October 31, 2024.

Conclusion: Start Here

Chikarmane, Poornima, et al. ILO-SNDT Study of Scrap Collectors, Scrap Traders and Recycling Enterprises in Pune: Preliminary Report of Findings. Pune: International Labour Organisation and SNDT Women's University, 2001. https://www.swachcoop.com/pdf/ILO%20Study.pdf

Chikarmane, Poornima. Integrating Waste Pickers into Municipal Solid Waste Management in Pune, India. WIEGO Policy Brief (Urban Policies) No. 8, 2012.

Gawade, Shatakshi. "Empowering Waste Pickers with Dignified Jobs for Environmental Change." Mongabay-India, January 2025. https://india.mongabay.com/2025/01/empowering-waste-pickers-with-dignified-jobs-for-environmental-change/.

Image Credits

The images opening each chapter were selected for the way they reflect or extend the ideas explored in the text. Full attribution, source, collection, accession details, and rights information are provided below. Titles and dates follow the source institution where available. All images are reproduced from public-domain or openly licensed sources.

Introduction. Gamochonia, plate 54, from Ernst Haeckel, Kunstformen der Natur, published in ten installment, Leipzig and Vienna, 1899-1904. Plate 54 belongs to instalment 6. Lithograph by Adolf Giltsch after Haeckel. Public domain, Wikimedia Commons.

Chapter 1. Ship in the Indian Ocean, 1237, Yahya ibn Mahmud al-Wasiti. Maqamat of al-Hariri, the Schefer manuscript, Bibliothèque nationale de France, MS Arabe 5847, acquired 1899. Reproduced here from a nineteenth-century reproduction after the miniature, published 1883. Public domain.

Chapter 2. Sagrada Família, Nativity façade, Barcelona, begun 1894, Antoni Gaudí. Photograph by Julian Lupyan, 4 August 2023, Wikimedia Commons, CC0 1.0 Universal. The architecture is public domain, Gaudí having died in 1926.

Chapter 3. A Cotton Office in New Orleans, 1873, Edgar Degas. Oil on canvas. Musée des Beaux-Arts de Pau, inv. 878.1.2, bought by the city of Pau in 1878. Public domain.

Chapter 4. The Courtyard of the Hospital at Arles, April 1889, Vincent van Gogh. Ink and pencil on paper. Sammlung Oskar Reinhart am Römerholz, Winterthur. Public domain.

landish Proverbs, 1559, Pieter Bruegel the Elder. Oil on galerie, Staatliche Museen zu Berlin, Ident. Nr. 1720. Public gle Art Project.

Chapter 6. The five classical orders, 1762. Encyclopédie, ou Dictionnaire raisonné des sciences, des arts et des métiers, of Diderot and d'Alembert, Recueil de planches, Tome I, Paris. Engraving. The title is a modern editorial one and not the plate's own. Public domain, Wikimedia Commons.

Chapter 7. A Number of People in the Street Going about Various Affairs, Meiji period, after Okumura Masanobu. Monochrome woodblock print, ink on paper. The Metropolitan Museum of Art, New York, MJP28, H. O. Havemeyer Collection, Bequest of Mrs. H. O. Havemeyer, 1929. Open Access, public domain.

Chapter 8. The Colosseum, eighteenth century, Giovanni Battista Piranesi. Etching from the Vedute di Roma, Rome, about 1748 to 1778. Public domain, Wikimedia Commons.

Chapter 9. Too Early, 1873, James Tissot. Oil on canvas. Guildhall Art Gallery, City of London Corporation. Public domain.

Chapter 10. Atlas catalan, about 1375, attributed to Cresques Abraham, Majorca. Bibliothèque nationale de France, MS Espagnol 30. The caravan is a detail from the eastern sheets. Public domain.

Chapter 11. Plaza Mayor de Mexico, 1836, after Carl Nebel, lithographed by P.-F. Lehnert. From Voyage pittoresque et archéologique dans la partie la plus intéressante du Mexique, Paris, 1836. Public domain.

Chapter 12. Undark (Shines in the Dark), magazine advertisement for the Radium Luminous Material Corporation (later United States Radium Corporation), 1921. Public domain.

Chapter 13. The Syndics of the Drapers' Guild, 1662, Rembrandt van Rijn. Oil on canvas. Rijksmuseum, Amsterdam, SK-C-6, on loan from the City of Amsterdam. Public domain.

Chapter 14. Garden Scene, Tomb of Ipuy, Dynasty 19, facsimile by Norman de Garis Davies. Tempera on paper. The Metropolitan Museum of Art, New York, 30.4.115, Rogers Fund, 1930. Facsimile of a wall painting in the Tomb of Ipuy at Deir el-Medina, Thebes, reign of Ramesses II, about 1295 to 1213 BC. Open Access, public domain.

Chapter 15. Study of Clouds, 5 September 1822, John Constable. Oil on paper. Victoria and Albert Museum, London, 590-1888, given by Isabel Constable. Public domain.

Chapter 16. The Turkish Letter Writer, begun 1840 and left unfinished, Sir David Wilkie. Oil on panel. Aberdeen Archives, Gallery and Museums, ABDAG003535. Public domain.

Chapter 17. The Geographer, 1669, Johannes Vermeer. Oil on canvas. Städel Museum, Frankfurt am Main, inv. 1149. Public domain, Google Art Project.

Chapter 18. Farhad Carves a Milk Channel for Shirin, folio 71 from a Khamsa of Nizami, 1524 to 1525, painting attributed to Shaikh Zada. Ink, opaque watercolor and gold on paper. The Metropolitan Museum of Art, New York, 13.228.7.5, Gift of Alexander Smith Cochran, 1913. Made at Herat, dated 931 AH. Open Access, public domain.

Conclusion. Wiosna, Spring, 1933, Leon Wyczółkowski. Watercolor, ink and crayon on paper, 71 x 79 cm. Muzeum Okręgowe im. Leona Wyczółkowskiego, Bydgoszcz. Painted at Gościeradz. Public domain, the artist having died in 1936.